Europe for Free

EUROPE

FOR
free

Brian Butler

Maps by Bonnie Kuster Butler

Mustang Publishing
New Haven

For Bonnie,
whose ardent support, encouragement,
and assistance made this book possible

Distributed to the trade by Kampmann and Co., New York.

Library of Congress Cataloging-in-Publication Data

Butler, Brian, 1950-
    Europe for free.

    1. Europe--Description and travel--1971-   --Guide-
books.   2. Free material.   I. Title.
D909.B83   1987   914'.04558   86-62920
ISBN 0-914457-15-2 (pbk.)

10 9 8 7 6 5 4 3 2 1

Acknowledgements

Many people have contributed to this book—European and American friends, helpful people in tourist offices throughout Europe, fellow travelers and kindred spirits from around the world, the kind staff of countless hotels, hostels, and campgrounds, and congenial Europeans from every country on that fair continent. Without the generous assistance of these people—and their patience in answering questions, giving directions, and providing information—this book would not have been possible.

And, to those friends in Europe who went above and beyond, a special thanks: the entire Pomi family, Gregor and Jette Herberhold, Laila Erikson, Hildegard Muller, Pia Purra, Pera Ikonen, Birgitte Randments, Christina Wirz, and Mr. Schroder.

Contents

FUN

No hotels.
No museums.
No historic sights.
Just the best bars, nightclubs, restaurants, beaches, flea markets—from London to Athens. Just the **fun** stuff, day and night, all over Europe.

Europe: Where the Fun Is contains nothing boring, like listings of the 83 hotels in town, or descriptions of 92 semi-famous cathedrals. Need to know where the train station or the nearest American Express office is? Check with Frommer or Birnbaum, because *Europe: Where the Fun Is* won't tell you.

But, if you want to know the latest about the punk scene in London, the truth about Amsterdam's Red Light District, the most fun restaurant in Paris, and the best way to navigate the Oktoberfest, then you need *Europe: Where the Fun Is.* Want free beer in Copenhagen, or a tan from the best beaches in Spain? Get this book.

Europe: Where the Fun Is costs $8.95 and should be available at bookstores, or use the coupon below.

*Named one of the 25 best European
travel guides by ''Changing Times'' magazine.*

Mustang Publishing • Box 9327 • New Haven, CT • 06533

Please send _____ copy(ies) of **Europe: Where the Fun Is** to the address below. I have enclosed a check or money order for $8.95 plus $1.00 postage *per book.*

Name _____

Address_____

City _____ State _____ Zip _____

*Allow 3 to 4 weeks for delivery. For one week delivery, include
$2.50 postage per book. Conn. residents add 7.5% sales tax.*

Introduction

This book is designed to burst the lingering myth that European travel has to be expensive—it doesn't! Hundreds of the best attractions, museums, events, and activities in Europe are absolutely **free**. Thousands more are free a day or two each week. Just about every city, town, or village in Europe has something interesting or amusing happening that won't cost you one cent. All you need to know is where and when.

In *Europe for Free*, you'll find hundreds of entries on free museums, castles, concerts, festivals, zoos, wine tastings, art treasures, brewery tours, natural wonders, ancient monuments, historic buildings, gardens, films, cultural events, and much more. These free attractions should make your trip more interesting—and definitely more affordable.

The book is organized alphabetically by country and by cities and towns within each nation. Each entry is headed by the name of the closest municipality and includes a brief description. Whenever possible, each listing specifies the hours, address, and phone number of the attraction.

Of course, the events and attractions in this book are just a fraction of the things to do and see throughout Europe. I've listed only the free things, so don't write-off Barcelona just because there are only six listings. There's a plethora of fun and fascinating attractions all over Europe, but, alas, not everything is free.

Finally, I want to emphasize that *Europe for Free* is intended for all European travelers, whatever their budget, and not just for backpackers or students. The francs, marks, or lira that you save on entry fees can be put to better use sampling the wines, beers, and exotic foods found only in Europe, and they can defray the cost of all those souvenirs you'll inevitably buy.

I sincerely hope that this book will help make your European trip more affordable and memorable.

Author's Note

A simple caveat before you begin: Hours and admission policies are not chiseled in granite, and if you find that an attraction has changed its hours or now charges a fee, I apologize. Please drop me a postcard with the details, and I will delete or change the entry in future editions.

Also, if you discover interesting free attractions, please let me know about them. If I use your tip in future editions of the book, I'll send you a free, autographed copy. Write to me in care of Mustang Publishing, P. O. Box 9327, New Haven, CT, 06533.

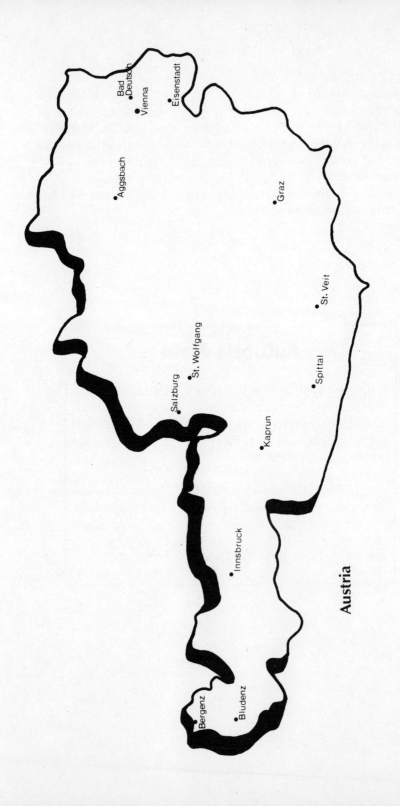

Austria

Aggsbach

Derelict Castle

The melancholy ruins of Aggstein Castle stand on a cliff 1,800 feet above the Danube. Built in the 12th century, the once formidable stronghold was destroyed in 1529 by the Turks, reconstructed in 1605, and severely damaged again. Although the footpath from the village is a bit steep, the panorama of the Wachau region and the castle remains make the hike worthwhile.

Time: April-Oct.: daily, 8am-sunset
Contact: Aggsbach Fremdenverehrsverein, ph. 2-753-8269 for directions

Bad Deutsch-Altenburg

Convenient to Vienna, this pleasant spa town on the threshold of the Little Carpathian Mountains owes its modern prominence to the ancient Romans, whose ruined Carnuntum is nearby.

Roman Capital

Just outside of town, you'll find the partially excavated site of Carnuntum, the ancient Roman capital of Pannonia. So far an 8,000-seat amphitheater, a military garrison, numerous homes, and

the Heidentor (a four gateway arch), have been discovered.
Time: Mon.-Sat., 9am-4:30pm
Contact: Verkehrsverein, ph. 2-165-2478 for information

Bludenz

Situated at the junction of three alpine valleys, Blundenz is a lively town too often neglected by travelers, who rush through on the way to mountain resorts. With its splendid old district of cobbled lanes and medieval buildings, Bludenz is a town of quiet but distinctive charms.

Free Concerts
Throughout the summer, free outdoor concerts are held in the main square of Bludenz's Altstadt. The music is often provided by brass bands in colorful folk costumes. After the performances, the audience retires to nearby beergardens to continue the festivities.
Time: June-Sept.: weeknights, 7:30pm
Place: Altstadt
Contact: ph. 5-552-2170

Bregenz

Clinging to sylvan hills along the shore of the Bodensee, Bregenz is a town with two distinguished faces. The lovingly preserved Oberstadt, with its ancient houses, steep narrow lanes, and hushed squares, watches over the modern Innerstadt, a stylish lakeside resort of garden promenades, boutiques, and sandy beaches.

Summer Festival
The month-long Bregenz Festival revolves around music of every description, from oom-pah-pah to opera. Although many events charge admission, there are daily concerts, exhibitions, parades, dances, and shows presented free.
Time: July to August
Contact: Bregenz Verkehrsverein, Inselstrasse 15, ph. 5-574-23391

Forest Rambles
Nestled between the shore of Lake Constance and forests, Bregenz

makes an excellent base for hikes in the Bregenzerwald of the Voralberg Alps. The regional tourist office has brochures on dozens of day hikes which take you through meadows of wildflowers, to tiny villages, and along easy trails with panoramas of Austria, Switzerland, and Germany.
Contact: Landsverkehrsamt Voralberg, Romerstrasse 7, ph. 5-574-22525

Dürnstein

This little fortified town is one of the loveliest on the Danube. Sheltered beneath a vineyard-covered ridge, Dürnstein has managed to preserve its ancient walls and gateways, medieval houses, and its exceptional Baroque church.

Legendary Castle

Durnstein is celebrated for its fine white wines and its crowning castle. According to local legend, Richard the Lionhearted was imprisoned here in 1193 while attempting to pass through on his way back to England from the Third Crusade. As the story goes, Richard had besmirched the honor of Leopold, Duke of Austria, and he was jailed until an enormous ransom was arranged by his faithful friend, Blondel. The fabled castle is reached by a pathway which begins at the eastern gateway on the Hauptstrasse.
Time: daily, 9am-6pm

Eisenstadt

Burgenland's provincial capital shows another side of Austria: far removed from the alpine heights and Tirolean valleys, Eisenstadt seems to belong to the Balkan steppes. Dominated by the Baroque splendor of its Esterhazy Palace, the little town faces nearby Hungary and Neusiedler Lake. Gypsy violinists play while patrons sip robust Magyar wines in Eisenstadt's rustic, thatched-roofed inns and taverns, adding to the Central European atmosphere. Long identified with the great composer, Josef Haydn, who lived at the Esterhazy court, Eisenstadt proudly boasts a rich cultural heritage, as alive today as it was under the Empire.

Composer's Tomb

Haydn lies in a carved mausoleum in Eisenstadt's unusual Berg-kirche. Across from Haydn's tomb, there's a unique manifestation of religious devotion called the Kalvarienberg. This curious reconstruction of Calvary Hill and the Via Dolorosa is populated by figures carved by monks in the 18th century and punctuated by little chapels and dioramas.
Time: Mon.-Sat., 8am-5pm
Place: Esterhazystrasse

Wine Festival

Early each September, Eisenstadt celebrates the grape harvest with the exuberant Weinwoche, a week-long paean to the local red wines. Fireworks fill the skies as costumed revelers dance, sing, parade, and, of course, drink their way around town.
Contact: Fremdenverkehrsverein Eisenstadt, Hauptstrasse 16, ph. 2-682-2507

Jewish Heritage

Housed in the old ghetto synagogue, Eisenstadt's Jewish Museum presents displays and memorabilia examining Jewish life in the Burgenland through the Holocaust.
Time: Mon.-Fri., 9am-3:30pm
Place: Wertheimerstrasse

Graz

Set in a countryside of rolling hills festooned with vineyards, Graz is Austria's second-largest city and best-kept travel secret. A showplace of the Baroque, this capital of the Steiermark manages to maintain a small town charm and strong artistic tradition, even though the surrounding suburbs are fast becoming an industrial center.

Renaissance Parliament

The Landhaus, seat of the Steiermark Landtag, is an outstanding Renaissance palace, built in the 1560's. The simple facade, which fronts on the elegant Herrengasse, belies the palace's dramatic innercourt, with its tiered arcades, ornate stairway, loggias, and

balconies. Be sure to visit the beautiful Landstube inside.
Time: Mon.-Fri., 9am-4:30pm
Place: Herrengasse
Contact: ph. 76591

Botanical Garden
Founded in 1888, Graz University Botanical Garden covers near-
ly five acres with greenhouses, floral beds, and a garden special-
izing in alpine plants from around the world.
Time: April-Oct.: Mon.-Fri., 7am-7pm; Sat. & Sun., 7am-1pm
Place: Schubertstrasse

Alternative Graz
A group of young Grazers have recently opened an exciting cultural
center called Fabrik in a former meat-packing plant. Many of the
events that they sponsor are free of charge, and there's a flea market
every Saturday morning in the courtyard.
Time: Mon.-Sat., 11am-?
Place: Plüddemanngasse 47

Innsbruck

No Austrian city is more dramatically situated than Innsbruck, with
alpine peaks rising literally within the city limits. The political,
economic, and cultural capital of the Tirol, Innsbruck is within easy
reach of snow-capped mountains, dark forests, wild meadows, and
resort villages. The inner face of Innsbruck is no less attractive, with
a medieval core huddled along the banks of the River Inn. Along
the Gothic arcades of the cozy Altstadt, you'll discover Baroque
churches, shops with vaulted ceilings, and swarms of tourists.

Hapsburg Pantheon
The Hofkirche (Palace Church) was built in 1563 to house the grandiose mausoleum of the Holy Roman Emperor Maximillian I of
Austria. Even though Maximillian is now interred near Vienna, his
tomb is one of the most important works of German Renaissance
sculpture. Both sides of the sarcophagus are lined by the famous
Swarzer Mander: 28 larger-than-life bronze statues representing the

Emperor's royal ancestors. In some cases, they are imagined forebearers, such as King Arthur of Britain, whose statue is by Durer. Don't let the grandeur of the mausoleum make you miss the Hof-kirche's other treasures, especially the tableaux of alabaster saints.
Time: Sundays, 9am-noon
Place: Universitatsstrasse 2
Contact: ph. 24302

Guided Hikes
Club Innsbruck provides free guided mountain hikes throughout the summer for anyone registered at a hotel, hostel, *pension*, or campground in town. If you're interested in the Club's outings, stop by the tourist office and register one day in advance.
Time: Mon.-Fri., 8am-noon & 2pm-5:30pm; Sat., 9am-noon
Contact: Verkehrsverein, Burggraben 3, ph. 25715

Enchanting Tirolia
The Karwendel Nature Protection Area, just north of Innsbruck, is famed for its scenery. Enticingly beautiful, it contains majestic mountain peaks, ancient forests, alpine pastures, glacial lakes, and wild mountain streams.
Time: unrestricted access
Contact: Tiroler Fremdenverkehrswerbung, Boznerplatz 6, ph. 20777

Baroque Gem
Dom zu St. Jakob is an ancient Gothic cathedral redecorated between 1717 and 1720 in a truimph of Baroque style by the renowned Assam Brothers of Munich. Cosmas, the painter and Egid, the stucco artist, worked their magic on churches and palaces throughout central Europe. St. Jakob's superb Mariahilf Altarpiece, however, is by Lucas Cranach the Elder.
Time: daily, 6am-noon & 2pm-6pm
Place: Domplatz

Garden Concerts
Innsbruck's Hofgarten was established in 1410 as a garden for the palace kitchen. Today, it covers 25 acres on the edge of the Altstadt and has glasshouses, flowerbeds, and a pavillion. Each evening in

the summer, free concerts are given at the pavillion by classical, pop, and jazz groups.
Time: June-Sept.: daily, 7:30pm-9pm
Place: Rennweg

Kaprun

Hydro-Power
The Kaprun Valley of the Tauern Alps is the site of Austria's most remarkable hydroelectric projects. These spectacular dams rise in tiers above the valley floor. The Kaprun Hydro-Power Station welcomes visitors for tours of one installation. For specific directions and appointment times, contact the Kaprun Tourist Office, just one mile away.
Contact: Fremdenverkrsverein Kaprun, ph. 654-7644

St. Veit An Der Glan

Fifteen castles on the hills around St. Veit testify to the power of the Dukes of Carinthia, who ruled there for 1,000 years. The medieval nucleus of St. Veit is preserved around the harmonious Hauptplatz, with its splendid homes and public buildings.

Town Hall
St. Veit's Gothic Rathaus was given a complete Baroque make-over during the 18th century. Entered from a Gothic passageway, the inner courtyard is appointed with tiered arcades and unusual decoration. Inside, the Great Hall is adorned with Baroque stucco and scroll work.
Time: Mon.-Fri., 8am-4pm
Place: Hauptplatz
Contact: ph. 4-212-2326

St. Wolfgang

This lovely lakeside town pays a heavy price for its superb scenery—it's mobbed by tourists. Still, it's worth a visit, especially in the spring or fall. If possible, try to arrive by lake steamer—the trip is unforgettable!

Gothic Marvel

St. Wolfgang's principal tourist attraction is its famous pilgrimage church. Built in the 15th century, the church possesses one of the finest examples of Gothic wood-working surviving today. This altarpiece by Michael Pacher was nearly removed in the late 17th century, when the church underwent Baroque remodelling. Happily, the artist commissioned to replace the altar recognized Pacher's genius and saved it.

Time: Mon.-Sat., 9am-5pm; Sun., 11:30am-5pm
Contact: ph. 6-138-2239

Salzburg

Salzburg has a storybook quality that immediately captures the traveler's imagination. Sharp spires, bulbous belfries, and copper domes tower above the Baroque Alstadt, while hundreds of feet above, the ancient castle is silhouetted against the sky. The old town's labyrinthine lanes leave romantic memories that linger long after you leave.

Situated between forested mountains on both banks of the Salzach River, Salzburg has been occupied for over 2,000 years. The city owed its splendor to ruling archbishops, who enjoyed vast powers as Princes of the Holy Roman Empire. These ecclesiastic despots turned the city into the "Rome of the North," with grand palaces, churches, and the mighty Hohensalzburg fortress.

Combine the attraction of the marvelous Altstadt with the surrounding landscape and a rich cultural tradition, and you've got a tourist mecca. Salzburg lures throngs of visitors throughout the year and is overwhelmed during the summer, when thousands come for the renowned music festival.

Ancient Convent

Founded by St. Rupert in 700, the Nonnberg Convent shares the Monchsberg mountain with the Hohensalzburg fortress. The old church is enclosed by a tranquil courtyard, while inside there are beautiful windows by Peter von Andlau, 12th-century frescoes, and a high altar. The views from the entranceway are spectacular.

Time: Mon.-Sat., 8am-11:30am & 1:30pm-4pm
Place: Nonnbergstrasse

Keeping in Touch
One of the many free services and activities offered by Salzburg University is the Lesesaal, or Public Reading Hall. This comfortable library and social hall has periodicals and newspapers from around the world. While you're getting in touch with the news of the world, check out the wide variety of events sponsored by the university.
Time: Mon.-Fri., 9am-7pm
Place: Hofstallgasse 4

Baroque Palace
Prince-Bishop Wolf Dietrich built the stunning Schloss Mirabell in 1606 for his mistress, Salome Alt. Alas, little is left of the original palace, which was remodelled in 1721 and after a fire in 1818. The marble staircase (the scene of many local weddings) is adorned with playful cupids by Raphael Donner. Throughout the year, chamber music concerts are held in the Marble Hall. The gardens feature fountains, pools, a maze, and statuary, including the mischievous Zwerglgarten with marble dwarves by Callot. With all of this Baroque splendor and the Festung Hohensalzburg as a back-drop, the Mirabell Gardens are ideal for taking memorable travel photos.
Time: daily, 7am-sunset
Place: Mirabellplatz

Immense Cathedral
It's often said that 10,000 people can easily fit inside Salzburg's mammoth Dom. The cathedral's early Baroque design by Santino Solari provides soaring twin towers and a noble marble facade. The impressive interior is noteworthy, not only for its majestic proportions but for the richness of Baroque stucco, marble, and painting. Every Sunday afternoon during the annual music festival and on August 15th, the *Jederman* (*Everyman*) play is performed in front of the Dom.
Time: daily, 8am-6pm
Place: Domplatz

Spittal An Der Drau
This pleasant old city occupies an expansive site at the foot of Mount Goldeck. As the main town of the Ober Karnten, it's a cultural and commercial center for the region.

Renaissance Palace

Schloss Porcia is one of the most beautiful Renaissance buildings in all of Austria. Built by the Imperial treasurer in 1527, the castle-like palace is framed by corner turrets. The inner courtyard is lined on three sides with graceful galleries and embellished with fine Renaissance decoration.

Time: May-Sept.: Mon.-Sat., 9am-6pm
Place: Schlosspark
Contact: ph. 4-762-3420

Vienna (Wien)

Two thousand years ago, Roman legionnaires discovered a little Celtic village on a small Danube tributary. They quickly settled in and constructed the fortified town of Vindobona to defend their eastern frontier. Over the centuries, the history of Vienna has been determined by its situation on the Danube and the natural frontier between East and West.

Traders who plied the Danube from the Black Forest to the Black Sea met there, as well as travelers from the Baltic to the Adriatic. The Crusaders passed through on their way to the Holy Land, and it was there that marauding Asian tribes and invading Turks were finally halted. A multi-lingual, multi-national empire—which for centuries decided the fate of Europe—was governed from Vienna. East and West, ancient and modern, meet and merge in this city, making "Vienna Gloriosa" an intriguing and exciting place to explore and discover.

Today, the medieval heart of Austria's capital is encircled by the famous Ringstrasse, built along the route of Vienna's ancient defensive walls. Inside the Ring, the winding streets and alleys of Old Vienna maintain the congenial, Old World charm for which the city is famous. Though tinged with a melancholy for its vanished imperial grandeur, Vienna still basks in its cultural heritage. It is mellow and cozy, stunning and enchanting.

Imperial Palace

The Hofburg, favored residence of Hapsburg Emperors, was begun around 1215 and continuously enlarged until the 1913 completion of the Neue Burg Palace. This more contemporary addition to the complex houses five museums: the Collection of Arms and Armor;

the Neue Gallerie, with European paintings of the 19th and early 20th centuries; the Musical Instrument Collection; the Ethnographic Museum, with Asian, African, and South American art and artifacts; and the Ephesos Museum, exhibiting Roman finds from the town of Ephesus.
Time: Oct.-March: Sun., 9am-4pm
Place: Neue Burg, Heldenplatz
Contact: ph. 934541

Dürer and More
Built in 1781, the Albertina contains the world's largest collection of graphic arts, with more than one million engravings, drawings, and sketches, along with a celebrated collection of work by Albrect Dürer. The palace gallery takes its name from Duke Albert of Saxony-Teschen, the son-in-law of Empress Maria Theresa, who began the esteemed collection in 1778.
Time: Sept.-April: Sun., 10am-1pm
Place: Augustinerstrasse 1
Contact: ph. 524232

From Time to Time
The Uhrenmuseum has a remarkable collection of 3,000 timepieces, from the earliest-known clocks to modern wrist calculators.
Time: Tue.-Sun., 8:45am-4:30pm
Place: Schulhof 2
Contact: ph. 632265

Baroque Palace Set
The marvelous Belvedere Palaces, along with their terraced gardens and Orangerie, comprise one of the world's most splendid ensembles of Baroque design. Built by the famed architect Lukas von Hildebrandt, the Palaces today house museums of Austrian, Baroque, and medieval art. Begin your visit at the Upper Belvedere, which Prince Eugene used for regal balls and banquets. After admiring the Hall of Titans, head directly to the upper galleries for the collection devoted to Austrian Jugendstil and Sezession artists. Next, stroll through the gardens to the Lower Belvedere to visit the Baroque Museum in the Prince's former apartments. The highlight is the glorious Gold Room—don't miss it! Then visit the Orangerie

and the Museum of Austrian Medieval Art, with rare works by Michael Pacher.
Time: Sun., 9am-noon
Place: Oberes Belvedereschloss, Prinz Eugenstrasse 27, Unteres Belvedereschloss, Rennweg 6
Contact: ph. 784-1580

Fine Arts

Housed in a monumental building on the Ring, the Kunsthistorisches Museum possesses one of the most impressive art collections in the world. The first floor galleries alone are a treasure of German, Dutch, and Flemish art, with entire halls devoted to Bruegel, Van Dyck, Dürer, Hals, Rubens, and Rembrandt. In the Right Wing, there are paintings from the French, Italian, and Spanish schools, with masterpieces by Raphael, Velazquez, Titian, and Rini. The museum also holds exceptional collections of ancient art and sculpture, along with displays of coins and medals.
Time: Sun., 9am-6pm
Place: Maria-Theresien Platz
Contact: ph. 934541

Natural History

Located directly across from the Kunsthistorisches is the Naturhistorisches Museum. This institution has enormous collections of prehistoric artifacts, fossils, botany, and zoology.
Time: Sept.-May: Sat. & Sun., 9am-3pm
Place: Maria-Theresien Platz

Municipal History

You'll discover fascinating details about Vienna and her people at the Historisches Museum der Stadt Wien. The displays include artifacts from the Roman era, stained glass and banners from St. Stephensdom, war trophies taken in battle with the Turks, period furnishings, and much more.
Time: Tue.-Sun., 10am-4:30pm
Place: Karlsplatz 4
Contact: ph. 42804

Free Concerts

Afternoons and evenings during warm weather months you can enjoy nostalgic concerts featuring Strauss waltzes in the Stadtpark. This green oasis is dotted with statues of famous composers and musicians and populated by noisy peacocks.
Time: May-Sept.: 3pm & 7:30pm
Place: Parkring at Johannesgasse

Magnificent Cathedral

The focal point of medieval Vienna is the spectacular St. Stephansdom. Built from 1147 to 1611 and completely restored after WWII, St. Stephans is one of Europe's most impressive cathedrals. Today, the Romanesque Riesentor (Giant's Tower) is all that remains of the original cathedral. Flanked by the Heidenturme (Pagan Tower), it is adorned with statues and carvings. Inside, you'll find the 15th-century Neustadt altarpiece, a masterpiece representing St. Barbara, St. Catherine, and the Virgin Mary. The chancel altar has a powerful altarpiece depicting the stoning of St. Stephan. In the apsidal chapel, the tomb of Emperor Frederick III symbolizes the eternal struggle between good and evil. From May through September, there are free organ recitals every Wednesday evening at 7pm in the cathedral.
Time: daily, 7:30am-8:30pm
Place: Stephansplatz

Academy of Fine Arts

Founded in 1692, the Akademie der Bildenden Künste presents paintings by Europe's finest artists: Bosch, Rubens, Van Dyck, Holbein, Titian, and Rembrandt. Stop by, if only to see Bosch's astonishing *Last Judgement*.
Time: Oct.-April: Tues., Thurs., & Fri., 10am-2pm; Wed., 10am-1pm & 3pm-6pm; Sat. & Sun., 9am-1pm
Place: Schillerplatz 3
Contact: ph. 579516

Town Hall Tours

Every weekday morning there are one-hour tours of Vienna's Rathaus. The tour includes public reception halls, council

chambers, the immense banquet hall, and seven inner courts.
Time: Mon.-Fri., 11am
Place: Rathausplatz at Dr. Karl Lueger Ring

Austrian Folklore
The Museum fur Volkskunde provides entertaining displays of traditional domestic life in Austria through the ages. The collections include costumes from various regions, home furnishings, musical instruments, and much more.
Time: Oct.-April: Sat. & Sun., 9am-1pm
Place: Laudongasse 15

Sarajevo Remembered
Vienna's Heeresgeschichtliches Museum will intrigue history buffs with its collections exploring the military history of the Austro-Hungarian Empire. One gallery details the fateful assassination of Archduke Franz Ferdinand and his wife in Sarajevo—an act which led to World War I.
Time: Oct.-April: Sat. & Sun., 10am-4pm
Place: Arsenalstrasse

The Giant Wheel
Looking for Harry Lime, or just some cheap thrills? Head for the Prater Amusement Park with its Riesenrad, the giant ferris wheel. Movie fans will recall the behemoth from *The Third Man*. There's no charge for admission to the park, but the rides cost money.
Time: daily
Place: Praterstein

Coach Museum
When you visit the Schönbrunn Palace and its public gardens, don't overlook the adjoining Schloss Wagenburg. This carriage museum has a terrific collection of Imperial coaches from the 16th through 20th centuries. Along with ornate Hapsburg vehicles, there are coaches which belonged to Napoleon and his son, the ill-fated King of Rome.
Time: Oct.-April: Sun., 10am-4pm
Place: Schonbrunner Schloss Strasse
Contact: ph. 833646

Tramology
Streetcar fans will enjoy the Wiener Tramway Museum, which displays old Vienese public transport, from horse-drawn streetcars to jaunty red trams.
Time: May-Sept.: Mon.-Fri., 9am-5pm; Sun., 10am-noon
Place: Maroltingergasse 53

Historic Strudel
The Alte Backstube may be the only combination cafe-bakery-museum in Europe. This 17th-century bakery illustrates Vienese baking over the last three centuries. The original ovens and bakers' equipment are on display.
Time: Tues.-Sat., noon-11pm; Sun., 3-11pm
Place: Lange Gasse 34

Maps and Agenda
Vienna's City Tourist Office, in the Opernpassage (on the Ring by the Opera House), furnishes city maps and programs of events in and around town. Be sure to request *This Week in Vienna*, a list of weekly attractions. They also sell the helpful three-day transit pass—it's a bargain that saves time and confusion for first-time visitors.
Time: daily, 9am-7pm
Place: Operpassage
Contact: ph. 431608

NOTE—The City of Vienna and the national government periodically change the admission price and free days of their museums and exhibits. It's possible that in the near future all museums will be free on Sundays throughout the year.

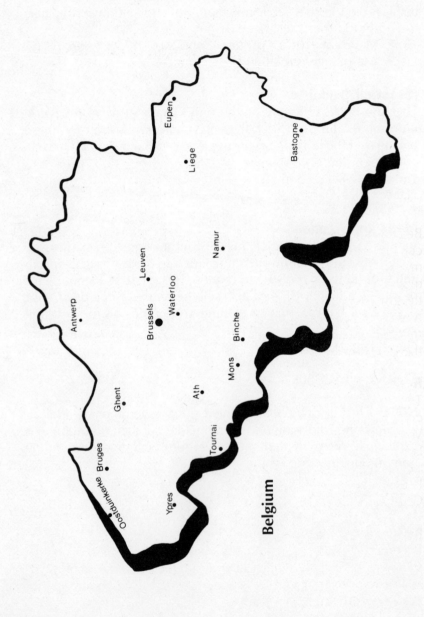

Belgium

Belgium

Antwerp

Belgium's second city is a paradox—a bustling port and industrial center, and a city of superb architecture and art. Past and present mingle in Antwerp, where Rubens coexists with modern commerce. In many ways, Antwerp's distinctive appeal derives from the convergence of epochs and styles. So don't be put off by Antwerp's frenetic hustle. Rather, head for the Old Town, where medieval guildhalls stand next to gabled homes and shops, all in the shadow of Belgium's largest Gothic cathedral.

Royal Museum of Fine Arts
The Musee Royal des Beaux-Arts houses one of the world's finest collections of Flemish art, featuring works by Rubens, Memling, Van Dyck, and Hals. There is also a fine collection of contemporary European art.
Time: Tues.-Sun., 10am-5pm
Place: Leopold de Waelplaats 9
Contact: ph. 03-232-2284

Medieval Fortress
Belgium's Maritime Museum is situated in Antwerp's oldest standing building, the 10th-century Castle Steen. Visitors interested in Europe's seafaring tradition can browse through exhibits of ship models, cartography, and ancient navigational devices. The im-

posing Castle Steen is well worth a visit on its own merits.
Time: Tues.-Sun., 10am-5pm
Place: Steenplein 1
Contact: ph. 03-233-7422

Jewels and Gems
Don't miss Antwerp's famous Diamond Center, where you can see
how precious gems are mined, cut, and polished. Also on display
are colorful exhibits exploring Antwerp's 500-year history as a center
of the international diamond trade.
Time: Tues.-Sat., 9:30am-5pm
Place: Jezusstraat 28
Contact: ph. 03-232-0103

Rubens' House
The 17th-century world of Peter Paul Rubens comes to life in the
restored home and studio of the master. Besides memorabilia and
art by Rubens, the museum contains paintings by some of his more
illustrious pupils: Jordaens, Van Dyck, and Snyder. Take time to
linger in the gardens and enjoy the atmosphere of Renaissance
Antwerp.
Time: Mon.-Sun., 10am-5pm
Place: Wapperstraat 9

Plantin-Moretus Museum
The refurbished home and printshop of Christopher Plantin, 16th-
century Europe's premier printer, is a charming museum for
bibliophiles and art lovers. From a Guttenberg Bible to working
16th-century printing presses, the museum contains a unique
collection.
Time: Tues.-Sun., 10am-5pm
Place: Vrijdagmarkt 22
Conta ct: ph. 03-231-1690

Ath

Carnival of the Giants
Dances, parades, games, and rides are just some of the events when
the village of Ath celebrates the Carnival of the Giants. The highlight

of the festival is the marriage between Goliath and the colossal Carnival Queen.
Time: last Sunday in August
Place: Grand Place
Contact: ph. 06-822-1094

Bastogne

Nestled on a high plateau in the Ardennes, Bastogne grew at the crossroads of three Roman thoroughfares. By the Middle Ages, it was an important way station on the Flanders-to-Lombardy route. Though seriously damaged during World War II, Bastogne still proudly bears its 17th-century nickname, "Paris of the Ardennes."

Battle of the Bulge Memorial

Built in the shape of a five-pointed star, the Mardasson American War Memorial overlooks the site where the Nazis launched their final counter-offensive. You can climb the arms of the memorial for a panoramic view of the battlefield and visit the nearby Bastogne Museum with its collection of war memorabilia.
Time: Mon.-Sat., 9:30am-5pm
Place: Mardasson Hill
Contact: ph. 06-221-1002

Walking Tours

Maps and route descriptions for two short hikes in the Ardennes are available from the tourist office. Promenade I follows an ancient Roman road through lovely Belgian scenery. Promenade II passes quaint villages and the Battle of the Bulge site.
Contact: Bastogne Tourist Office, rue de Marche 16, ph. 06-221-2711

Brugge (Bruges)

Brugge is northern Europe's loveliest medieval city. With footbridges arching across placid canals, medieval spires soaring above cobbled squares, and ancient houses lining romantic lanes, Brugge is breathtaking. Frozen in time like a gem in amber, Brugge is one place where you won't have to imagine how Europe looked in the Middle Ages.

Magnificent Michelangelo

Inside the Church of Notre Dame, you will find the exquisite statue *Madonna and Child* by Michelangelo. Completed in 1503, the work is his only sculpture in Belgium and his only work to leave Italy during the master's lifetime.

Time: Mon.-Sat., 10am-noon & 2:30pm-5:30pm; Sun., 2:30pm-5pm
Place: Sinte Katelijnestraat and Mariastraat

Walking Tour

More than a thousand years old, Brugge is a living museum of medieval European life. One of the best ways to get to know this intact medieval city is to take a self-guided walking tour. For details contact the city tourist office.

Office hours: Mon.-Sun., 9am-noon & 1pm-5pm
Place: Grote Markt
Contact: 05-033-0711

Jerusalem Church

Visit a replica of the Church of the Holy Sepulchre of Jerusalem, noted for its rare, sculptured altarpieces. Despite a devastating fire in the 15th century, the chapel retains most of its original curiosities and features the oldest stained glass windows in Flanders.

Time: Mon.-Sat., 10am-noon & 2pm-5pm
Place: corner of Jeruzalemstraat and Balstraat
Contact: ring bell for admittance

Lake of Love

For a lovely stroll, head for the Minnewater, or "Lake of Love." Once a bustling harbor, this waterway with weeping willows and swans is the most picturesque spot in Brugge.

Place: end of Wijngaardstraat

Carillon Concerts

Soaring above Brugge's central square is an octagonal belfry with a 49-bell carillon. Free concerts are given year-round, so take a

seat on the steps of the Provincial Palace and enjoy the music.
Time: June 15-Sept. 30: Mon., Wed., & Sat., 9pm-10pm; Sun.,
11:45am-12:30pm. Oct. 1-June 14: Wed., Sat., & Sun.,
11:45am-12:30pm
Place: Grote Market

Begijnhof
Founded in the 13th century, the Begijnhof (or Beguinage) is an
oasis for visitors. Originally a cloistered community for lay sisters,
the Begijnhof is now home to Benedictine nuns. The sisters can
be seen in their traditional habits on their way to prayers in the
14th-century chapel. The peaceful courtyard, enclosed by the
whitewashed, gabled houses of the nuns, invites you to wander
the paths between trees and fields of wild flowers.
Time: Mon.-Sun., daylight hours
Place: Wijngarstraat

Windmills
No need to go to Holland to find windmills; Brugge has three of
its own. Perched on an earthen dike along the Ghent Canal, the
red windmills evoke a bygone era in the low-countries.
Time: Mon.-Sat., 9am-5pm
Place: Kruisvest near the Ghentpoort

Brugge Town Hall
The 14th-century Stadhuis (Town Hall) is one of the oldest and finest
Gothic city halls in Europe. Its facade is lined with statuary and
topped by storybook turrets. Inside, you'll see murals depicting
Brugge's history and a majestic ceiling.
Time: Mon.-Sat., 9:30am-4:30pm
Place: the Burg
Contact: ph. 05-033-0711

Ancient Pageantry
Each year since 1311, the people of Brugge have commemorated
the arrival of the Relic of the Holy Blood with a colorful pageant.
The annual event centers around a parade of hundreds of costumed
townspeople. Heralded by marching bands and followed by choirs,
mounted knights, and groups depicting Biblical scenes, the

townspeople follow the Golden Reliquary of the Holy Blood through the winding streets.
Time: Ascension Day, May, 3pm
Place: starting at the Burg

Brussels

Brussels, a city of contrasts and diversity, rewards exploration with memorable discoveries. Much of the town is stark and modern, but there are still lanes so narrow that rooftops almost touch across the street, broad avenues lined with Art Nouveau townhouses, districts crammed with stylish galleries, and neighborhoods of faded but proud homes and shops. For the museum connoisseur or the lover of fine churches, there's a reward waiting around most every corner.

Panorama
The terrace of the immense Palais de Justice affords a panoramic view of Brussels. Designed by the Belgian architect Poelaert, the Palais de Justice is the largest edifice constructed during the 19th century and is located on the former site of Brussels' gallows hill.
Time: Mon.-Fri., 9am-5pm
Place: Place Poelaert

Musical Instruments
The Museum of Musical Instruments has an excellent collection of ancient and modern instruments from around the world. Unfortunately, only 1,200 of the museum's 5,000 instruments are on display at any one time.
Time: Tues., Thurs., & Sat., 2:30-4:30pm; Wed., 4:30-7pm; Sun., 10:30am-12:30pm
Place: Place du Petit Sablon 17
Contact: ph. 02-513-2554

Gothic Cathedral
Begun in the 13th century, Saint Michael's Cathedral is seated on a hill in the heart of Brussels. The inspiring Gothic church is the national cathedral and the site of royal weddings and funerals. The

treasure of St. Michael's is the set of stained glass windows by the 16th-century artist Bernard d'Orley.
Time: Mon.-Sat., 9am-5pm; Sun., 2:30pm-5pm
Place: rue des Paroissiens & rue de la Banque

Grand' Place
The heart of Brussels is the incomparable Grand' Place, one of the loveliest squares in Europe. Dominated by the stately Hotel de Ville, the square is enclosed by opulent guildhalls, each sporting a colorful banner and adorned with gold leaf. Weekdays, the square is the site of a flower market, and on Sundays, it's the locale of a fascinating bird market. Above all, don't miss the chance to wander the Grand' Place at night when it is illuminated by romantic floodlights.
Place: Grand' Place

Free Map
If you arrive in Brussels by air, be sure to get a free city map from the Acotra booth in the airport. This map furnishes touring information and an essential street index.
Time: Mon.-Sun., 8:30am-6:30pm
Place: lower arrival hall, Zaventem International Airport
Contact: ph. 02-513-8940

Cheeky Statue
Often called Brussels' oldest citizen, the Mannekin Pis is an irreverent statuette of a little boy urinating into a fountain. More than 350-years old, the audacious little fellow is the work of Jerome Duquesnoy, and it remains the source of numerous folk tales. Although stolen many times, the Mannekin Pis has always been restored to its place of honor.
Place: corner of rue de l'Étuve & rue du Chens

Old Masters
The Musee d'Art Ancien has a magnificent collection of Flemish and Dutch paintings, including works by Breughel, Bosch, Rubens,

and Van Dyck. This gallery should be on every art lover's itinerary.
Time: Tues.-Sun., 10am-5pm (free only on Wed., Sat., & Sun. afternoons)
Place: rue de la Régence 3
Contact: ph. 02-513-9630

Elegant Mall
Built in 1846, the historic Galleries St. Hubert is the oldest shopping mall in Europe. This marble, glass-roofed arcade (actually made-up of two shopping promenades, Galerie du Roi and Galerie de la Reine) houses some of Brussels' finest shops and cafes.
Time: Mon.-Sun., 9am-11pm
Place: between rue Marché-aux-Herbes & rue des Bouchers

African Art
The Royal Museum for Central Africa maintains a collection devoted to the arts and cultures of Central Africa. This outstanding museum, located in Tervuren Park, exhibits paintings, crafts, gems, and primitive artifacts.
Time: (winter) Mon.-Sat., 10am-4:30pm; (summer) 9am-5:30pm
Place: Leeuvensteenweg 13, Tervuren
Contact: ph. 767-5401

Historic Pageant
Brussels' most colorful pageant takes place each July in the fabled Grand' Place. The Ommergang, or literally the "Walk-Around," originated in the 15th century to commemorate a young girl's miraculous discovery of a statue of the Virgin Mary. Members of Brussels' aristocracy, garbed in medieval costume, parade around the square and then participate in medieval games and jousts.
Time: first Thurs. evening in July
Place: Grand' Place
Contact: Ommergang Society of Brussels, rue de Flandre 46

What's Going On
To find out what's happening in Brussels, get a free copy of the English language guide *The Bulletin* at the city tourist office. It is an informative weekly guide to entertainment and cultural life in

Belgium's capital and the surrounding districts.
Place: Brussels Tourist Office, rue Marche-aux-Herbes 61
Contact: ph. 02-512-3030

Eupen

Standing at the threshold of the dark Hertogenwald Forest, Eupen
is a city of unique flavor and atmosphere. Part of Belgium only since
the end of World War I, it remains a multi-cultural town. Originally a dependency of the Duchy of Limburg, Eupen came under the
sway of Burgundy, the Hapsburgs, France, and finally Prussia in
the 19th century. Eupen boasts many splendid old buildings, as
well as fine Renaissance and Baroque churches.

Rhine Carnival
Each winter, Eupen celebrates a Rhine Carnival weekend
culminating in Rosenmontag (Rose Monday). A flamboyant parade
of marching societies, elaborate floats, and brass bands follows the
Carnival Prince and his entourage through the historic districts of
town.
Time: weekend prior to Shrove Tuesday
Contact: City Tourist Office, Bergstrasse 6, ph. 08-755-3450

Gaasbeck

Storybook Castle
Definitely worth a visit, this 13th-century marvel has diverse
displays: Renaissance tapestries, Russian icons, medieval furniture,
sacred relics, and much more. Prior to the free guided tour, an
audio-visual show provides a terrific introduction to the Castle.
Time: Tues.-Thurs., Sat., & Sun., 10am-5pm
Place: Gaasbeck Park, 12 km. from Brussels
Contact: ph. 02-513-8940

Ghent

Less spectacular perhaps than its neighbor Brugge, but extraordinary
in its own right, this former capital of the Counts of Flanders still
deserves a visit. Ghent has old canals and streets lined with

medieval houses, fine churches, historic guildhalls, and enchanting castles.

Medieval Shrine

Named for a highwayman-turned-saint, the Cathedral of Saint Bavos blends Romanesque, Baroque, and Gothic styles. The church boasts a fine interior and is renowned for the Van Eyck brothers' painting, *The Adoration of the Mystic Lamb*, along with an elaborate pulpit by Delvaux.
Time: Mon.-Sat., 9:30am-noon & 2pm-6pm; Sun., 2pm-6pm
Place: Botermarkt

Museum of Antiquities

For the flavor of historic Ghent, visit the Museum van Oudheden in the ancient Cistercian Bijloke Abbey. The museum houses a collection of Flemish art, weapons, and everyday items, along with restored rooms from Ghent's homes and guildhalls.
Time: Mon.-Sat., 10am-noon; 1pm-4:30pm
Place: Godhuizenlaan
Contact: ph. 09-124-1555

Recreation Area

The Watersportbaan Recreation Area in Ghent's western suburbs offers extensive recreational opportunities, with swimming, fishing, windsurfing, tennis, rugby, soccer, biking, picnicking, and boating facilities.
Time: Mon.-Sun., 6:30am-8:30pm
Place: Watersportbaan
Contact: ph. 09-125-3641

Hekelgem

Masterpieces in Sand

In the village of Hekelgem, several cafes exhibit sand carpets, or *zandtapitjen* as they are called in Flemish. Practioners of this dying art can be found in some shops, creating copies of works by great masters in colored sand.
Contact: Tourist Office, ph. 02-513-9090

Leuven (Louvain)

Although this old university town was sacked and burned twice by Teutonic hordes, Leuven's rich medieval character has been beautifully restored. Today, the lively streets are again crowded with students and lined with old houses, Gothic churches, university halls, and magnificent public buildings.

Brewery Tour
Stella Artois, Belgium's largest brewer, offers free tours of their Leuven brewery, with an invitation to sample the product at the end of the tour.
Time: Mon.-Fri., 10am-4pm
Contact: ph. 01-622-9411

Municipal Elegance
Don't miss Leuven's Stadhuis (Town Hall). This Gothic marvel is embellished with Brabantine stonework, ornamentation, and carving. Miraculously, the 15th-century building survived the German bombardment of Leuven during both World Wars.
Time: Mon.-Sat., guided tours at 11am & 3pm
Place: Naamsestraat 1
Contact: ph. 01-623-4941

Liege

Following the winding course of the River Meuse, Liege is Belgium's third-largest city and the gateway to the northern Ardennes. The busy streets of this old industrial city are as capricious as the meandering river. Despite extensive World War II damage, Liege has restored much of its heritage.

Walloon Folklife
Housed in an old convent, the Musee de la Vie Walloon retraces everyday life in 19th-century Liege, with local crafts, costumes, toys, and art. During the winter, the museum hosts puppet shows.
Time: Sat. & Sun., 10am-4pm
Place: Cours des Mineurs

Old Liege

The charming Musee d'Ansembourg is a nobleman's residence built in 1735, with a collection of 18th-century arts and furniture from the workshops and studios of Liege.
Time: Sat., 10am-5pm; Sun., 10am-4pm
Place: En Feronstrèe 114

Glass Museum

Housed in a 16th-century palace, the Glass Museum of Liege displays a magnificent collection of Belgian, Roman, Venetian, Islamic, and Asian glassware.
Time: free on Sat., Sun., and holidays, 10am-12:30pm & 2pm-5pm
Place: Curtius Palace, Quai de Maestricht
Contact: ph. 04-152-4419

Historic Walking Tour

Discover the historic heart of Liege by taking the self-guided walking tour provided by the city tourist office. The 3 km. tour passes medieval buildings, ancient markets, and lovely neighborhoods.
Time: Mon.-Fri., 9am-6pm; Sat.-Sun., 10am-2pm
Place: Gare des Guillemins or En Feronstree 92
Contact: ph. 04-122-2456

Namur

Dominated by its Citadel atop a rocky cliff where the Meuse joins the Sambre, Namur is an immaculate town with brick houses and quaint shops. It's hard to imagine that this peaceful town has been the scene of dozens of battles since the Roman era.

Sacred Art

The Convent of Notre Dame has a splendid collection of religious art. Highlights of the exhibit are the 12th-century, jewel-studded reliquaries by the monk Hugh d'Oignies.
Time: Wed.-Sat., 10am-noon; 2pm-5pm
Place: rue du Pont

Stilt Wars

For the Festival Grand Feerie, the citizens of Namur revive the an-

cient art of stilt-walking. Costumed teams of warriors on stilts battle each other until only one remains aloft.
Time: early July
Place: Place Leopold
Contact: ph. 08-122-2859

Oostduinkerke

Oostduinkerke is a modest family resort with wide beaches and great seafood restaurants.

Shrimp Festival
The village celebrates the shrimping season with an annual carnival that features games, parades, fireworks, and shrimp eating and catching contests. The festivities culminate with an enormous beach bonfire.
Time: first Sunday in July
Place: Oosterduinkerke Beach
Contact: ph. 05-851-1189

Horseback Fishermen
A traditional way of life still survives on the Flemish coast, where local fishermen on horseback dredge the shallows of the North Sea at low tide for shrimp.
Time: July-Sept.
Place: Oosterduinkerke Beach

Tournai

Tournai is one of the most historic towns of Belgium. Already settled when the Romans arrived, it became a royal seat during the Frankish era. During the Middle Ages and again during the 18th-century, Tournai was absorbed by France. And despite destruction during World War II, the town still retains the oldest inhabited private homes in Europe, dating from 1175.

French Folklore
The Musee du Folklore evokes the popular life of Tournai with a series of reconstructed interiors. There are artisan's studios, a farm

kitchen, and small retail shops.
Time: Wed.-Mon., 10am-noon & 2pm-5:30pm
Place: Maison Tournaisienne
Contact: ph. 222045

Waterloo

Napoleon's Downfall
The site of the fateful clash on June 18, 1815 between Napoleon and the Duke of Wellington is a pastoral scene today. See the panoramic view of the battlefield that played such a decisive role in the history of Europe by climbing the steps to the top of the Lion Monument that commemorates the battle.
Time: Mon.-Sun., 8:30am-7pm
Place: Waterloo Battlefield
Contact: ph. 02-354-4900

Wingene

Breughel Festival
The village of Wingene honors the Flemish painter Pieter Breughel with a festival each autumn. The entire village dresses in costume and recreates scenes from Breughel's paintings. After the living tableau, everyone gathers in the town square for a feast of regional dishes.
Time: second Sunday in Sept.
Place: Grote Markt

Ypres

During the Middle Ages, Ypres was one of the great cities of Flanders, with a population of almost 200,000. Unfortunately, none of Ypres' original buildings survived the destruction of World War I. Today, the town of 35,000 lacks the splendor of Brugge or Ghent, but it has managed to resurrect many of its landmarks and the facades of its finest old homes and shops.

Flying Cats
Ypres is the site of one of Europe's most bizarre festivals. The Kat-

tenwoendag (Cat Festival) includes costumed paraders, Belgian folklore giants, and cat floats, and it culminates with the town jester tossing toy cats from the belfry to the revelers below. People who catch a flying feline win prizes and get free drinks all day.
Time: second Sunday in May
Place: Grote Markt
Contact: ph. 05-720-2623

World War I Memorial
The Menin Gate in Ypres is an enduring memorial to the 250,000 British troops who died during World War I on the western front. Panels on the Gate are inscribed with the names of 55,000 soldiers who fell in the defense of Ypres. Every evening, traffic through the Gate is stopped for five minutes as a Belgian bugler plays in honor of fallen allies.
Time: sunset

Nationwide

Beaches
For fun in the sun, head for Belgium's North Sea coast. One hour from Brussels by car or train, 70 kilometers of white sandy beaches offer all the usual beach-related activities, as well as casinos and nightclubs.
Contact: Belgian Tourist Office, rue Marche-aux-Herbes 61, ph. 02-512-3030

Allinge
Rønne

Skagen

Lindholm Høje
Alborg
Rebild

Arhus

Jelling
Fredericia

Ribe

Odense
Kvaerndrup

Ærø

Fredenborg
Helsingør
Hillerød
Roskilde

Copenhagen

Haslev
Naestved

Denmark

Denmark

Aalborg

On the shore of the icy-blue Limfjord, Aalborg blends the best of old and new Denmark. Originally a Viking settlement, Denmark's fourth-largest city has a preserved Old Town of narrow lanes and medieval houses, and modern districts with boulevards, parks, and modern buildings.

Ancient Hospital

Denmark's oldest hospital and social service institution is housed in the ancient Monastery of the Holy Ghost, Aalborg's oldest standing building. Call the tourist office to arrange a visit to see the tranquil white cloisters, the vaulted cellars, and the 16th-century frescoes of the monastery, which is still used as a retirement home.
Time: weekdays, 2pm-4pm
Place: C.W. Obels Plad
Contact: Touristbureauet, Ostergade 8, ph. 126022

Medieval Church

The beautiful whitewashed St. Budolfi Kirche stands in the city center. The 18-bell carillon plays a tune every hour from 9am to 10pm, and the interior boasts a Rennaissance pulpit and altarpiece, along with colorful frescoes.
Time: Mon.-Sat., 9:30am-4pm
Place: Budolfi Plads

City Castle
Built in 1539, the Aalborghus Castle overlooks the Limfjorden. Now occupied by government offices, the castle's courtyard, dungeon, and ramparts can be toured during business hours.
Time: Mon.-Fri., 9am-4:30pm
Place: Slotspladsen

Aarhus

With records stretching back to 928, Denmark's second city is a bustling seaport on the Kattegat and a lively university town. Despite Aarhus' mostly modern face, the city has preserved many old buildings and churches.

Monsoon House
One of the many interesting features of the Aarhus Botancial Garden is the glass Monsoon House with its tropical plant collection from Southeast Asia. Flower Valley, a terraced area planted with Scandinavian flowers, is also interesting. A creek flows through the garden forming four ponds for aquatic plants and birds.
Time: Mon-Sat., 1:30pm-3:30pm; Sun., 10am-noon & 1:30pm-4pm
Place: Mollevejen 10

Tower Views
There are fine views of Aarhus, the harbor, the Kattegat, and beaches from the tower of the controversial Town Hall. Built in 1941 to commemorate the 500th anniversary of the city charter, the Radhuset's architecture has been a source of dispute ever since.
Time: daily, noon-2pm
Place: Radhus Plads
Contact: ph. 121600

Organ Recitals
Frequent organ concerts are held during the summer months on Denmark's largest pipe organ in St. Clemens Cathedral. The immense brick church, built in 1201, has a carved altarpiece with a crowd of religious figures, 15th-century frescoes, and beautiful stained glass.
Time: Mon.-Sat., 9:30am- 4pm
Place: Clemenstorv

Castle Garden

On the outskirts of Aarhus is the Marselisborg Castle, a royal summer residence. In the woods that surround the castle, there is an arboretum with 1,500 trees and shrubs, along with a variety of wild flowers.
Time: daily, 8am-7pm
Place: Carl Nielenvej

Aeroskobing

Gingerbread Village

One of Denmark's loveliest villages, Aeroskobing, on Aero Island, has been called a "fairytale town with Lilliputian gingerbread houses." Thirty-five of the buildings are classified as ancient monuments. Don't miss the 13th-century chapel with its octagonal steeple and ancient art.
Contact: Touristbureauet, Torvet, ph. 521300

Allinge-Sandvig

This twin resort village at the northern tip of Bornholm Island is a holiday spot for trendy Europeans, but it's rarely visited by Americans. The alliance of medieval and modern on Bornholm, along with the island's natural attractions, make this area one of Denmark's top destinations.

Craggy Ruins

There are magnificent views of Bornholm Island and the sea from the ruins of Hammerhus Castle, perched on a crag near Allinge-Sandvig. Built in 1250, the castle was the scene of many battles between Danish and Swedish forces. The ruins were used as a quarry until the 19th century, when it was designated a historic monument. For directions to the walking path to Hammerhus Castle, contact the tourist office.
Contact: Turistforeningers Bureau, ph. 980001

Copenhagen (Kobenhavn)

One in four Danes makes Copenhagen his home, and it won't take you long to see why. With its lively pedestrian zones, appealing architecture, expansive parks, and colorful waterfront, Denmark's capital is a charming city, built on a human scale. Visitors are often surprised to discover that most of Copenhagen's sights are within a relatively small area. Even Tivoli Garden, the world's loveliest amusement park, is right in the heart of town. In spite of devastating fires during the 18th century and British naval bombardment in the 19th century, Copenhagen's skyline is still punctuated by ancient steeples, castles, and copper-clad roofs.

But Copenhagen is not a museum town; instead, it reflects a special blend of modern elegance and historic charm that epitomizes Scandinavia's capital cities. Copenhagen has an exuberant social scene and nightlife, and the city is Denmark's cultural center, rich in art, music, theater, and great museums. The best way to get in touch with this special town is to wander, get lost, have a beer at an outdoor cafe, and meet some good-humored Danes.

Brewery Tour
Don't miss the tour of the Carlsberg Brewery, which makes some of the best beer anywhere. Glib tourguides deliver monologues on the entire brewing process while escorting visitors around the brewery. The tour includes a visit to the company museum and gallery and ends at the beerhall, where tables are laid with dozens of bottles of the Carlsberg beers and soft drinks—all free, of course.
Time: Mon.-Fri., 9am, 11am, & 2:30pm
Place: Ny Carlsbergvej 140
Contact: ph. 211221, ext. 1312

More Beer
Tuborg Brewery, affiliated with Carlsberg, also offers an interesting tour. Copious free samples follow the tour.
Time: Mon.-Fri., 8:30am-2:30pm
Place: Strandvejen 54
Contact: ph. 293311, ext. 2212

National Museum
Denmark's National Museum displays a collection of artifacts from Danish history. This depository of national treasures maintains an excellent Viking-era department and a fine collection of northern

European religious art. The antiquities section includes treasures from Greece, Rome, Asia, and Egypt, while the ethnographic wing houses artifacts from Greenland's Eskimo cultures.
Time: June-Sept.: daily 10am-4pm; Oct.-May: daily, 11am-3pm
Place: Frederiksholm Kanal 12
Contact: ph. 134411

Marble Church

The immense Frederikskirche begun in 1749 wasn't completed until 1894 due to a lack of funds. The facade of the Baroque church is decorated with statues of Biblical and religious figures, while the interior features golden candelabra, elaborate carvings, and an ivory crucifix.
Time: Mon.-Fri., 9am-4pm; Sat., 9am-noon
Place: Frederiksgade 1
Contact: ph. 153763

Fine Arts

The Statens Museum for Kunst houses the most extensive collection of Danish art in the world, plus collections of European art from the 13th to 20th centuries, including works by Rembrandt, Reubens, Titian, Picasso, and Dürer.
Time: Tues.-Sat., 10am-5pm
Place: Solvegade

Arms and Armor

The Royal Danish Arsenal Museum, situated behind the Christianburg Palace, is one of the world's great military museums. The 16th-century arsenal displays artillery, swords, armor, and battle standards.
Time: May-Sept.: Mon.-Sat., 1pm-4pm & Sun., 10am-4pm; Oct.-April: Mon.-Sat., 1pm-3pm & Sun., 11am-4pm
Place: Tojhusgade 3

Christiania

The adventurous traveler will want to investigate Copenhagen's Free State of Christiania on Christianshavn. In 1970, squatters on an old military base in the Badsmandsstraede district proclaimed Christiania's independence as a free state, and for a while they received official recognition as a social experiment. Today, the

district is shared by idealists trying to build a progressive community and drug-dealing counter-culturists. The resulting mix is one part street theater, one part utopian settlement, and one part slum— it's anything but boring. Although occasionally threatened with eviction and often the subject of parliamentary debate, this community's existence is a good example of the legendary Danish tolerance.
Place: Christianhavn, south of Prinsessegade

City Museum
The Kobenhavn Bymuseum contains artifacts and art which illustrate the history of Denmark's capital through the ages. There are detailed models of the city, costumes, and an exhibit dedicated to the Danish philosopher Soren Kierkegaard, with memorabilia and personal documents.
Time: Tues.-Sun., 10am-4pm
Place: Vesterbrogade 59

University Garden
Set on the old city ramparts, the University of Copenhagen Botanic Garden contains nearly 25,000 plant species. There are sections devoted to roses, rock plants, and native Danish species. Behind the Geology Museum (also in the Garden), there are extensive greenhouses with tropical plants—one houses an amazing giant water lily.
Time: daily, 10am-3pm
Place: Gothersgade 128

Applied Arts
The Kunstindustrimuseet (Museum of Applied Arts) houses a collection of international decorative arts from the Middle Ages to modern times. The museum is noted for its excellent wood carvings, tapestries, furnishings, and porcelains.
Time: Tues.-Sat., 1pm-4pm
Place: Bredgade 68

Musical History
The Music History Museum provides a variety of musical experiences at the press of a button. You can hear ancient and modern instruments: lutes, drums, pianos, harpsicords, zithers, and more

in the demonstration halls. There are also memorabilia and unusual instruments from around the world.
Time: Tues., Wed., Fri., Sat., & Sun., 1pm-4pm
Place: Abenra 34

Changing of the Guard
When Denmark's Queen is in residence at the Amalienborg Palace, the changing of the Royal Guard is held in the Palace Square. The soldiers of the Royal Guard start from Rosenborg Castle at 11:30am and march to the palace for the presentation of arms. Following the ceremony, there is a concert by the regimental band.
Time: daily, 11:30am-noon
Place: Amalienborg Slot

War Heros
The Frihedsmuseet chronicles the Danish resistance to Nazi occupation and repression. The museum displays relics of the resistance, from homemade weapons to Nazi torture devices.
Time: May-Sept.: Tues.-Sun., 10am-4pm; Oct.-April: Tues.-Sun., 11am-3pm
Place: Churchill Parken on the Langelinie

Oriental Art
Asian art, Middle Eastern ceramics, and decorative furnishings can be found in the eclectic C. L. David Collection, along with a variety of European works.
Time: Tues.-Sun., 1pm-4pm
Place: Kronprinsessegade 30

Den Permanente
Copenhagen's Permanent Exhibition of Art and Design displays and sells a selection of Denmark's furnishings and handicrafts, all chosen by a special selection committee. Everything from fine jewelry to hand-loomed rugs is guaranteed to be top quality.
Time: Mon.-Sat., 9am-5:30pm; Sun., 9am-2pm
Place: Vesterbrogade 8
Contact: ph. 124488

Classical Arts
The Carlsberg beer fortune endowed the Ny Carlsberg Glyptotek

with a vast collection of antiquities and 19th-century art. The upper floors house French Impressionist paintings by Cezanne, Monet, Degas, and Gaugin, along with sculpture by Rodin.
Time: free on Wed. & Sun., 10am-4pm
Place: Dantes Plad 7

Natural History
Copenhagen's Zoological Museum is a fun and educational natural history museum with intriguing working models, colorful displays, and changing exhibits on ecology and bionomics.
Time: daily, 10am-4pm
Place: Universitetsparken 15

Copenhagen Cathedral
Completed in 1829, the Vor Frue Kircke, Copenhagen's neo-classical cathedral, is unimpressive from the outside but graceful and beautiful inside. The poignant sculptures by Bertil Thorvaldsen, particularly his *Christ and Apostles*, are well worth a visit.
Time: daily, 8am-5pm
Place: Norregade 6
Contact: ph. 144128

Sculpture Museum
The Thorvaldsen Museum displays sculpture by Denmark's greatest sculptor, Bertil Thorvaldsen. In addition to his classical sculpture, the museum contains the artist's personal collection of ancient statuary and paintings by his contemporaries.
Time: Wed.-Mon., 10am-3pm
Place: Porthusgade

Fredensborg

Palace Gardens
The gracious Fredenborg Palace is the spring and autumn residence of the Danish royal family. The surrounding Peace Park was patterned on the gardens of Versailles. With its radiating avenues and sculpture gardens, the Palace garden is one of Denmark's most impressive parks. When the Queen is in residence, there is a col-

orful changing of the guard daily at noon.
Time: daily, 6am-sunset
Place: Slotsgade

Fredericia

Fredericia was established in the early 17th century as a military town to protect the Island of Fyn and lower Jutland from German incursions. Today the small city is an important railway junction and port town.

Memorial Day

Each July 7th, ceremonies are held to honor Danish troops who fell in battle against German invaders in 1849. Following the formal observance, there is a dramatic procession by troops in authentic 19th-century uniforms.
Time: July 7th
Place: Gothersgade 24
Contact: Fredericia Touristforening, ph. 921377

Rampart Walks

Fredericia retains well-preserved rampart walls, which give excellent views of the town and countryside.

Haslev

Rococo Mansion

Hans Christian Andersen was just one of the many influential guests to visit the enchanting Bregentved Estate, one of Denmark's loveliest private homes. With its distinctive spire, the manor occupies a large formal garden open to visitors. The stately home has been owned by the family of Count Moltke since 1746.
Time: Wed. & Sun., 9am-8pm
Contact: ph. 03-692120

Helsingor

Lovely Kronborg Castle has dominated Helsingor and guarded the Oresund Passage for more than 500 years, and the busy seaport

itself its older still by 500 years. Hamlet's ficticious home is graced
by many half-timbered houses, medieval churches, and promenades
from Helsingor's halcyon days, when ships paid to sail through the
narrow waterway separating Denmark from Sweden.

Medieval Monastery

Helsingor's Carmelite Monastery, dating from 1430, is one of Denmark's finest examples of medieval architecture. The arcaded
cloisters, refrectory, and chapel hall are open for visits.
Time: daily, 1:30pm-4:30pm
Place: Havnegade

Neo-Classical Mansion

The 18th-century Marienlyst Mansion, occupying the site of
Frederik II's former Lundehave Castle, is a beautiful neo-classical
manorhouse, now the home of Helsingor's Municipal Museum.
The original furnishings and decor have been preserved on the
third floor, while the remainder of the mansion serves as an ex-
hibition hall.
Time: May-Sept.: daily, 1pm-4pm; Oct.-April: daily, 1pm-3pm
Place: Marienlystallee
Contact: ph. 211333

Hillerod

Hillerod is a pleasant North Zealand town toured mainly for its
double-moated Fredriksborg Castle.

Money Museum

Numismatists won't want to miss Hillerod's small but entertaining
Money Museum. The collection of coins, banknotes, and objects
relating to currency is housed in the Fredriksborg Bank.
Time: Mon.-Fri., 10am-4pm
Place: Slotsgade 16
Contact: ph. 262852

Castle Park

The immense Frederiksborg Castle, one of Europe's most sensational Renaissance palaces, is encircled by Baroque gardens created
in the early 18th century by Johann Kreiger. The garden remains

one of Scandinavia's most enchanting parks.
Time: daily, 6am-sunset
Place: Slotsgade
Contact: ph. 260489

Jelling

One of Scandinavia's most important antiquarian sites, Jelling is dominated by the burial mounds of Viking kings and the nation's oldest surviving church. During its heyday, Jelling was the seat of Denmark's first united monarchy under Gorm the Old, progenitor of a Viking dynasty that eventually conquered Britain and Norway.

Viking Kings

Nowhere is Denmark's Viking heritage more apparent than in Jelling, with two 10th-century burial mounds and ancient rune stones. The mounds contain the remains of King Gorn and his queen, Thyra Danabod. Nestled between the mounds, a tiny 11th-century chapel contains the oldest frescoes in Denmark. Two rune stones lie beside the church—the larger was erected by King Harald Bluetooth; the other set up by King Gorm to honor his queen. The basement of the chapel houses the remains of a wooden church built by King Harald, who introduced Christianity to Jutland.
Time: Church: Mon.-Sat., 10am-4pm
Contact: ph. 871310

Kvaerndrup

Island Fortress

Outside of Kvaerndrup, you will find one of Europe's finest island fortresses, Egeskov Castle. Erected in 1525 on a foundation of oak pilings in a small lake, the castle rises sheer above its moat. The renowned Egeskov Gardens are Denmark's most elaborate, with a 200-year old maze, fruit trees, hedges trimmed into animal forms, rare roses, and the gorgeous Baron's Garden.
Time: daily, 8am-sunset
Contact: ph. 622323

Lindholm Hoje

Viking Village
Overlooking the Limfjord in northern Jutland are the graves of Scandinavia's most important Viking burial ground. Many of the graves are set in the shapes of Viking boats. Here, too, are the remains of a Viking village, with 15 excavated dwellings from the 8th and 9th centuries.
Contact: Turistbureauet Norresundby, ph. 171718

Naestved

This South Zealand industrial town's medieval days are recalled by the many old homes and Gothic churches in the city center.

Classic Glass
The Holmegard Glassworks, just north of Naestved, produces glassware of unsurpassed quality and design. Visit the workshops for a tour and see the artisans turn molten glass into beautiful products.
Time: Mon.-Fri., 9am-1:30pm; Sat. & Sun., 11am-1:30pm
Place: Holmolstrup 54
Contact: ph. 721667

Odense

Denmark's third-largest city traces its origins back almost a thousand years. Despite this antiquity, Odense is mostly a modern industrial town with few reminders of its heritage. But if you do come in search of Hans Christian Andersen, its possible to discover a few corners of Odense where the author would feel at home.

Magnificent Gothic
Built in the 13th century, the commanding St. Knud Cathedral is named for King Knud, who was assassinated in Odense in 1086. The Cathedral features a 16th-century altarpiece with 300 figures, and the somber crypt contains the tombs of kings Knud and Hans.
Time: Mon.-Sat., 10am-4:15pm
Place: Klingenberg
Contact: ph. 127520

Rebild

National Park

In 1911, Danish-Americans purchased a tract of rolling, heather-covered hills and presented it to the Danish government for use as a park that would link the two countries. In the park you'll find a replica of Abraham Lincoln's log cabin, which houses a Museum of Emigration. Each year, to emphasize the cultural ties, the largest 4th of July celebration outside the United States is held in the park. Festivities feature singers, dancers, and speakers from both countries. The celebration culminates with a sing-along of American and Danish songs and a dazzling fireworks display.
Place: 17 miles south of Aalborg
Contact: ph. 08-392222

Ribe

Oldest Town

Enchanting, ancient Ribe is Denmark's oldest town. Founded around 840 AD, Ribe is a charming place, with narrow lanes lined with homes and shops from the 15th through 18th centuries. Besides its delightful architecture, Ribe is known for the storks which nest on chimneys around town and for the ruined Riberhus Castle.
Contact: Ribe Turistbureauet, Overdammen 10, ph. 421500

Romanesque Cathedral

Ribe's dominant landmark is the Vor Frue Cathedral. Built partly of Rhineland stone and Danish brick, the church soars above the square. Begun in 1130, the cathedral stands on the site of Denmark's first Christian church. The belltower offers a magnificent view of Ribe and the surrounding marshlands, and the carillon plays four times daily, at 8am, noon, 3pm, & 6pm.
Time: Mon.-Sat., 10am-noon & 2pm-4pm; Sun., 2pm-4pm
Place: Torvet

Quintessential Abbey

Although the St. Catherine Church and Monastery dates from 1228, the present buildings were built in the 15th century. Since its restora-

tion in 1930, St. Catherine's has been recognized as one of Scandinavia's best-preserved monasteries. Be sure to look for the graffiti in the monks' cubicles in the church.
Time: Mon.-Sat., 10am-noon & 2pm-4pm
Place: Dagmarsbro

Ronne

Ronne Days
During the tourist season, Ronne, Bornholm Island's capital, celebrates its visitors with many free activities. Each Thursday, the city sponsors free concerts, exhibits, shows, and carriage rides around town. With its quaint homes and shops, Ronne is a charming, lively town.
Contact: Bornholmske Turistforeningen, Havn, ph. 950806

Roskilde

This attractive old town, overlooking its namesake fjord, was once Denmark's greatest city. Capital of the nation until the 15th century, Roskilde was also an important ecclesiastical center, evidenced by its immense cathedral. Roskilde's fisherman's quarter is rich in medieval atmosphere, with steep lanes, thatch-roofed cottages, and magnificent views.

Viking Ships
Since the wrecks of 51,000-year old Viking ships were discovered in the Roskildefjord in 1957, the town has been a center for the study and reconstruction of Viking ships. Although the Viking Ship Museum charges admission, at its annex you can see craftsmen constructing replicas of Viking boats, utilizing ancient methods and tools. Behind the shipyard there is often a replica of a Viking warship at anchor in the fjord.
Time: Mon.-Fri., 9am-5pm
Place: Havnen
Contact: ph. 352700 or 356555

Skagen

Church of the Dunes

Just west of Skagen, Denmark's northern-most town, the tower of a 14th-century church lies half-buried in a sand dune. The rest of the church was abandoned to the drifting sand in 1795.

Contact: Skagen Turistbureauet, Sct. Laurentivej 18, ph. 441377

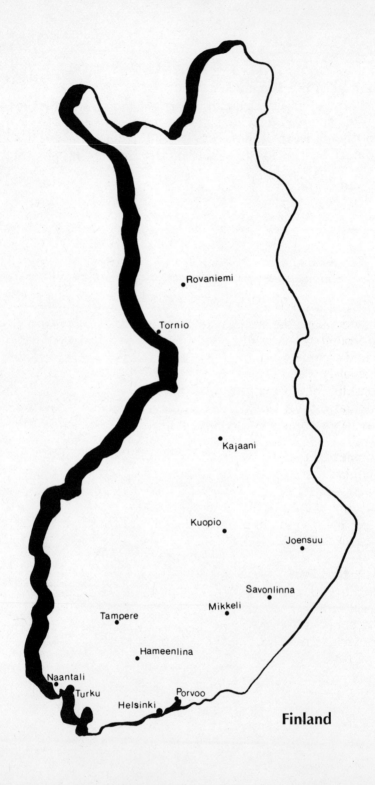

Rovaniemi

Tornio

Kajaani

Kuopio

Joensuu

Savonlinna

Mikkeli

Tampere

Hameenlina

Naantali

Turku

Porvoo

Helsinki

Finland

Finland

Hämeenlinna

Situated along the shore of Lake Vanajavesi, Hämeenlinna grew up around the Tavastehus Castle. This historic town, birthplace of famed composer Jean Sibelius, has experienced considerable industrial development in recent years, but it retains an intimate relationship with the wooded lakeland around it. Boats of the celebrated Silver Line sail daily from the docks, offering a unique way to experience Finland's harmony of water and forest.

Ancient Church
Hattula Church, built in the late 13th century, is one of Finland's oldest remaining stone churches. The interior is decorated with fearsome paintings and beautiful carvings.
Time: daily, 10am-5pm
Place: Pälkäme Road

Beautiful Park
On the outskirts of town, the Aulanko National Park has extensive facilities for both summer and winter sports. In warm weather, plays and concerts are performed at the park's castle.
Contact: Kanta-Hameen Matkailutoimisto, Raatihuoneenkatu 13, ph. 202233

Helsinki

The heart of this sparkling capital clusters on a rocky peninsula and a series of harbor islands on the northern Gulf of Finland. Called the "Daughter of the Baltic," Helsinki's liveliest districts ring the seafront harbor.

Proclaimed capital of Finland in 1812, the city reflects 19th- and 20th-century urban planning, where architectural genius and civic pride has produced one of Europe's most liveable cities. The central city, rebuilt after a fire in 1808, is an open-air museum of 19th-century neo-classical design, while the encompassing districts of boulevards and parks reflect the finest in contemporary architecture.

Contemporary Arts

The Helsinki City Art Museum houses an interesting collection of modern Finnish and European arts.
Time: Wed., 11am-6:30pm
Place: Tamminiementie 6

Parliament

The austere Eduskuntatalo (Parliament House) allows visitors to take guided tours and witness plenary sessions from the visitors' gallery. Visits with representatives can be arranged by phoning in advance.
Time: Tour: Mon.-Fri., 2pm; Sat., 11am
Place: Mannerheiminitie 30
Contact: ph. 440051

City Museum

Helsinki's City Museum has a collection of art, furnishings, photographs, and municipal archives—all illustrating the city's vigorous history.
Time: free on Thurs., noon-8pm
Place: Karamzininkatu 2

Free Concerts

Throughout the summer, free concerts are held daily at various locations around Helsinki. Some of the best free shows are held at the Esplanade Park bandstand near the harbor market each weekday afternoon. Jazz, rock, pop, and classical groups from

throughout Scandinavia perform. To find out the times and locations of the shows, pick up a free copy of *Helsinki This Week* at the tourist office.
Contact: Helsinki Tourist Office, Pohjoisesplanadi 19, ph. 174088 or 169-3757

Golden Domes
The golden-domed Russian Orthodox Uspensky Cathedral is an imposing presence above Helsinki's harbor district. Inside the cathedral you will find mosaics, gilded icons, and other religious art.
Time: daily, 10am-4pm
Place: Kanavakatu 1
Contact: ph. 634267

City Landmark
Dominating the Senate Square and harbor like an enormous wedding cake, the Tumiokirkko (Lutheran Cathedral) is Helsinki's most beloved landmark. Designed by Carl Engel in 1830, the cathedral's stark interior is a marked contrast to the rich Uspensky Cathedral nearby.
Time: daily, 9am-7pm
Place: Senate Square

National Museum
Folk costumes, coins, art, archeological finds, and historic exhibits are among the many displays in the Kansallismuseo (National Museum of Finland). A collection of Finno-Ugric artifacts and an ethnological section are particularly interesting and unusual.
Time: free on Tues., 11am-9pm
Place: Mannerheimintie 34
Contact: ph. 402-5229

Gibraltor of the North
Built in the 18th century to defend Helsinki Harbor, the Suomen-Linna Fortress, sometimes called the "Gibraltor of the North," is a short excursion from the city. You can explore the fortifications guarding the harbor, swim in the Baltic, picnic, sunbathe, and enjoy terrific views of Helsinki.
Place: Susisaari Island

Ateneum Art Museum
The most extensive collection of graphics, paintings, and sculpture in Finland is found at this gallery. The museum specializes in works by Finnish artists and European masters.
Time: free on Sat., 11am-5pm
Place: Kaivokatu 4

Botanical Gardens
The University of Helsinki Botanical Gardens were founded in 1833, with the greenhouses for tropical plants added in 1890. Along with the summer flowers, there are more than 1,200 species of plants in the gardens. Special tours can be arranged by phoning ahead.
Time: daily, 9am-sundown
Place: Unioninkatu 4
Contact: ph. 631150

Stunning Glass
In the land of outstanding glass and ceramic design, Arabia is one of the finest manufacturers of all. Anyone can visit the downtown showroom and shop, but tours of the factory and company museum must be arranged by appointment in advance.
Time: Shop: Mon.-Sat., 9am-5pm
Place: Shop: Pohjoiseplanadi 25; Factory: Hameentie 135
Contact: Shop: ph. 170055; Factory: ph. 177611

Walking Tours
Begin your visit to Helsinki by taking one of the tourist office's self-guided walking tours. These brochures provide excellent orientation to the city.
Time: Mon.-Fri., 8:30am-6pm; Sat., 8:30am-1pm
Place: Pohjoisesplanadi 19
Contact: ph. 169-3757

Rock Church
Chiseled out of a granite hillside, the Temppeliaukio Church (which looks like a flying saucer about to take off) is one of the most unusual

churches in Europe. Topped by a copper dome, the interior of red and grey granite is moving in its grace and symmetry.
Time: Mon.-Sat., 10am-9pm; Sun., 5pm-9pm
Place: Lutherinkatu 3
Contact: ph. 494698

Design Center
Admirers of Scandinavian design will want to visit the Finnish Design Center. The exhibition displays glassware, textiles, jewelry, rugs, and much more by Finland's leading artisans and designers.
Time: Mon.-Fri., 10am-5pm; Sat., 10am-3pm; Sun., noon-4pm
Place: Kasarmikatu 19B
Contact: ph. 626388

Senate Square
Helsinki's Senate Square is probably the finest grouping of neo-classical architecture in the world. The airy and harmonious plaza is surrounded by the Cathedral, the University, and the Government Palace. Film fans will recognize this 19th-century square immediately, since it has been the set for numerous movies that pretend to be in the Soviet Union.

Garden City
Tapiola, the Garden City, is a utopian community in the suburbs of Helsinki. Planned, designed, and funded by non-profit organizations during the early 1950's, Tapiola today is a self-contained community with all housing and city services within walking distance.
Contact: ph. 9-046-7652

Sibelius Memorial
Finland's composer Jean Sibelius is memorialized by a controversial monument. The massive grouping of steel tubular piping is most impressive at night when it is illuminated.
Place: Sibelius Park, Mechelininkatu

Joensuu
The cultural, commercial, and administrative capital of North Karelia, Joensuu is a busy city. Founded in 1848, this modern town is situated where the rushing Pielisjoki flows into Lake Pyhäselka.

Regional Culture
The Soviet annexation of much of this region prompted the establishment of the Karelian Culture House to preserve and promote the Karelian culture. The collection in this small museum on the island of Ilosaari includes local handicrafts, folk costumes, and art.
Time: Mon.-Sat., 10am-4pm
Place: Ilosaari Island
Contact: ph. 201318

Kajaani

In the forested country of the northern Lake District, Kajaani is an interesting old town with attractive 18th- and 19th-century buildings. Its main attraction for travelers is its proximity to the beautiful Kainuu countryside.

Swedish Castle
On the island of Linnasaari you will find the restored Kajanebogr Castle. Often the scene of Russian-Swedish conflicts, the castle was destroyed in the early 18th century and reconstructed in 1938.
Time: Mon.-Fri., 10am-5pm; Sat., 11am-4pm
Contact: ph. 25079

Kuopio

Kuopio is the capital of Savo Province and the former capital of old Karelia (now mostly in the Soviet Union, and not by choice). Built on a peninsula in Lake Kallavesi, Kuopio is a busy commercial town and family resort for summer and winter sports. Even though few of the city's early buildings remain, it's a neat, satisfying town and makes an excellent base for exploring the surrounding lakes and forests.

Icon Collection
Kuopio's Orthodox Church Museum houses a collection of Russian Orthodox icons, Bibles, vestments, and other religious artifacts.

This is one of the finest displays of Russian religious art outside of the Soviet Union.
Time: May-Sept.: Tues.-Sun., 10am-4pm
Place: Karjalankatu 1
Contact: ph. 121411

Mikkeli

Capital of the province of the same name, Mikkeli is an attractive old town at the edge of Lake Saimaa. Although the area has been inhabited for more than a thousand years, Mikkeli first acquired municipal status in the 18th century. Consequently, most of the town's buildings are relatively modern, with the exception of some fine old homes and the 14th-century Savilhiti Church.

Military Museums

The strategic location of Mikkeli made it the headquarters for Finland's national military hero Marshall Mannerheim. Today you can visit the headquaters and see a collection of historical memorabilia.
Time: Tues.-Sat., 11am-5pm
Place: Paamajankatu 7
Contact: ph. 13938

Naantali

Sleepyhead Day

Sleepyhead Day has been celebrated in Naantali for more than 100 years. The celebration involves awaking early in the morning and dressing in costume. One person is named "Sleepyhead of the Year" and tossed into the town harbor. Bearers of this honorable title have included the Mayor, a member of Parliament, and a Bishop.
Time: July 27, very early
Place: Boat Harbor
Contact: ph. 755388

Medieval Convent

The Convent Church of St. Birgitta has been restored to its 15th-

century appearance, although little remains of the Convent of Vallis Gratiae itself. On a hill above the harbor, the church possesses an interior with beautiful frescoes, carvings, and candelabra.
Time: June-Sept.: daily, noon-6pm; Oct.-May: Sun., noon-3pm
Place: Nunnakatu

Old Town
The old town quarter of Naantali should be considered a living museum. Growing up around the Convent walls, the houses and shops have remained on their original medieval sites. After the town was devastated by fire in the 17th century, new houses were built on the same sites. Today the town is a living example of medieval Finnish culture and history. All of the buildings in the old quarter are local monuments, and 20 are official national monuments.
Contact: Naantali Tourist Office, Tullikatu 12, ph. 755388

President's Villa
Kultaranta, the summer residence of Finland's president, is across the harbor from Naantali. The estate has lovely gardens where flowers and vegetables are cultivated to supply the president's household. The inner Medallion Park contains a rose garden and sculpture. Set on a rocky hill, the estate provides a priceless view of old Naantali and the Convent.
Time: May-Aug.: Fri., 6pm-8pm only
Place: Luonnonmaantie, on Luonnonmaa Island

Free Concerts
Each summer, free concerts are held in Kaivopuisto Park. Situated directly below the old Convent, the tranquil park with its quaint bandstand evokes a gentler time.
Time: Daily
Place: Maariankatu

Porvoo (Borga)
Crowded with colorful wooden houses, Porvoo is a splendid Baltic port town, just 30 miles east of Helsinki. Established in 1346 by a Swedish king, Porvoo today attracts many artists and writers with its Old World charm.

Historic Church

Rising above the twisting, narrow streets, Porvoo's 15th-century cathedral has a startling rococo interior. The bronze statue of Tsar Alexander commemorates the 1809 meeting of the Diet of Porvoo, which guaranteed the Finnish constitution.
Time: Tues.-Sat., 9:30am-5pm
Place: Rauhankatu 20
Contact: ph. 140145

Rovaniemi

Barely five miles from the Arctic Circle, Rovaniemi is the capital of Finnish Lapland and the gateway to the wild north. The city owes its contemporary design to architect Alvar Aalto, who created the unique layout of the post-war town. Situated at the confluence of the Kemijoki and Ounasjoki Rivers, Rovaniemi attracts a surprising number of travelers during the short summer season. Although there's a lot to do in this friendly town, it's primarily a base for Arctic adventurers.

Lapp Culture

In Lappia Hall there are extensive exhibits relating to all aspects of Lapp Culture. Within the same building you will find the Lappland Provincial Museum, Lapp Library, and concert hall.
Time: June-August: Mon.-Fri., 11am-7pm; Sat., 11am-4pm
Place: Hallituskatu 9
Contact: ph. 23821

Arctic Church

Built to replace the church destroyed by Nazis in 1944, this beautiful church is noted for its outstanding carvings. The Rovaniemi Seurakunta's real treasure is Lennart Segerstahl's alterpiece, *The Tree of Life*.
Time: daily, 9am-7pm
Place: Kirkkotie 1
Contact: ph. 16270

Savonlinna

Dating back to 1475 when its storybook Olavinlinna Castle was built, Savonlinna is the most attractive and interesting town of the Saimaa Lake District. The romantic old town quarter is set on an island in the shadow of the magnificent castle, while the city's modern districts spread along the shore of the lake. With excellent train and boat connections, Savonlinna makes an ideal base for exploring the Saimaa Lake District.

Cathedral Tours
The stately Lutheran Cathedral, set on the Savonniemi Peninsula, was restored after World War II. Throughout the summer, student guides provide tours of the imposing Cathedral, diplomatically skipping over the details of the deliberate bombing of the church.
Time: Mon.-Fri., 9:30am-3:30pm
Place: Kirkokatu

Summer Festival
Each July, the Savonlinna hums with festival activities. Most events occur in Olavinlinna Castle in the lake, but there are open-air concerts and dances all around town. Art exhibitions are also a prominent feature of the three-week festival.
Contact: Municipal Tourist Office, Olavinkatu 35, ph. 13458

Handicraft Market
Savonlinna's market attracts artisans from throughout the Saimaa Lake District and Karelia. You can find great bargains on Finnish handicrafts, jewelry, and ceramics.
Time: Mon.-Fri., 8am-1pm
Place: Boat Harbor

Tampere

Finland's second-largest city is located on a long stretch of rapids between Lake Nasijarvi and Lake Pyhäjärvi. Tampere, the nation's leading industrial city, is modern and attractive, with a number of museums and cultural events.

Lenin Museum

Historically-minded tourists will want to visit Tampere's Trade Union House, a cultural and political center with a collection of Lenin memorabilia.
Time: Tues.-Sat., 11am-5pm
Place: Hallituskatu 19
Contact: ph. 27313

Free Concerts

All summer, free concerts and folk-dancing exhibitions are staged in Tampere's parks. Most parks either front the foaming river or one of the surrounding lakes. Check with the tourist office for times and locations of events.
Contact: Municipal Tourist Information, Aleksis Kivenkatu 14B, ph. 26652 or 26775

Tornio

White-Water Festival

European white-water enthusiasts converge on Tornio each July for the White-Water and Whitefish Festival. Even the losers can enjoy the good eating. The contest takes place a few miles north of the city at the Kukkolankoski rapids.
Time: last Sunday in July
Contact: Municipal Tourist Office, Valikatu 3, ph. 40623, or Regional Tourist Office, Laivurinkatu 2, ph. 40048

Turku (Abo)

Founded in the 13th century, Turku is Finland's oldest city, third-largest metropolis, and former capital. Lying at the mouth of the River Aura on the Gulf of Bothnia, Turku is closer geographically and culturally to Sweden than other Finnish cities. The old seaport is protected by the massive Turku Castle, once called the "Key to Finland." After the devastating fire of 1827, much of the city was redesigned with avenues of tall buildings and spacious parks. But the liveliest part of town is still the ancient market place, bustling with activity from dawn till late at night.

Windjammers

Two venerable sailing vessels are moored on the River Aura at St. Martin's Bridge in downtown Turku. The *Suomen Joutsen* is a training ship for the Finnish Navy; the windjammer *Sigyn*, recently restored, is open to the public during the summer.
Time: June-Aug., 11am-3pm
Place: Ostra Strandgatan
Contact: ph. 303563

Dazzling Church

Turku's Russian Orthodox Church, built by Carl Engel in 1840, is a treasury of Eastern religious art. Don't miss the gem-studded, gilded icons.
Time: Mon.-Fri., 9am-6pm; Sat., 10am-3pm
Place: Kauppatori
Contact: ph. 15262

Forest Park

Turku's Ruissalo Park has something for everyone. Located on an island on the city outskirts, the park has sandy beaches, the largest oak forest in Finland, hiking and riding paths, golf, boating, gardens, and swimming pools.
Contact: Tourist Assoc. of SW Finland, Lantinen Rantakatu 13, ph. 11333

Ancient Cathedral

Turku's Tuomikirkoo (St. Henrik's) looms above the River Aura on Unikankari Hill. Constructed in the early 13th century, this edifice is in late Romanesque style, with Gothic and Renaissance additions. The interior contains many tombs of famous Swedes and Finns, plus the sarcophogus of Queen Karinna Mänsdotter.
Time: May-Sept.: Mon.-Fri., 9am-7pm; Sat., 10am-3pm; Sun., 2pm-4pm. Oct.-April: Mon.-Fri., 10am-4pm; Sat., 10am-3pm; Sun. 1pm-4pm
Place: Cathedral Square
Contact: ph. 336366

Nationwide

Midsummer Festival

On the last Friday in June, Finland celebrates the longest day of the year with singing, dancing, parades, and bonfires. The bonfires become open-air theaters, as plays and recitals are performed around them. Midsummer's Eve is also a choice time for weddings all over the country.

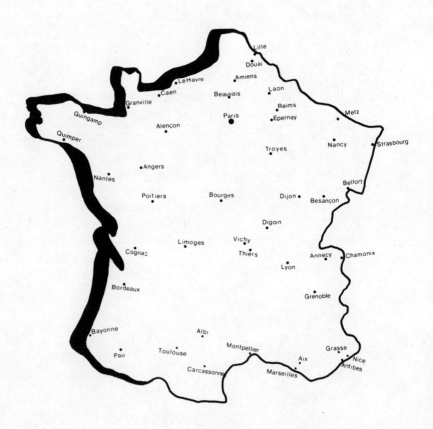

Lille
Douai
Le Havre
Amiens
Laon
Caen
Beauvais
Granville
Reims
Guingamp
Paris
Epernay
Metz
Quimper
Alençon
Nancy
Strasbourg
Troyes
Angers
Nantes
Belfort
Poitiers
Bourges
Dijon
Besançon
Digoin
Cognac
Limoges
Vichy
Thiers
Annecy
Chamonix
Lyon
Bordeaux
Grenoble
Bayonne
Albi
Pau
Toulouse
Montpellier
Grasse
Carcassonne
Aix
Nice
Marseilles
Antibes

France

France

Aix-en-Provence

This ancient capital, nestled below Monte Sainte-Victoire, embodies the finest aspects of Provencal civilization. Patrician mansions, tranquil squares, and elegant fountains preserve the past grandeur. Aix's main boulevard, the Cours Mirabeau, is one of the world's great avenues. Behind the Baroque townhouses which flank the boulevard, you'll find narrow lanes that open unexpectedly onto enticing plazas.

Founded by the Roman general Sextius 2,100 years ago, Aix reached its true glory in the 17th and 18th centuries. Its famous university has attracted scholars since 1409. Each July and August, the city hosts a music and arts festival, drawing artists and visitors from around the world.

Remarkable Library
On the first floor of the Hotel de Ville is the Bibliotheque Mejanes, with 300,000 volumes and rare illuminated manuscripts. The town hall also hosts exhibits of contemporary art in the library.
Time: Tues.-Sat., 10am-noon & 2pm-6pm
Place: Place de Hotel de Ville
Contact: ph. 261293

Eclectic Architecture
The Cathedral of St. Sauveur has architecture and ornamentation

from the 5th to 17th centuries. The interior houses tapestries and the fantastic triptych, *The Burning Bush*, by Nicholas Froment.
Time: Mon.-Sat., 9am-6pm
Place: Place de L'Universite
Contact: ph. 260293

Albi

Albi is known as *la ville rouge*—the red city—because of its colorful brickwork and roofing. Every shade of red is represented in Albi's architecture. Albi's brick cathedral, Renaissance gardens, and noble squares create a town of harmony and majesty.

Film Festival
Each summer Albi hosts a week-long International Amateur Film Festival. The tourist office provides free tickets to all of the screenings.
Time: first week of August
Contact: Syndicat d'Initiative, Place Ste. Cecile 19, ph. 542230

Alencon

Aristocratic and amiable, this one-time ducal city retains its reputation as the "lace capital of Normandy." Long famous for its exquisite point lace, Alencon is the administrative center of the Sarthe Valley. The heart of old Alencon is a treasure of Gothic churches and ornate townhouses. In the 18th-century, Madame Perriere, a local lace-maker, developed an unusual hexagonal pattern, scattered with tiny florets and blossoms. Her innovation is still evident in bonnets worn by women on festival days.

Lace-Making
Alencon maintains a lace-making school—Ecole Dentelliere—and a lace museum. The 15th-century Maison d'Oze houses both the tourist office and the lace museum.
Time: Tues.-Fri., 10am-noon
Place: Museum: Place Lamagdaleine; Ecole Dentelliere: Rue du Pont Neuf
Contact: ph. 261136

Amiens

Perched on the banks of the Somme, Amiens has been wealthy since the Middle Ages, thanks to the textile trade and its famous velvets. The modern Tour Perret and the tower of the 13th-century cathedral of Notre Dame vie for dominance on town's skyline. North of the cathedral, a section, reminiscent of Venice, is criss-crossed with romantic canals.

Sublime Gothic

With its slender spire and 126 pillars, the Notre Dame Cathedral of Amiens is one of the world's paramount Gothic structures. The main facade has three doorways decorated with statues and bas-relief sculptures of Old Testament figures. The interior has magnificent iron grill work and carved choir stalls. The largest cathedral in France, Notre Dame was the model for the Cologne Cathedral.
Time: daily, 7:30am-7pm
Place: Place Parmentier & Place Notre Dame
Contact: ph. 917928

Angers

With its teal rooftops, wide boulevards, and charming gardens, Angers is a beautiful city. Protected by a massive feudal chateau, the old district is a delight to explore on foot. The region around Anger offers perfect conditions for fruit and wine production, making the town the market for Anjou wines and produce.

Wine Tastings

Wine lovers won't want to miss the opportunity to sample the famous rose d'Anjou and with other fine wines at the Maison du Vin de L'Anjou. Tradition has it that the wines of Anjou are favored by royalty, from the Plantagenets to the Kings of England.
Time: Wed.-Sun., 10am-1pm & 2pm-6pm
Place: Place Kennedy 5
Contact: ph. 886389

Vineyard Visits

The association of growers in the region provides the addresses of vineyards and wine cellars that welcome visitors. Many growers are happy to have you tour their facilities and sample the product. Contact: Conseil Interprofessional des Vins d'Anjou, Blvd. Foch 21, ph. 876257

Liqueur Tour
The makers of Cointreau receive guests at their facilities in the suburbs of Angers. Twice daily they provide tours of the plant and offer free refreshment.
Time: Mon.-Fri., 10am & 2pm
Place: Carrefour Moliere, St.-Barthelemy-d'Anjou
Contact: ph. 432521

Annecy

Set against an alpine backdrop on the edge of Lake Annecy, this popular resort town traces its roots to prehistoric times. The town center is a pedestrian district with arcades, romantic passageways, and colorful shops. Annecy has a busy tourist trade year-round.

Summer Festival
Each July, Annecy holds a week-long Festival de la Vielle Ville. The free activities include concerts, films, parades, fireworks, and outdoor plays.
Time: mid-July
Contact: Tourist Office, Rue Jaures 1, ph. 450033

Ancient Castle
On an island in the swirling waters of the River Thiou, the 12th-century Palais de l'Ile provides unbeatable views of the Alps and Annecy's flower-filled streets. This former prison also hosts shows and exhibits.
Contact: Tourist Office for *Le Mois a Annecy*, a free listing of local events of all types.

Antibes

Originally a Greek trading settlement, Antibes is a vibrant Mediterranean resort town and a major center for the commercial production of flowers. Facing Nice across an azure bay, it's a city of ancient seaside ramparts, great art, and aquatic sports.

Picasso
The Picasso Museum is housed in the Chateau Grimaldi and perched on a cliff overlooking the Mediterranean. The master lived in the villa for many years and produced an amazing volume of work here. Ceramics, lithographs, drawings, and engravings—inspired chiefly by the Mediterranean environment—comprise the display.
Time: free on Wed., 10am-noon & 3pm-6pm
Place: Place du Chateau
Contact: ph. 339564

Baccarat
A small town on the edge of the Vosges Mountains, Baccarat owes its renown to the illustrious glassworks established there in 1764.

Crystalworks
Lovers of fine crystal will want to visit the home of France's leading maker of crystal, Cie des Cristalleries de Baccarat. Tours of the facility are limited, so call first for an appointment.
Time: Mon.-Fri., 10am-4:30pm
Place: rue des Cristalleries
Contact: ph. 375-1247

Banyuls-sur-Mer
Encircled by rugged, vine-clad hills, Banyuls-sur-Mer is known as a sunny resort spot and for its delectable wines. Set on a bay near the southern end of the Côte Vermeille, Banyuls is a picturesque seaside village with all the amenities of larger Mediterranean resorts.

Wine Cellar
The Languedoc-Roussillon region produces nearly 60% of France's wine. The wines are as different as the varied landscapes—whites from Narbonne, reds from Corbieres, blanquette from Limoux, and sweet apertifs from Banyuls. You can visit the cellars of Banyuls'

Cooperative l'Etoile and taste the local product after touring the facilities.
Time: daily, 9am-noon & 2pm-5:30pm
Place: Ave Puig-del-Mas
Contact: ph. 880010

Bayonne

Cut in thirds by its waterways, Bayonne is the bustling, animated center of le Pays Basque. Grand Bayonne quarter, with the 13th-century Ste.-Marie Cathedral and the old chateau, features a pedestrian precinct, while Petite Bayonne across the Nive has the grandiose Chateau Neuf and the city's excellent museums.

Basque Festival

The Bayonne Country Folk Festival, held early each August and running for a week, provides an excellent introduction to Basque traditions. Besides the continuous feasting on local specialties, there are bullfights, concerts, fireworks, and parades.
Time: first week of August
Contact: Syndicat d'Initiative, Place de la Liberté, ph. 593131

Port Tour

Bayonne's position at the confluence of the Adour and Nive Rivers has helped make the town a major port since the 12th century. The people at the port installation office are happy to give tours to visitors.
Time: Mon.-Fri., 10am-noon & 2pm-4pm
Place: Allees Marines
Contact: ph. 558408

Cordial Visits

If the local liqueurs strike your fancy, stop by at the Izarra Distillery for a free tasting and a short tour of the facilities.
Time: Tues.-Sat., 2pm-5pm
Place: Admiral Bergeret Quay 9
Contact: ph. 550945

Beaune

Beaune, in the heart of Burgundy, is one of France's most charming cities. With a host of architectural and historic treasures, Beaune is famous for the colorful Hôtel Dieu, Romanesque churches, fine townhouses, and the regal Hôtel des Ducs. And in this center of the Côte d'Or wine region, you're never far from a glass of France's best wine.

Flemish Tapestries
The Collegiate Church of Notre Dame houses 15th-century silk and wool tapestries from Flanders. Titled *The Life of the Virgin*, the tapestries are exhibited behind the altar. The church also has some beautiful old frescoes.
Time: Mon.-Sat., 8am-5pm
Place: Place Monge

Wine Show
While many of Beaune's wine cellars provide free wine tastings, the Maison Calvet has an audio-visual show. The presentation explains the production process and is followed by a tour of the facilities.
Time: Tues.-Sat., 10am-noon & 2pm-5pm
Place: Blvd. Perpreuil 6
Contact: ph. 222605

Besancon

The old town of Besancon, situated in a bend of the River Doubs, is full of character. Tracing its history from a Roman settlement, this cultural center preserves its history in fine architecture and museums. There are unforgettable views from the ramparts of the old citadel.

Botanical Gardens
This hillside city has had a botanical garden since 1575. Today, the

gardens include an arboretum, greenhouses, an amusing rookery, and even an artificial peat bog.
Time: Mon.-Fri., 8:30am-4:30pm; Sat., 8:30am-noon
Place: Place Marechal Leclerc
Contact: ph. 809255

Fantastic Clock
The Cathedral St. Jean houses a wonderful astronomical clock with 30,000 moving parts, 70 dials, and dozens of fanciful characters. The clock's mechanical parade six times a day is a show you won't want to miss.
Time: daily at 9:50am, 10:50am, 11:50am, 2:50pm, 3:50pm, and 4:50pm
Place: Porte Noire

Bordeaux

Thanks to planning by 18th-century administrators, Bordeaux's town center remains a handsome architectural whole. In the 1700's, Bordeaux was transformed into a city of boulevards, plazas, and gardens. The town is the center of the Bordelais, the world's largest area of vineyards, which produce over 500 million bottles of wine each year.

French Art
The Musée des Beaux-Arts contains a collection of French art from the 15th century to the present. Highlights of the gallery are works by Renoir, Matisse, Delacroix, and Degas.
Time: free on Wed. & Sun., 10am-noon & 2pm-6pm
Place: rue Montbazon
Contact: ph. 442841

Wine Museum and Tastings
The Bordeaux region is the world's leading producer of wine. At the Hotel des Vin, you can learn all about the production process and the history of the vineyards, plus you can buy and sample some of the seven local wines.
Time: Mon.-Sat., 10am-5pm
Place: rue Abbe-de-l'Epee 106
Contact: ph. 480129

Bourges

Saint Etienne Cathedral stands watch over old Bourges. The city's medieval grandeur is expressed in the homes and public buildings of the old quarter. Bourges was occupied by Julius Caesar in 52 BC and served as capital of France from 1422 to 1427. The university, founded by Louis XI in 1463, is John Calvin's alma mater.

Spring Festival
Bourge's Festival Printemps is primarily a series of concerts held throughout town. Many of the jazz, rock, and pop shows are free and very good. Contact the Culture House for ticket information and schedules.
Time: first week in April
Contact: Maison de la Culture, Place Seraucourt, ph. 201384

Supreme Gothic
The 13th-century Cathedral St. Etienne, a superb example of French Gothic architecture, is famous for its doorways, tapestries, and stained glass windows. The crypt, France's largest, houses the tomb of Jean, Duke of Berry.
Time: daily, 8am-7pm
Place: Rue du Guichet
Contact: ph. 247533

Caen

Caen, capital of Basse-Normandie, grew from a small island village at the confluence of the rivers Orne and Odon. As a favored town of William the Conqueror, the city prospered, attracting abbeys, chateaux, and a university. Although much of the town was devastated in 1944, most of the great churches survived unscathed. Caen today is a thriving city with modern districts and medieval treasures.

University Gardens
Founded in 1689, Caen's Jardin des Plantes serves as a city park and a botanical garden of Caen University. It contains alpine plants,

rare trees, greenhouses, and an herb garden.
Time: Garden: daily, 8am-7pm; Greenhouses: Wed., Sat., & Sun.,
8am-7pm
Place: Place Blot 5
Contact: ph. 862765

Ancient Citadel
There are excellent views of Caen from the Castle of William the
Conquerer, built in 1060. The Citadel, restored extensively since
World War II, has beautiful promenades, gardens, museums, and
a chapel.
Time: daily, 7:30am-7pm
Place: Porte sur la Ville

Camaret

Megaliths
Outside of the port of Camaret-sur-Mer, there is a grouping of 150
megaliths at Lagatjar. The intersecting lines of standing stones were
built between 5000 and 2000 BC. Because the stones align with
the sunrise and sunset at the solstices, scientists believe the stones
were the work of sun-worshippers.
Contact: Syndicat d'Initiative, Place Kleber, ph. 279360

Carcassonne

Medieval Town
The walled town of Carcassonne is one of Europe's best-restored
fortress towns. Dating back to Roman times, the old Cité is surrounded by a double ellispe of walls and watch towers. Within the
ramparts are a castle and winding lanes with ancient houses.
Contact: Syndicat d'Initiative, Blvd. Camille-Pelletan, ph. 254132

Fireworks Display
There is a magnificent pyrotechnical exhibition each Bastile Day
in Carcassonne. The old city makes a lovely setting for the display.
Time: July 14th

Carnac

Mysterious Megaliths
The area around Carnac is crowded with thousands of megaliths and dolmen dating from the Neolithic and early Bronze Age periods.
Contact: Syndicat d'Initiative, Ave des Druides 74, ph. 521352

Chamonix

Mountain Walks
Chamonix, renowned for its skiing, hiking, and superb scenery, has over 200 miles of mountain paths around the town that have been posted for walks and hikes.
Contact: Office of Tourism, Place de l'Eglise, ph. 530024

Chartres

Crowded with old gabled houses, the medieval upper town clusters around the Chartres Cathedral. The lower town, with its old bridges across the River Eure, provides great views of the cathedral.

Chartres and Its Cathedral
The soaring Cathedral at Chartres is a masterpiece of Gothic architecture. The building, the sculpture, and the stained glass combine to make an attraction of grandeur and beauty.
Time: daily, 7am-7pm
Place: Place de la Cathedral
Contact: ph. 215403

Cognac

Cognac was once a sleepy port on the Charente. But when brandy was invented in the 17th century, the town was changed by English and Dutch wine merchants who cornered the new market. Over the years, the houses of the old quarter have become blackened by a veneer of fungus, caused by the fumes from brandy production.

Cognac Tour

Begin your visit to Cognac with a tour of the cellars of the producers of France's favorite *eau-de-vie*. Each year the region produces nearly 250,000 bottles of the liqueur. The tourist office can
provide a complete list of facilities open for tours and tastings. Most
cellars are open for visits Monday through Friday from 9am-4:30pm.
Contact: Syndicat d'Initiative, Place Monnet, ph. 821071

Dijon

Dijon owes its grandeur to the Dukes of Burgundy, who turned
this capital into a center of art and regal pomp 500 years ago. Today, Dijon blends medieval charm and modern planning into a
pleasant whole. Many of the old streets have been converted into
pedestrian districts, perfect for aimless wandering.

Botanical Garden

Established in 1770, the Arquebus Botanical Garden contains one
of France's oldest arboretums, with many exotic trees from Asia.
Time: daily, 7am-5pm
Place: Ave. Albert I

Fine Arts

Dijon's Musée des Beaux-Arts has one of France's wealthiest fine
arts collections, with works by Reubens, Titian, Monet, and Cor-
ot. On the ground floor, a sculpture hall has works by Rude and
Pompon.
Time: free on Sun., 9am-noon & 2pm-6pm
Place: Place de la Liberation
Contact: ph. 431212

Period Mansion

The Magnin Museum is furnished in elegant period decor, much
of it original. The real prize of the collection is a masterpiece by
Hieronymous Bosch entitled *Christ Crowned with Thorns*.
Time: free on Sun., 9am-noon & 2pm-5:30pm
Place: rue des Bon-Enfants 4
Contact: ph. 321854

Douai

Douai is the capital of France's coal country, as well as home to the former Flanders Parliament. Not part of France until 1713, Douai has many old Flemish homes and public buildings. The Maison du Dauphin, with its wrought iron balcony, is particularly attractive.

Big Bells

With 62 bells, Douai's Hotel de Ville has the largest carillon in Europe. Carillon concerts are held each weekend and on national holidays.
Place: Place d'Armes & rue de la Marie

Folk Festival

Every July since 1530, the people of Douai have feted the folk giant Gayant and his family with bands, dancing, and wicker giants paraded through the streets. During the two-week Fete de Gayant, the carillon plays each evening.
Time: first two weeks of July
Contact: Tourist Office, Hotel de Ville, rue de la Marie, ph. 872663

Epernay

Champagne Tours

Epernay is in the heart of champagne country, and many champagne cellars have headquarters there. Moët et Chandon hosts an excellent tour, ending with a free sample.
Time: Mon.-Fri., 9:30am-12:30pm & 2pm-5:30pm; Sat. 9:30am-noon
Place: Caves Dom Perignon, Ave. de Champagne 18
Contact: ph. 517111

Gerardmer

Forest Walks

Surrounded by lakes and mountains, Gerardmer is the center for 200 miles of marked trails through the Vosges Mountains and Alsace. The tourist office provides information on dozens of hikes.
Contact: Place des Deportes, ph. 630874

Granville

A popular seaside resort since the early 19th century, this old pirate haven perches on a rocky promontory above the Atlantic. The upper town has preserved its old military installations, including the 15th-century Grande Porte drawbridge. The lower town presents a 19th-century face in its narrow lanes and pleasant cafes.

Dior's Garden
This beautiful public garden once belonged to the family of Christian-Dior. A rugged path with gorgeous views takes you from the upper terrace of the garden to the beach at Donville.
Time: daily, 8am-sunset
Place: rue d'Estouteville

Grasse

Perfume Tours
For years, Grasse has been the hub of France's perfume industry. Many of the perfumeries are open for tours. Molinard at Boulevard Victor Hugo, Fragonard at Boulevard Fragonard, and Galinard on Route de Cannes are three of the companies that welcome visits. For others, check the local tourist office.
Contact: Office de Tourisme, Place Foux, ph. 360356

Grenoble

Grenoble, a growing industrial center, manages to balance modern districts with a historic old quarter. A lively pedestrian zone at the heart of the city incorporates Gothic churches and Renaissance townhouses. With one of France's largest universities and a big tourist trade, Grenoble is a robust city year-round.

Outstanding Collection
Grenoble's Museum of Painting and Sculpture has one of the finest art collections in France. Besides the old masters—Goya, Durer,

Tintoretto—the collection of modern art is remarkable. Don't miss the gallery of contemporary sculpture.
Time: Wed.-Mon., 1pm-7pm
Place: Place de Verdun
Contact: ph. 543436

Mountain Views
There are magnificent views of Grenoble and the surrounding mountains from the Fort de la Bastille on Mount Rachais. A series of marked paths pass through caves, tunnels, and over bridges.
Contact: Office de Tourism, rue de la Republic

Folk Museum
Housed in a 17th-century convent, the Dauphinois Museum provides an overview of the folk traditions of the region.
Time: Wed.-Mon., 10am-noon & 2pm-6pm
Place: rue Maurice Gignoux

Haras du Pin

Chateau Farm
The 18th-century Chateau Colbert is a horse-breeding center with history and charm. The Le Pin Stud farm breeds English thoroughbreds, Arabians, French trotters, Percherons, and Norman cobs. Visitors are welcome to the daily workouts and the harness demonstrations every Thursday from April 15th to October 15th.
Time: Mon.-Sat., 9am-noon & 2pm-6pm
Place: Colbert Court
Contact: ph. 671248

Le Havre

France's second-largest port suffered 146 World War II air-raids and had to be rebuilt completely. Very few old monuments remain. Still, Le Havre is worth a visit for the tourist interested in modern architecture and urban planning.

Monumental Church
The modern Church of St. Joseph was designed by Auguste Per-

ret, the pioneer of reinforced concrete architecture. A bell tower tops the stark chapel, and a stunning wall of stained glass overlooks the harbor.
Time: daily, 9am-noon & 2pm-7pm
Place: rue Morlent

Power Station

You can tour Le Havre's power station, one of Europe's largest and most powerful, with a capacity over 1.5 million kilowatts. The tours are quite interesting, but note that most tours are in French only.
Time: Mon.-Fri., 10am-noon & 2pm-5pm
Place: Bassin Theophile-Ducrocq
Contact: ph. 212288

Jarnac

Cognac Cellars

Jarnac is the home of the cognac producer, Couvoisier. The liqueur is aged in the cellars of the distiller, where your tour takes you prior to a free tasting.
Time: Mon.-Sat., 10am-noon & 2pm-4pm
Place: Place du Chateau
Contact: ph. 810411

Laon

Laon is an amalgam of ancient and modern France. The *haute ville* (upper town), a network of medieval lanes bordered by old houses and encircled by time-worn ramparts, is connected to the *basse ville* (lower town) by France's most advanced public transportation system, the POMA-2000.

Early Gothic

Towering over the plain of Champagne, the Cathedral of Notre Dame is one of Europe's finest Gothic churches. The interior is noted for its stained glass, especially the two rose windows, and its rich treasury. The Cathedral introduced many architectural

novelties which were used on later buildings, such as Rheims Cathedral and Notre Dame de Paris.
Time: daily, 8am-5pm
Place: Place du Parvis
Contact: ph. 234587

Limoges

Often overlooked by travelers, Limoges has Gallo-Roman antiquities, the ancient la Boucherie quarter, and fine museums. Although primarily associated with porcelain, Limoges was known first for the exquisite enamels made there since the 12th century.

Famous Porcelain
To learn about the production process of world-famous Limoges porcelain, contact the tourist office for information on tours of the porcelain workshops.
Time: Tours: Mon.-Fri., 9am-noon & 2pm-5pm
Contact: Syndicat d'Initiative, Blvd. de Fleurus, ph. 344687

Enamel Workshop
Tradition says that residents of Limoges have been producing enamel-work since the 7th century. You can see the two processes, *cloisonné* and *champlevé*, demonstrated at the Limoges Enamel workshop on the rue des Tanneries.
Time: Mon.-Sat., 10am-noon & 2pm-4pm
Place: rue des Tanneries 31
Contact: ph. 327056

Cathedral Gardens
The botanical garden and park is behind St. Etienne Cathedral. The gardens, with over 1,500 varieties of plants, surround the Municipal Museum of Limoges, which has a collection of enamels that dates back to the early 12th century.
Time: daily, 8am-sunset
Place: rue de la Cathedral

Locronan

This town clusters around its well-preserved Grand Place. Once a Breton textile center, Locronan prospers today from tourists drawn by its rare architectural unity. The Renaissance homes and businesses around the town square are adorned with elegant dormer windows and carved doorways.

Artisan Workshops

Locronan has an excellent exhibition hall with a variety of Breton crafts. There are frequent demonstrations of weaving and displays of pottery, leatherwork, silk, and textiles.
Time: Mon.-Sat., 9:30pm-noon & 1:45pm-5pm
Place: Maison des Artisans, Place de l'Eglise, ph. 917014

Lyon

Lyon is one of Europe's least-known great cities. France's third-largest metropolis stretches for miles along the parallel banks of the rivers Rhône and Saône Lyon's modern districts rub shoulders with restored Renaissance and medieval quarters.

By the 16th century, Lyon was wealthier and more populous than Paris. It flourished until the French Revolution, when mobs destroyed large areas of the town and killed over 5,000 citizens. Today, Lyon's only mobs come in the form of tourists—over five million a year.

Beaux-Arts

The St. Pierre Palace is home of one of France's finest museums, the Musée des Beaux-Arts. The collection includes Rembrandt, El Greco, Picasso, Monet, Renoir, Van Gogh, Matisse, and Degas, plus a sculpture gallery with works by Rodin.
Time: Wed.-Mon., 10am-noon & 2pm-6pm
Place: Place des Terreaux
Contact: ph. 8422575

Riverside Park

Lyon's Parc de la Tete d'Or contains many fun attractions. The park has lakes, a zoo, a botanical garden, mini-golf, and a rose garden

with hundreds of varieties.
Time: daily, 6am-11pm (summer); 6am-8pm (winter)
Place: Boulevard des Belges

Marseilles

Modern Marseilles is flanked by the ancient remains left by Phoenician mariners of 3,000 years ago, and France's second-largest city
bustles with commotion and color. Always looking seaward,
Marseilles was long ruled by local aristocrats and bishops. Half its
population died in the Great Plague, and the town was demolished
in World War II.

Today, Marseilles stretches along the limestone cliffs that hug the
Mediterranean shoreline. The heart of city life is the Vieux Port,
an inlet used as a harbor since Phoenician times. Radiating from
the old port, the Canebiere is lined with bistros, shops, and hotels,
a great place for evening strolls and people-watching.

Marine Museum
Ship lovers shouldn't miss the Musée Marine, with models and
displays illustrating the history of Marseilles through its maritime
associations.
Time: Mon.-Sat., 10am-noon & 2:30pm-7pm
Place: rue Paradis

Fine Arts
The Musée des Beaux-Arts has a collection of paintings from the
15th to the 20th centuries, with works by Reubens, David, Corot,
and Watteau. On the first floor, France's first children's museum
introduces children to pictorial art.
Time: free on Sun., 10am-noon
Place: Boulevard Longchamp
Contact: ph. 622117

Cité Radieuse
The Cité Radieuse, designed by Le Corbusier, is an avant-garde
housing complex. Built in the early 1950's, it remains a landmark
in modern architecture.
Place: Boulevard Michelet 280

Provencal Art
The Cantini Museum is housed in an elegant 17th-century mansion. The focus of the collection is 17th- and 18th-century Provencal ceramics, displayed amidst period furnishings.
Time: free on Sun., 10am-noon & 2:30pm-6:30pm
Place: rue Grignan 17

Metz

Originally the Roman town of Metis, Metz became part of France in 1552. Its vulnerable position near the German border has ensured a history of war and political dislocation. Though Metz suffered during both World Wars, it remains a lively city with a picturesque old town and ancient monuments.

Stunning Glass
The Cathedral of St. Etienne contains a treasure of stained glass. The ancient windows are supplemented by marvelous 20th-century panels by the genius Marc Chagall. Be sure to visit the museum of religious statuary in the Cathedral's crypt.
Time: daily, 9am-6pm
Place: Place d'Armes
Contact: ph. 775-6521

Montbeliard

Auto Factory
Until the 19th century, Montbeliard was an independent principality, but today this small city near the Swiss border is an industrial center. You can tour the Peugeot auto plant on the edge of town and see their 19th-century steel foundry.
Time: Mon.-Fri., 8:30am-noon
Place: rue Bonal

Montpellier

Known for its sunny climate, fine wines, and university, Montpellier began as a trading post on the spice route from the Middle East. This city owes its handsome countenance to development during the 17th and 18th centuries and much of its fame to its university. Distinguished scholars have been educated at Montpellier since medical schools were first established there in the 11th century. Today, Montpellier rivals Paris in the prestige of its medical college.

Ancient Gardens

Montpellier's Jardin des Plantes is France's oldest university botanical garden, founded in 1593 by Henri IV. The glasshouses contain a stunning collection of orchids.
Time: daily, 8am-noon & 2pm-6pm
Place: rue Auguste Broussonnet

Regional Art

Occupying an 18th-century Jesuit school, the Fabre Musée has a fine collection of regional paintings and drawings.
Time: Tue.-Sun., 9am-noon & 2pm-5pm
Place: Blvd. Montpellieret & Blvd. Sarrail
Contact: ph. 929003

Old Town Walk

Throughout Montpellier's Vieux Ville are many lovely Italianate townhouses. These *hotel particulier*, with ornate balconies, central courtyards, and grand staircases, are often concealed behind plain exteriors. To find these gems you'll need the walking tour plan from the tourist office.
Contact: Tourist Office, rue Maguelone 6, ph. 582604

Baroque Art

The restored Abbey of St. Benoit houses the Musée Atger, with its small, yet substantial, assemblage of Baroque and Renaissance drawings and sketches.
Time: Mon.-Fri., 10am-noon & 2pm-7pm
Place: rue del'Ecole de Medecine

Mortain

Waterfall

In a rocky ravine behind the 12th-century Abbey Blanche, the Grand Cascade tumbles through the woodland. The local tourist office can provide directions for the Grand Cascade, the Petite

Cascade, a natural ampitheater, and many other lovely sites in the
Cance Valley.
Contact: Tourist Office, rue du Bourg-Lopin 1, ph. 590051

Nancy

Royal Park
The Parc de la Pepiniere was created for Louis XIV and transformed
into a public park in the 19th century. The enchanting park contains a floral clock, fountains, and a rose garden. Each summer there
are free outdoor concerts; check with the tourist office.
Time: daily, 5am-11pm (summer); 6am-9pm (winter)
Place: Place De Gaulle

Crystal Works
Nancy's premiere manufacturer of fine crystal, Daum Cristalleries,
welcomes guests to their facilities for a short tour. Sorry, no free
samples.
Time: Mon.-Fri., 9:30am-noon
Place: rue des Cristalliers
Contact: ph. 335-2241

Nantes

Ancient Nantes, Brittany's largest city, is a town of art and culture,
an industrial center, and a busy port. During the early Middle Ages,
Nantes came under attack from Vikings and the British, but by the
16th century, the city's position on the Loire led to a rich shipping
trade. Today, Nantes is a city of fine boulevards, quaint medieval
quarters, and delightful mansions.

Ducal Palace
The massive Chateau Ducal fortress of Nantes, with its pinnacled
gables, round towers, and surrounding moat, dates from the
mid-15th century. Today, the Ducal Palace houses three entertaining museums. The Musée des Salorges is a maritime museum with
a collection of ancient navigational instruments, models of old sailing vessels, and documents relating to nautical history. In the Gover-
nors Palace, the Musée des Arts Populaire provides an excellent

introduction to Breton culture. The Musée Tour de Fer-a-Cheval exhibits contemporary regional arts.
Time: free on Sun., 10am-6pm
Place: Place de la Duchese-Anne
Contact: ph. 47051

Classy Mall
The Passage Pommeraye is an ornate shopping arcade. Built in 1843, this intriguing gallery is decorated with colorful plasterwork, classical statuary, and charming balconies.
Time: daily, 9am-10pm
Place: rue de la Fosse

Nemours

Forest Rambles
Nemours, just south of Paris in the Forest Fountainbleau, has a network of walking paths. The rambles through the tranquil forest lead to many deserted ruins and picturesque natural sites.
Contact: Syndicat d'Initiative, rue de Tanneurs 17, ph. 428-0395

Nevers

Bernadette of Lourdres
The Convent of St. Gildard, where Bernadette of Lourdres secluded herself as a nun, contains the saint's embalmed body in a glass casket, which makes for a rather grisly tourist attraction.
Time: Mon.-Sat., 9am-5pm
Place: rue de Lourdres
Contact: ph. 590703

Nice

Named in honor of the goddess Nike, Nice grew under Roman rule as a military port and administrative center. As a possession of the House of Savoy, Nice did not become French until 1860. The mild Riviera weather drew the English to winter here by the Bay of Angels in the 18th century. The main attractions are still a superb Mediterranean locale, beautiful gardens, and the old city of winding streets and fine esplanades.

Marvelous Matisse

The Musée Matisse's collection of paintings, sculpture, drawings, and tapestry spans the artist's entire career. The engrossing exhibit also includes Matisse's personal art collection, home furnishings, and memorabilia.
Time: Tues.-Sat., 10am-noon & 2:30pm-6:30pm
Place: Ave. des Arenas-de-Cimiez

Massena Museum

The Museum of Prince Victor Massena, housed in a 19th-century villa, contains a collection of Provencal art, Nicois folk art, antique jewelry, and religious objects from the region.
Time: Tues.-Sun., 10am-noon & 2pm-5pm
Place: Promenades des Anglais 35
Contact: ph. 870707

Chagall Treasure

Hidden among the trees on Cimiez Hill, the Musée Marc Chagall displays 17 large paintings which comprise the lyrical *Biblical Message*. The gallery uses glass and space to focus the Mediterranean light on Chagall's work.
Time: free on Wed., 10am-noon & 2pm-5:30pm
Place: Blvd. de Cimiez
Contact: ph. 876060

Fine Arts

The Jules Cheret Musée des Beaux-Arts owns a collection of Italian primitives, French Impressionists, and regional art. Works by Renoir, Degas, Monet, and Dufy are highlights. Be sure to see the Picasso ceramics and the Oriental print rooms.
Time: Tues.-Sun., 10am-noon & 2pm-5pm
Place: Ave. des Baumetts 33

Orbec

Cheese and Crackers

Lovers of Camembert cheese won't want to miss the Lanquetot Fac-

tory in the Norman town of Orbec. See how the product is made and sample some at the source. Set in the Auge Valley, Orbec is a small but lively town with numerous old houses.
Time: Mon.-Fri., 9:30am-noon & 2pm-4pm
Place: rue de Vimoutiers 8
Contact: ph. 328002

Oradour-sur-Glane

Grim Ruins
In June 1944, 250 children and 400 adults—the entire population of Oradour-sur-Glane—were slaughtered by Nazi SS troopers in retaliation for Resistance harassment in the area. After killing the populace, the SS set fire to the village. Today the charred remains stand as a grim memorial.
Contact: Syndicat d'Initiative in nearby St. Junien at Place du Champ-de-Foire, ph. 021793

Paris

Paris is the consummate European city. It's the capital not only of France, but also of fashion, art, gastronomy, and style. But, grand as it is, Paris remains a city of neighborhoods and ancient villages, all ripe with quiet pleasures and illustrious monuments.

The Rive Droite extends from the walls of Chateau Vincennes in the east to the woodlands and gardens of the Bois de Boulogne in the far west. Within this crescent are l'Étoile (with the Arc de Triomphe at its heart), the Louvre, Haussmann's grand boulevards, Centre Georges-Pomoidou, Les Halles, and Monmarte, crowned by the Basilica of Sacre-Coeur.

The Rive Gauche sweeps from Eiffel's "Shepherdess of the Clouds" in the west through the imposing Champ de Mars and Invalides. Then it swings down the chic Boulevard Saint-Germain to the Latin Quarter, with its community of students and artists. South of St. Germain is Montparnasse, known for its nightlife.

In the heart of the city are two islands, Île St. Louis and Île de la Cite. There, Caesar's army found the small Celtic fishing village of Lutetia in 53 BC. Taking the name of a local tribe, the Parisii, for their new town on the left bank, the Romans built a thriving river trade on the Seine.

Paris owes much to Phillipe Auguste II, who built the first city walls in 1180 and the first Louvre Palace in 1190. The town continued to grow and prosper in the 13th century, with the founding of the Sorbonne and the construction of Sainte Chapelle. Later, the Black Death and the Hundred Years War brought the city to the brink of ruin, but by the early 16th century the Louvre was rebuilt, major avenues were laid out, and the ornate Hotel de Ville was constructed.

Napoleon turned Paris into an imperial capital with significant public building projects, such as the Madeleine, the Carrousel Arch, the Bourse, Place Vendome, and the Arc de Triomph at l'Étoile. But Napoleon's most grandiose visions weren't realized until 1853, when his nephew Louis-Napoleon appointed Baron Haussmann the Prefect of the Seine. Haussman remade Paris, driving great thoroughfares through crowded ancient quarters, giving the city a modern plan. He also planned public parks and gardens, the Opera, railway stations, and the arrondissemont system.

During the halcyon days between the Franco-Prussian debacle and the Great War, Paris blossomed. The face of the city still bears witness to la Belle Epoque in the unrivaled showpiece of the Paris Exposition, la Tour Eiffel, and in the first Metro lines with their sumptuous Art Nouveau stations.

Paris grew still greater between the two World Wars, but nothing to compare with the postwar modernization of the 50's and 60's. The international style of architecture made its first appearance as Parisian suburbs were transformed by vast tower blocks, such as La Defense. In 1971 the ancient Les Halles market was pulled down, and in 1979 an ultra-modern shopping and recreational precinct opened on the site.

Still, even as the futuristic Centre Pompidou rises in the middle of ancient Beaubourg village and "le fast food" appears on the Champs-Elysees, Paris remains the quintessential European city, a joy to discover.

Porcelain Museum

The finest collection of porcelain, ceramics, and faience in Europe is housed in the Musée National de Ceramique. Since 1824, the

museum has documented the history of the Royal Porcelain Factory and has collected ceramics from around the world.
Time: free on Wed., 9:30am-noon & 1:30pm-5:15pm
Place: rue Sevres 4
Contact: ph. 534-9905

National Archives
The Palais Soubise houses the Archives Nationales and the Musee de l'Histoire de France. The collection of documents includes original letters from Napoleon, Voltaire, Richelieu, and de Gaulle. Don't miss the apartments of the Prince Soubise—they comprise some of the most elaborate rococo ensembles in Paris.
Time: free on Wed., 2pm-5pm
Place: rue des Francs-Bourgeois 60
Contact: ph. 277-1130

Palais de Tokio
The palatial Musée du Palais de Tokio serves as a catch-all museum—in addition to works from the Musée d'Art Moderne, it houses the Museum of Modern Art of the City of Paris, Musée d'Art et Essai (where the Louvre holds temporary shows), and the Musée d'Art Postimpressionisme.
Time: free on Wed., 9:45am-5:15pm
Place: Ave. du President Wilson 13

Cognacq-Jay Museum
The founder of the La Samaritaine department store chain endowed this museum of 18th-century France. The collection contains furniture, porcelain, paintings, jewelry, and other *objects d'art*.
Time: free on Sun., 10am-5:30pm
Place: Blvd. des Capucines 25
Contact: ph. 742-9471

Fine Arts
The Petite Palais houses the Fine Arts Museum of the City of Paris in an Art Nouveau exhibition hall of daring glass and metal design. The collection includes antiques, furnishings, and 19th-century paintings.
Time: free on Sun., 10am-5:40pm
Place: Ave. Winston Churchill

Oldest Church

The Church of St. Germain-des-Pres is probably the oldest standing church in Paris. The original structure was built in 558 by Germanus, then Bishop of Paris. The foundations of the present church were laid in 1004, and the massive bell tower dates from about ten years later. The interior reflects 12th-century remodeling.
Time: daily, 10am-5pm
Place: Place St. Germain-des-Prés
Contact: ph. 325-4171

Maison de Balzac

Documents relating to the life and literary work of Honoré de Balzac are displayed, along with first editions of his books, at the author's last Parisian residence.
Time: free on Sun., 10am-5:30pm
Place: rue Raynouard 47
Contact: ph. 224-5638

Musée Victor Hugo

The Victor Hugo Museum preserves the apartments of the author, along with a collection of memorabilia, drawings, photos, and furniture. An exhibit introduces the author and his works to the uninitiated.
Time: free on Sun., 10am-5:40pm
Place: Place des Vosges

Money Museum

Numismatists will enjoy a visit to the Musée de la Monnaie. The interesting collection of coins, tools, notes, and documents is housed in a Louis XVI-style mansion.
Time: Mon.-Sat., 11am-5pm
Place: Quai de Conti 11
Contact: ph. 329-1248

Cemetery of the Stars

If you're interested in tombs of famous people, go to the Pere Lachaise Cemetery. Just a few of the luminaries interred here in-

clude Chopin, Balzac, Piaf, Proust, Oscar Wilde, Jim Morrison, Moliere, and Gertrude Stein.
Time: daily, 8:30am-5pm
Place: Blvd. de Menilmontant
Contact: ph. 370-7033

Notre Dame

The masterpiece of Gothic architecture is more than a church; it's the heart of France. All distances are measured from Notre Dame. Begun in 1163, construction wasn't completed until the end of the 14th century. The glorious interior is composed of five naves lit by rose windows of 13th-century stained glass. Take the time to see the Cathedral from all angles, inside and out; it's truly a glory of human achievement. There are free organ concerts on Sundays at 5pm.
Time: daily, 8am-6:30pm
Place: Place du Parvis
Contact: ph. 326-0739

Memorial de la Deportation

On the Île de la Cité, directly behind Notre Dame, a monument to the French victims of Nazi concentration camps is a haunting reminder of the depths of human depravity.
Place: Square de l'Ile de France

French Heritage

The Musée National des Arts et Traditions Populaires is a center for the study of French culture and folklore. There is a poster gallery, a folk music archive, a print gallery, and a pictoral archive.
Time: free on Wed., 10am-5:15pm
Place: Route du Mahatma Gandhi 6
Contact: ph. 747-6980

Musée Rodin

This museum presents the work of France's foremost sculptor, Auguste Rodin. Housed in an 18th-century hotel, the collection

includes some of Rodin's most famous works in bronze and marble. *The Kiss, The Thinker,* and *The Doors of Hell* are all there.
Time: free Wed., 10am-5:45pm
Place: rue Varenne 77
Contact: ph. 705-0134

Eastern Art
The Musée Cernuschi has one of Europe's finest collections of Far Eastern art. The exhibit focuses on early Chinese art, dating back to 220 BC. The gallery also offers exhibitions and demonstrations of calligraphy.
Time: free on Sun., 10am-5:30pm
Place: Ave. Velasquez 7
Contact: ph. 563-5075

Paris' Past
The Musée Carnavalet provides an introduction to the history of Paris. The collection of artworks, furnishings, and memorabilia gives a picture of upper-class Parisan life in the 17th and 18th centuries.
Time: free on Sun., 10am-5:30pm
Place: rue de Sévigné 23
Contact: ph. 272-2113

Beaubourg
The Centre National d'Art et de Culture Georges-Pompidou, better known as ''The Beaubourg,'' incorporates permanent displays, changing exhibitions, a library, a cinema, a music center, experimental shows, a modern art museum, a computer center, a language lab, a sculpture studio—something for everybody. Most of the attractions are free. Don't miss the view of Paris from the external escalator and the top floor cafe.
Time: Mon., Wed., Thurs., Fri., noon-10pm; Sat. & Sun., 10am-10pm
Place: rue St. Martin
Contact: ph. 277-1233 or 277-1112

Modern Art Pioneer
Housed in the former stables of the Abbey St. Germain-des-Prés, the Musée Eugene Delacroix includes the home and studio of a

pioneer of modern art. The collection of paintings and drawings is a must for modern art lovers.
Time: free on Wed., 9:45am-5:15pm
Place: Place de Furstemberg 6
Contact: ph. 354-0487

The Louvre

With over 450,000 objects in its collection, the Louvre is one of the world's wealthiest museums. The collection includes European sculpture and painting, Greek, Roman and Egyptian antiquities, Oriental arts, prints, and applied arts. Housed in a former royal palace, the Louvre has been a national museum of art since 1791. A visit to the Louvre is a truly memorable experience, so go early and stay still the closing bell.
Time: free on Sun., 9:45am-5:15pm (some halls till 6:30pm)
Place: Place du Carrousel
Contact: ph. 260-3926

Medieval Art

One of the most important collections of medieval art in France is found at the Musée Cluny in its 15th-century abbey residence. The collection includes sculpture, crafts, and applied and decorative arts from the early Middle Ages to the 17th century. One of the great treasures of the museum is the amazing *Lady and the Unicorn* tapestry.
Time: free Wed., 9:45am-noon & 2pm-5:30pm
Place: Place Paul Painleve 6
Contact: ph. 325-6200

Modern Paris

The Maison de l'UNESCO was built in Paris in 1958 as a headquarters for the United Nations' organization and as a symbol of international cooperation. The complex was designed by a group of three architects from different nations, while the art for the interior was presented by some of the greatest artists of the day. There is a Calder mobile, ceramic murals by Miro, paintings by Picasso, sculpture by Moore, and a Noguchi garden.
Time: Mon.-Fri., 10am-noon & 2pm-5pm
Place: Place de Fontenoy

Napoleon's Triumph
Built between 1806 and 1836 to commemorate Napoleon's military triumphs, the Arc de Triomphe remains the world's largest triumphal arch. Beneath the monument is the Tomb of the Unknown Soldier and the Eternal Flame, which is ceremoniously rekindled each evening at 6:30.
Place: Place Charles de Gaulle de l'Etoile

Impressionists
The world's premiere collection of Impressionist art is housed in the Musée du Jeu de Paume. There are magnificent works by Degas, Manet, Monet, Renoir, Gauguin, Cezanne, Seurat, Toulouse-Lautrec, Van Gogh, and more.
Time: free on Wed., 9:45am-5:15pm
Place: Place de la Concorde
Contact: ph. 260-1207

Oriental Art
Centered around a collection donated by industrialist Emile Guimet, the Musée Guimet is France's leading museum of Oriental art. It also houses a research institute of Asian culture.
Time: free on Wed., 9:45am-noon & 1:30pm-5pm
Place: Place d'Iena
Contact: ph. 723-6165

Pau

Capital of the Pyrenees-Atlantic, Pau is a garden city set against the mountains of the Pyrenees. Pau didn't join France until the 17th century and grew in the early 19th century when it was "discovered" by British tourists drawn by the delightful climate. During recent years, Pau has flourished from exploitation of natural gas deposits.

Pyrenees Promenade
A free funicular carries sightseers from the Pau railway station to the elegant Boulevard des Pyrenees, which offers exceptional views over 75 miles of hills and mountains.

Fine Paintings

The Pau Musée des Beaux-Arts houses an excellent collection of 16th- through 20th-century European painting. There is a gallery of works by Degas, along with canvases by Velasquez and El Greco.
Time: Wed.-Mon., 10am-noon & 2pm-6pm
Place: rue Mathieu Lalanne
Contact: ph. 272708

Pauillac

Premiere Cru Classé

An appointment is required, but don't let that deter you from visiting the Chateau Mouton Rothschild. The wine museum contains tapestries, paintings, sculpture, and other art relating to wine-making and vineyards.
Time: weekdays by appointment
Place: rue Pouyalet
Contact: ph. 592222

Chateau Lafite-Rothschild

You can also visit the cellars at Chateau Lafite-Rothschild, along with the popular Vinotheque. Wine has been produced there since the 18th century.
Time: weekdays (except during fall harvest season)
Contact: ph. 590104

Perigueux

Dominated by its domed churches, Perigueux has preserved the atmosphere of its ancient past. The heart of the old town encircled by a loop of the River Îsle, sits upon the ruins of Roman Vesone. Judging by recent excavations, a wealthy city of luxurious villas and huge public buildings existed there until invasions decimated the population. Perigueux revived during the early Middle Ages, as evident in the restored homes and shops in the Quartier Saint-Front and the glorious churches of the old Cité. Today, the town is famous for its gastronomic specialities such as *foie gras* and truffles.

Paté Tours

The Factory Champion Foie Gras offers a guided tour of their production facility. Paté lovers can expect a small sample following the tour.
Time: Mon.-Fri., 9am-noon & 2pm-4pm
Place: Place Chateau St. Laurent-sur-Manoire
Contact: ph. 536900

Oriental Towers

Be sure to take the free guided tour of the Cathedrale St. Front. The white-domed church, with its Byzantine cupolas and Eastern bell towers, was remodelled in the 19th century by the architect of Sacre Coeur in Paris. The original 10th-century church, built in the Greek cruciform style, is barely visible beneath the many restorations.
Time: Mon.-Sat., 9am-noon & 3pm-5pm
Place: Place de la Clautre
Contact: ph. 531063

Pompadour

Royal Stud Farm

It is somehow fitting that the former chateaux of the infamous Madame Pompadour was turned into a royal stud farm by Louis XV after her death. Today, the farm breeds Anglo-Arabs and is open for visits on weekday afternoons. During the summer, there are frequent horse shows and races at the chateaux, which opens its gardens to guests on show and race days.
Time: July-Jan.: Mon.-Fri., 3pm-5pm
Place: Chateaux Pompadour
Contact: ph. 733043

Quimper

This ancient capital of Cornouaille, at the confluence of the Odet and the Steir, has managed to retain its traditional Breton flavor. On the winding, narrow lanes you'll see women in traditional dress and hear the Breton language spoken. In the old quarter around the 13th-century cathedral, many ancient houses are decorated with unusual caryatids.

Folk Festival
Each July, Quimper hosts the Festival de la Cornouaille. The week of activities includes concerts of Breton folk music, dances, costume parties, plays, markets, films, and feasting.
Time: third week of July
Contact: Office de Tourisme, rue du Roi-Gradlon 6

Ceramic Center
Since the 17th century, Quimper has been a center of ceramic pro-duction in Brittany. One of the finest local potteries, Faience Keraluc, offers free tours and demonstrations.
Time: Mon.-Fri., 8:30am-noon & 2pm-6pm
Place: rue de Benodet
Contact: ph. 902529

Breton Art
Quimper's former Bishop's Palace is home to a museum of the Department Breton. It contains Breton costumes, furnishings, woodcarvings, and regional painting.
Time: free on Wed. & Sun., 10am-noon & 2pm-6pm
Place: Place St. Corentin
Contact: ph. 950469

Reims

An important urban center since Roman times, Reims has been the site of many significant events in French history: in 496 AD Clovis, King of the Franks, was baptized there; from the 12th cen-tury to the 18th, all French monarchs were crowned there; and World War II in Europe officially ended there on May 8, 1945. Devastated repeatedly by war and fire, Reims endures as a vital and prosperous city. Modern Reims owes its continuing success to Dom Perignon, a monk who invented the method for produc-ing champagne at the Hautviller Abbey in the 17th century.

War Room
History buffs won't want to miss the Salle de Guere, the local

schoolroom where the Germans officially surrendered to the Allies in May, 1945. The room has remained the same since the signing, except for the photographs of the signers on the wall.
Time: March 15-Nov. 11: Wed.-Mon., 10am-noon & 2pm-6pm
Place: College Technique, 10 rue Franklin Roosevelt

Champagne Tours
Many of France's leading champagne producers are located in and around Reims. Most cellars are open for limited visitation by appointment. The tri-level Ruinart cellars are among the finest in Reims, but call first.
Place: rue des Crayeres 4
Contact: ph. 854029

Modern Cellar
For a tour of a modern champagne production facility, contact Besserat de Belle for an appointment to see their high-tech installation.
Place: Allee du Vignoble
Contact: ph. 060918

More Tours
To find out about other champagne cellar visits, contact the tourist office.
Contact: Syndicat d'Initiative, rue Jadart 1, ph. 472569

Elegant Cathedral
The huge Cathedrale de Notre Dame is so well-proportioned that it gives the impression of harmony and airiness. Add spectacular stained glass windows, and you have one of the world's most beautiful churches.
Time: daily, 9am-7pm
Place: Place de Cardinal Lucon

Superb Art
The Musée des Beaux-Arts contains a fine collection of European art. The galleries include enamels, tapestries, Flemish masters, and an extensive Impressionist collection.
Time: Wed.-Mon., 10am-noon & 2pm-5pm
Place: rue Chanzy 8

Ancient Reims
For a fascinating view of ancient Reims, visit the Musee Archeologique in the Abbeye St. Remi. The exhibits include religious artifacts, weapons from the 12th to 19th centuries, sculpture, antiques, and jewels.
Time: Tue.-Sat., 10am-noon & 2pm-5pm
Place: rue St. Simon 56

Strasbourg

Strasbourg is at the same time an old Alsatian town and a vigorous international city. The heart of Strasbourg is the medieval La Petite France district; at the heart of the district is the breathtaking Notre Dame Cathedral.

Ornate Gothic
The lofty Cathedrale Notre Dame, built of red sandstone, towers above the Petite France district of old Strasbourg. The lacework facade, astronomical clock (which plays at 12:30pm), 14th-century stained glass, and *Pillar of the Last Judgement* combine to make this church a treasure of the Middle Ages.
Time: daily, 8am-noon & 2pm-7pm
Place: Place de la Cathedrale
Contact: ph. 325707

European Parliament
Visitors are welcome to observe sessions of the European Parliament at the modern Palais de l'Europe, headquarters of the Council of Europe. The visitors' gallery has headsets for simultaneous translation of debates. To tour the facilities, call in advance for an appointment.
Time: Mon.-Fri., 9am-noon & 2:30pm-5pm
Place: Ave. de l'Europe
Contact: ph. 614961, ext. 3033

Vichy

Dignified Vichy preserves the turn-of-the-century charm of France's most renowned spa. The neat public gardens and spa establishments exemplify the leisurely pace of life which continues to attract a dedicated clientele. The name Vichy also evokes a darker vision of the town that served as the seat of France's collaborationist government from 1940 to 1944.

Missionary Momentoes

Vichy's Maison du Missionaire houses a collection of artifacts from religious missions in former French colonies and other tropical locales. There are stuffed animals, models of all sorts, crafts from far-flung corners of the earth, and fascinating old photos.
Time: Tue.-Sat., 3pm-6pm
Place: Ave. Thermale 36
Contact: ph. 987194

Nationwide

Wine Route

Alsace offers innumerable possibilities for free wine tastings in the towns of the region. By following the Wine Route from Thann to Marlenheim, one can sample each of the seven varietals and one blend produced in Alsace. For a list of cellars and vineyards, contact the office below.
Contact: Centre d'Information du Vin d'Alsace, Ave de la Forie-aux-Vin, Colmar, ph. 410621

England

Great Britain
(England and Scotland)

Abbotsbury

Abbey Ruins

This Dorset village of stone and reed-thatched cottages surrounds the ruins of St. Peter's Benedictine Abbey. The most impressive remains of the monastery, established by the Viking King Knut the Great in 1026, are the large tithe barn, dating from around 1400, and fragments of original abbey buildings.

Time: accessible during daylight hours
Place: Church St. & Abbey Rd.
Contact: ph.03058

Aberdeen

The "Granite City" is an unusual blend of commerce and culture. Development of North Sea oil and gas reserves has brought prosperity to this friendly old fishing port. World famous for its silvery, granite buildings, Aberdeen upholds its reputation as an attractive town with a variety of attractions, parks, and gardens.

Old Aberdeen

The restored Provost Skene House is home to a museum of Scottish history. This stately townhouse features exhibits on old town

Scotland

life, period furnishings, and art.
Time: Mon.-Sat., 10am-5pm
Place: Guestrow
Contact: ph. 641086

Scottish Art
Scottish paintings from the 16th century to the present—along with
English and French art, prints, and sculpture—are offered at the
Aberdeen Art Gallery and Museum. Special exhibitions and events
are held throughout the year.
Time: Mon.-Sat., 10am-5pm; Sun., 2pm-5pm
Place: Schoolhill
Contact: ph. 646333

High Seas
Ironically, Aberdeen's newest attraction, the Maritime Museum,
is housed in the city's oldest surviving home, the Provost Ross
House, dating from 1590. Aberdeen's nautical history is presented
through exhibits, models, and gear. The North Sea Gas and Oil
Gallery has high-tech models of oil rigs that show how those
modern behemoths work.
Time: Mon.-Sat., 10am-5pm
Place: Shiprow
Contact: ph. 585788

Summer Festival
Contact the tourist office at St. Nicholas House for details on Aberdeen's Summer Festival, held each July. Concerts, parades, shows,
and fireworks enliven Aberdeen for ten days.
Contact: St. Nicholas House, Broad St., ph. 632727

Botanical Garden
The six-acre Cruickshank Botanical Garden, established in 1898,
includes rock gardens, alpine flora, a sunken heath garden, water
gardens, and a collection of spring bulbs.
Time: May-Sept.: Mon.-Fri., 9am-5pm; Sat. & Sun., 2pm-5pm
Place: University of Aberdeen, St. Machar Drive
Contact: ph. 40241, ext. 5244

Contemporary Arts

The 18th-century James Dun House has been restored as a museum of local arts and interests, with changing exhibitions every month and weekly special events.
Time: Mon.-Sat., 10am-5pm.
Place: 61 Schoolhill
Contact: ph. 646333

Granite Cathedral

St. Machar's Cathedral, today a mostly 15th-century Gothic building, was erected in 1157 on the site of the saint's 6th-century chapel. Be sure to notice the oak ceiling in the nave, decorated with coats-of-arms of ancient Scottish kings.
Time: Mon.-Sat., 8:30am-6pm
Place: Chasonry St.

Abergavenny

Abergavenny, gateway to South Wales, is set in a lovely mountain-ringed valley. Although it dates from the Roman era, the present town grew up around its 11th-century Norman castle.

Castle of Deceit

To avenge the murder of his uncle, William de Braose invited the local gentry for Christmas dinner in 1177 and murdered them all as they dined. Then, he sent his soldiers to his guest's homes and had their male heirs dispatched. Today, little remains of his castle, but what's left is still impressive. Plus, the ruins have stunning views of Brecon National Park and the four peaks that guard Abergavenny.
Time: daily, 8am-6pm
Place: Castle Hill
Contact: ph. 4282

National Park

The mountains and moors of Brecon National Park begin at Abergavenny's doorstep. Stop at the Information Center for details

on points of interest in the park, with its sandstone mountains, swift rivers, and thundering cascades.
Time: Office: daily, 9:30am-6:30pm
Place: Monk St.
Contact: ph. 3254

Abergwili

Once the home of the Bishops of St. David, Abergwili is now a suburb of Carnarthen, near the coast of southern Wales.

Folklife and Archaeology
The Carmarthen Museum is rich in prehistoric, medieval, and Roman artifacts, with an emphasis on finds from the nearby Roman city of Moridunum. Welsh culture and folklife are also highlighted.
Time: Mon.-Sat., 10am-4:30pm
Place Old Bishop's Palace
Contact: ph. 231691

Welsh Stronghold
Remains of the 13th-century Llanstephen Castle stand on a site above the Towy estuary. Protected by cliffs, the fortress today consists of one curtain wall and tower, with a large gatehouse and inner ward.
Time: always accessible
Place: seven miles south on B4312

Aberystwyth

Trim pastel Victorian townhouses line the promenade above Cardigan Bay in this Welsh seaside resort. Along with its attraction as a vacation spot, Aberystwyth also has castle ruins, the oldest university in Wales, and the National Library.

Arts Center
The Aberystwyth Arts Center presents exhibits of painting, graphics,

and sculpture—both British and international—and an extensive collection of ceramics.
Time: Mon.-Sat., 9am-5pm
Place: Penglais Hill Campus
Contact: ph. 4277

New Museum
Recently opened in the restored Coliseum Theater, Aberystwyth's Coredigion Museum provides an eclectic collection encompassing country folklife, maritime artifacts, archaeological displays, mining machinery, and Welsh history.
Time: Mon.-Sat., 10am-5pm
Place: Terrade Rd.
Contact: ph. 617911

National Library
The National Library of Wales, one of six libraries that receive a copy of every book printed in Great Britain, is housed in an imposing neo-classical building surrounded by flowerbeds. Specializing in Celtic and Welsh literature, the library has most of the world's surviving medieval manuscripts in Welsh.
Time: Mon.-Fri., 9:30am-6pm; Sat., 9:30am-5pm
Place: Penglais Hill
Contact: ph. 3816

Alton

Alton's history dates back at least to the Roman era. Later, it developed along the medieval route from Winchester to Canterbury—called the Pilgrim's Way. The modern town's main street, aligned along this route, has a number of fine Georgian and Victorian buildings. During the English Civil War, Alton was the scene of bitter fighting; the parish church still has musket balls embedded in the doorway.

Unusual Abbey
Founded in the late 19th century to promote charitable work among British seamen, the Abbey of Our Lady and St. John remains incomplete. Based on the design of the famous Jervaux Abbey, the

monastic buildings have an appealing individuality.
Time: Mon.-Sat., 9am-4pm (or by appointment)
Place: Alton Rd.
Contact: ph. 83986

Museum and Gallery
The Curtis Museum contains collections of history, archaeology,
geology, crafts, and games. Adjoining is the Allen Gallery, hous-
ing English ceramics and exhibits by Hampshire artists.
Time: Tue-Sat., 10am-5pm
Place: High St.
Contact: ph. 82802

Avebury

Monumental Megaliths
Rising around the village are the great sarsen stones of Avebury
Circle, one of Britain's most important megalithic sites. Near
Avebury Henge are the related sites of Sillbury Hill, the greatest
manmade hill of antiquity in Europe; Windmill Hill, the campsite
of Britain's earliest Neolithic culture; and West Kennet Barrow, the
earliest site of the Avebury complex, begun about 3500 BC, with
burial chambers separated by huge stones.
Time: all sites are open 9am-sundown
Contact: ph. 06723

Axminster

A few miles from the Devon coast, Axminster is an ancient town
with two squares, Georgian homes, and a 700-year old church.

Mill Tour
You can observe every stage of carpet weaving at the Axminster
Carpet Factory. Thomas Whitby, a local tailor, brought the first loom
to town in 1755, and Axminster has been a carpet center ever since.
Time: Mon.-Fri., 9am-noon & 1:30pm-5pm (closed in July)
Place: King Edward Rd.
Contact: ph. 32244

Ayot St. Lawrence

This Hertfordshire village is best known as the former home of George Bernard Shaw, who lived and worked here from 1906 until his death in 1950.

Romantic Ruin

The ruined 14th-century Ayot St. Lawrence Church has stood unused since 1770, when the lord of the manor built a new church nearby. Set in the heart of the village, the ruin is overgrown with ivy. Beneath the tower is the lonely, romantic tomb of an unknown 14th-century knight and his lady.

Time: daylight hours
Place: High St.

Ayr

Ayr is a resort city on Scotland's Firth of Clyde Coast and a convenient center for exploring Robert Burns country. The nation's national poet was born in the suburb of Alloway, where enthusiasts will find Burns' home, museum, and monuments.

Gallery and Sculpture Park

Traditional, contemporary, and applied arts, along with regional exhibits, are on display at the Maclaurin Art Gallery at the Rozelle Mansion. The surrounding park's nature trail is dotted with sculpture by Henry Moore and others.

Time: Mon.-Sat., 11am-5pm
Place: Monument Rd.
Contact: ph. 45447

Aysgarth

Park Center

The Aysgarth National Park Center has interpretive displays, maps, and information on the Yorkshire Dales. Guided walks of the moors depart daily at 1:30pm from the Center during summer months.

Time: April-Oct., 10am-5pm
Place: Aysgarth Falls
Contact: ph. 09-693424

Balloch

A busy tourist town on the southern end of the Loch Lomond, Balloch is a popular place for outings from nearby Glasgow and for cruises on the Loch.

Castle Park

Set on the bonny banks of Loch Lomond, with magnificent views of the Loch and countryside, Balloch Castle County Park is an ideal spot to enjoy the Scottish scenery. The park has a nature trail and a charming garden.
Time: Park: daily, 8am-dusk; Garden: daily, 10am-6pm
Place: Alexandria
Contact: ph. 58216

Bangor

A pleasant university and resort town, Bangor is situated at the scenic entrance to the Menai Strait in North Wales.

Art and History

The Bangor Museum portrays Welsh history through crafts, documents, furniture, art, and prehistoric artifacts. Local painters and sculptors are exhibited in the Bangor Art Gallery.
Time: Tue.-Sat., noon-4:30pm
Place: University College, Fford Gwynedd
Contact: ph. 351151, ext.437

Venerable Cathedral

Bangor Cathedral's chief attraction is its disparate architectural styles. Although the diminutive cathedral's history dates back to the 6th century, it's far more Victorian than medieval in character. The chapterhouse contains a valuable collection of Welsh manuscripts and books, while the Biblical Garden has plants mentioned in the Bible.
Time: Mon.-Sat., 9am-6pm
Place: Glanafon
Contact: ph. 51693

Barnstaple

This historic town makes a delightful detour from North Devon's spectacular cliffs and beaches. Reminders of Barnstaple's history are found all about the friendly town.

Ancient Market

Early each Friday morning, the Panneir Market come to life as it has for over 1,000 years. Farmers, merchants, and peddlers from the countryside congregate to trade—as people have done since 930, when King Alfred granted Barnstaple its charter as a market town.
Time: Friday, 6:30am-2pm
Place: Butcher's Row

Leather Tours

Visitors are always welcome at Sanders and Son, where they can see the processes used to produce Devonshire sheepskins and leather goods.
Time: Mon.-Fri., 9:30am-4:30pm
Place: Pilton Bridge Rd.
Contact: ph. 42335

Devonshire Days

The North Devon Athenaeum contains a collection of regional antiquities, pewter, and Roman pottery. Its reference library has an English history collection of nearly 40,000 volumes.
Time: Mon.-Fri., 10am-1pm & 2:15pm-5pm; Sat., 10am-1pm
Place: The Square
Contact: ph. 42174

Barrow-in-Furness

This 19th-century town, on the western end of a long peninsula, has fine sandy beaches and a beautiful nature reserve close by.

Byegone Britain

Travelers heading for Britain's Lake District should stop by the Furness Museum. It has finds from regional Stone Age sites, plus

ship models, old furnishings, and seasonal exhibits.
Time: Mon.-Wed. & Fri., 10am-5pm; Thurs. & Sat., 10am-1pm
Place: Ramsden Square
Contact: ph. 20650

Bath

The Romans called Bath *Aquae Sulis*—"Waters of the Sun"—and
traveled far to bathe in the hot springs. Today, the restored Roman
baths and temple are the town's prized possessions. Bath never
ceased to be a spa town. After falling on hard times during the
Tudor era, it blossomed again in the 18th century. Much of present-
day Bath was designed by John Woods and William Pulteneny.
Their houses, bridges, and squares are unmatched in elegance,
making Bath a delight to visit.

Eminent Art

The collections at Bath's Victorian Art Gallery include paintings
by European masters, rare porcelain, antiques, etchings, and
graphics.
Time: Mon.-Sat., 10am-6pm
Place: Bridge St.
Contact: ph. 61111, ext.65024

Lantern of the West

Bath Abbey's windows have earned it the nickname "Lantern of
the West." Little remains of the Saxon abbey founded here in 676,
on the site of the present building. The present church, begun in
1499, is noted for its delicate windows and medieval carvings.
Time: Mon.-Sat., 8:30am-6pm
Place: High St.
Contact: ph. 330289

Botanical Gardens

Bath Botanical Gardens specializes in cherry trees, heather, flower-
ing shrubs, and herbaceous plants. You'll also find many rare plants.
Time: Mon.-Sat., 8am-sunset; Sun., 10am-sunset
Place: Royal Avenue
Contact: ph. 62831

Berwick-Upon-Tweed

This historic border town on the River Tweed is threaded by winding lanes which lead to the market and oldest barracks in Great Britain.

Civic Gallery
The Berwick Museum and Art Gallery houses collections of pewter, ceramics, local antiquities, and paintings, including some fine French works.
Time: May-Oct.: Mon.-Fri., 10am-5pm; Sat., 9am-noon
Place: Marysgate
Contact: ph. 307320

Tudor Ramparts
England's most northern town is still sheltered by Elizabethan walls, begun in 1555 as a bastion against the marauding Scots. Regarded as the best-preserved of all Tudor fortifications in England, they are the town's main tourist attraction.

Beverly

Often overlooked by visitors to neaby York, Beverly is an old market town surrounded by pastures and farms. Founded in 700 by St. John of Beverly, the town fourished during the Middle Ages as a center of the wool trade. Quietly prosperous over the centuries, Beverly retains many fine monuments, stately Georgian homes, and Victorian buildings.

Arts and Heritage
Beverly's Art Gallery and Heritage Center display local antiquities, pottery, and paintings, plus frequent exhibitions by local artists.
Time: Mon.-Wed., 9:30am-12:30pm & 2pm-5pm; Thurs., 9:30am-noon; Sat., 9:30am-4pm
Place: Champney Rd.
Contact: ph. 882255

Outstanding Church
The Beverly Minster equals many cathedrals in beauty and majesty. Built between 1220 and 1460, the church is an example of ear-

ly English architecture at its finest. Be sure to look for the Percy tomb and the gorgeous glass in the Lady Chapel.
Time: Mon.-Sat., 8:30am-6pm
Contact: ph. 867430

Bexley

Beastie Gardens
The grounds of Hall Place, a mansion in suburban London, include a sweeping display of gardening expertise. There are delightful ornamental gardens with topiary depicting the Queen's beasts, plus many gardens and a conservatory for exotic plants and flowers.
Time: Gardens: Mon.-Fri., 8am-sunset; Sat. & Sun., 9am-sunset; Conservatory: daily, 10:30am-4:30pm
Place: Bourne Rd.
Contact: ph. 303777, ext. 2322

Biddenden

Biddenden is a picturesque village of half-timbered houses and inns and brick cottages. The small village green is dominated by a curious sign depicting the "Biddenden Maids," 12th-century Siamese twins who lived in the village and left a fund to provide cheese and bread for the poor.

Carriage Collection
Located in a 15th-century manorhouse, the Baby Carriage Collection has 400 infant vehicles of the past. Amusing displays portray the history of the pram from the 16th century to the present.
Time: May-Sept.: Mon.-Fri., by appointment only
Place: Bettenham Manor
Contact: ph. 291343

Kentish Vineyard
Visitors are welcome to explore the Biddenden Vineyards, established in 1969. Planted primarily with German varietals, the vineyard

opens its pressing operation in late October and holds tastings year-round.
Time: Mon.-Sat., 11am-5pm; Sun.,noon-5pm
Place: Little Whatmans
Contact: ph. 291726

Birmingham

In recent years, Birmingham has initiated a huge urban renewal program, which the city fathers hope will erase the town's reputation as a souless, ugly city. Little remains of medieval Birmingham, but there are some fine 18th- and 19th-century buildings around the city. Many districts have charm, such as Gas Street Basin, where a houseboat community thrives, or Bournville, built as a model industrial settlement at the turn of the century.

Science and Industry

If you're intrigued by engines and machinery, you'll love the Birmingham Museum of Science and Industry. Displays from the Industrial Revolution to the present include steam, gas, and hot air engines, locomotives, vintage cars, and a superb aircraft section. The James Watt Building contains the world's oldest working steam engine, from 1779.
Time: Mon.-Sat., 10am-5pm; Sun., 10am-noon
Place: Newhall St.
Contact: ph. 236-1022

Arts and Antiques

The Birmingham Museum and Gallery ranks among Britain's best museums. The Fine Arts collection ranges from the 14th century on and includes a premier pre-Raphaelite exhibit. The Natural History department shows dinosaur replicas and British fossils. Frequent lectures, demonstrations, and special exhibits also enliven the museum.
Time: Mon.-Sat., 10am-5pm; Sun., 2pm-5pm
Place: Chamberlain Square
Contact: ph. 235-2834

Fine Arts

Often overlooked by visitors, Birmingham's Barber Institute of Fine

Arts has a small but exciting collection of such greats as Rubens, Van Dyck, Delacroix, Turner, Rodin, and Gauguin.
Time: Mon.-Fri., 10am-5pm; Sun., 10am-1pm
Place: Edgbastion Park Rd.
Contact: ph. 472-9062

City Hall

Designed by Joseph Hansom, inventor of the hansom cab, Birmingham's Town Hall is a masterpiece of Victorian architecture, modeled on the Temple of Castor in Rome. Surrounded by colossal Corinthian columns, it houses a collection of art illustrating the city's history.
Time: Mon.-Fri., 9am-4pm
Place: Victoria Square
Contact: ph. 235-3411

Blackburn

This textile city was founded by the Romans, who built an outpost there to guard their road across the moors.

Textile Tales

The Lewis Museum of Textile Machinery portrays the development of Blackburn's textile industry. The galleries contain models of the famous Spinning Jenny, Arkwright's Frame, and Kay's Flying Shuttle.
Time: Mon.-Sat., 9:30am-5pm
Place: Exchange St.
Contact: ph. 667130

Eclectic Collections

Blackburn's Museum and Art Gallery presents a variety of interesting exhibits that include icons, paintings, Japanese art, local antiquities, old books, a time tunnel, and militaria.
Time: Mon.-Sat., 9:30am-5pm
Place: Library St.
Contact: ph. 667130

Bradford

Bradford is an interesting old Yorkshire city not far from Leeds. Prosperity from a textile trade during the 19th century endowed Bradford with some fine Victorian buildings—the Wool Exchange and City Hall are especially noteworthy. St. Peter's Cathedral has gorgeous windows by William Morris, as well as a number of medieval monuments.

Films and Photos
The National Museum of Photography, Film, and Television presents exhibits which explore the world of photography. Many of the displays require visitor participation.
Time: Tues.-Sat., noon-8pm; Sun., 2:30pm-6pm
Place: Prince's View
Contact: ph. 727488

Stately Hall
Dating from the 15th century, Bolling Hall contains exquisite furnishings, including an unusual Chippendale bed and rare heraldic glass. The manorhouse also is home to the local Museum of Yorkshire Folklife and History.
Time: Tues.-Sun., 10am-5pm
Place: Bolling Hall Rd.
Contact: ph. 723057

Twisted Textiles
Housed in an old mill, the Bradford Industrial Museum is devoted to the development of the local worsted textile industry.
Time: Tues.-Sun., 10am-5pm
Place: Moorside Rd.
Contact: ph. 631756

Art in the Dales
Cartwright Hall incorporates painting, sculpture, prints, and graphics, plus programs based on inter-museum loans. The oddly-designed mansion was donated to the city as a memorial to Edmund Cartwright, inventor of the powerloom.
Time: Tues.-Sun., 10am-5pm
Place: Lister Park
Contact: ph. 493313

Brighton

Britain's most popular family resort is a curious place—part Regency promenade, part tawdry funhouse, part Victorian village. Brighton has something for everybody: miles of beach, amusement arcades, a warren of streets filled with antique shops, restaurants, and pubs, and the extravagant Royal Pavilion.

Summer Fest

Brighton hosts a rousing, two-week festival each May, with torch-light parades, concerts, fireworks, art shows, special markets, dances, and much more.
Contact: Brighton Festival Office, 54 Old Steine, ph. 29801

Birds of Britain

Booth Natural History Museum is renowned for its displays of British birds in their natural habitats. Butterfly and vertebrate galleries round out this fine museum.
Time: Mon.-Sat., 10am-5pm; Sun., 2pm-5pm
Place: 194 Dyke Rd.
Contact: ph. 552586

Diverse Collections

The Brighton Museum and Art Gallery exhibits Art Nouveau furnishings, works by Salvadore Dali, Sussex folk art, and British archaeology.
Time: Tues.-Sat., 10am-5:45pm; Sun., 2pm-5pm
Place: Church St.
Contact: ph. 603005

Bristol

Originating as a settlement by a River Avon bridge, Bristol grew to be one of England's leading cities during the Middle Ages. The city's wealthy merchants endowed the town with glorious churches and public buildings, as well as grand private mansions. Sadly, bombings in WWII devastated Bristol's architectural heritage. Dedicated rebuilding and renewal has made Bristol, still an important port, a city of charm and character—everything is now "shipshape Bristol fashion."

Blaise Castle

The "castle" in Blaise Castle is a Gothic folly set on the estate grounds. The mansion houses a superb folk museum with toys, costumes, crafts, and timepieces. Blaise House also has many woodland trails and picnic spots.
Time: Mon.-Wed., Sat., & Sun., 10am-1pm & 2pm-5pm
Place: Henbury
Contact: ph. 506789

Oldest Chapel

Bronze statues of John and Charles Wesley flank the entrance to the oldest Methodist Chapel in the world. Built in 1739, both John Wesley's Chapel and apartments are preserved in their 18th-century form.
Time: Mon., Tues., Thurs.-Sat., 10am-4pm
Place: The Horse Fair
Contact: ph. 24740

Cars and Concordes

A dockside warehouse in the heart of Bristol houses the Bristol Industrial Museum. The collection displays vehicles from horse-drawn trolleys to the Concorde, plus locomotives, a steam tug, and vehicles produced in the Bristol area over the centuries.
Time: Sat.-Wed., 10am-1pm & 2pm-5pm
Place: Prince's Warf
Contact: ph. 299771, ext.290

Lustrous Glass

At the Bristol City Museum and Gallery, glassware is the focus of interest. The story of glass through the ages is highlighted by Bristol's vitreos ware.
Time: Mon.-Sat., 10am-5pm
Place: Queens Rd.
Contact: ph. 299771

Historic House

The Georgian House, once the home of West Indian merchant John Pinney, is now a handsome museum kept as though the Pin-

ney family were still in residence. Mahogony furnishings and other Georgian decor fill the house.
Time: Mon.-Sat., 10am-1pm & 2pm-5pm
Place: 7 Great George St.
Contact: ph. 299771, ext.237

Church Museum
St. Nicholas Church has been converted into a museum with ecclesiastical art, vestments, silver, and exhibits on Bristol history through the Reformation. The real treasure is the Hogarth altarpiece.
Time: Mon.-Sat., 10am-5pm
Place: St. Nicholas Street
Contact: ph. 299771, ext.243

Arnolfini
This converted tea warehouse overlooking the harbor is now a center for contemporary arts. The complex features galleries for avant-garde artists, cinemas, and a concert hall.
Time: Tues.-Sat., 11am-8pm; Sun., 2pm-7pm
Place: Narrow Quay
Contact: ph. 299194

Caernarfon
Edward I, who subdued the Welsh during the 13th century, built a castle and walled town at Caernarfon to protect his territory and to demonstrate England's might to recalcitrant subjects. Ironically, the castle and city have become one of the showpieces of Welsh tourism. The town also has attractive homes and shops built during the region's mining boom.

Roman Fortress
Substantial ruins remain of the Roman fort at Segontium, which was built to accommodate 1,000 men. The fort's walls enclosed a barracks block, workshops, a bath house, a granary, and a Mithraic temple. The National Museum of Wales maintains an excellent museum on the site.
Time: Mon.-Sat., 9:30am-5:30pm; Sun., 2pm-4pm
Contact: ph. 5625

Cambridge

Set between marshlands to the south and the wild fens to the north, Cambridge was established as a ford over the River Cam. It soon became a bustling Celtic trading village, and when the Romans built a bridge over the river, the city got its name. How the University began at Cambridge is still a mystery. Traditionalists suggest that the monks from nearby Ely established the first school in the 11th century, and other religious orders followed. It is known, however, that the first college proper, Peterhouse, was founded in 1284. Other colleges sprang up to house the growing number of students who came to town.

Today, Cambridge is the quintessential university town, with a wealth of historic buildings, winding passages lined by medieval cottages, and the peaceful, willow-strewn "Backs." The University owns much of the town and takes great care to preserve its 700-year old tradition.

Polar Research

The Scott Polar Research Insitute is a memorial museum to the explorer and his companions. It presents diaries, mementoes, and photos of Robert Scott's expedition to the South Pole. Exhibits also include Eskimo art, souvenirs of other Arctic expeditions, and information on current polar exploration.
Time: Mon.-Sat., 2:30pm-4pm
Place: Lensfield Rd.
Contact: ph. 66499

Treasured Bequest

The Fitzwilliam Museum contains Egyptian, Greek, and Roman antiquities, Islamic art, European porcelain, illuminated manuscripts, and antique furnishings. The upper gallery has one of the finest collections of paintings and drawings—from Old Masters through French Impressionists—in the United Kingdom.
Time: Tues.-Sat., 10am-5pm; Sun., 2pm-5pm
Place: Trumpington St.
Contact: ph. 69501

Norman Church

Built in 1130 as a replica of the Holy Sepulcher Church in Jerusalem,

Cambridge's Round Chruch is one of five round churches still surviving in Great Britain.
Time: Mon.-Sat., 9am-5pm
Place: Bridge St.

University Colleges
Visitors are welcome to wander around the colleges and grounds, although many are closed during exam periods. Without a doubt, King's College Chapel is the one place not to miss. Considered one of Britain's most beautiful buildings, it is a Gothic marvel of fan vaulting and carved stone. The stained glass windows are breathtaking, while the altar is graced by Ruben's *Adoration of the Magi*.
Time: Chapel: Mon.-Sat., 9am-3:45pm
Place: King's Parade
Contact: ph. 350411

Anthropology and Archaeology
The Museum of Archaeology and Anthropology explores human development from prehistory to the present. The fascinating gallery covers the people of Asia, Africa, and the Americas.
Time: Mon.-Fri., 2pm-4pm; Sat., 10am-12:30pm
Place: Downing St.
Contact: ph. 359714

Canterbury
This cradle of English Christianity has attracted flocks of pilgrims since St. Augustine arrived from Rome, converted King Ethelbert, and built the first cathedral in 597. Sadly, historic Canterbury has been ravaged three times: first by Danish Vikings in 1011, then by Roundheads during the English Civil War, and finally by German bombing in WWII. But the city has retained a medieval flavor, with ancient buildings and winding streets now thick with tourists.

Ancient Hospice
One of Canterbury's oldest buildings is the Hospital of St. Thomas the Martyr, opened in 1080 for poor pilgrims. Inside the building, which has been used as an almshouse since the 16th century, there

are medieval murals and a dual chapel in the vaulted crypt.
Time: Mon.-Sat., 10am-1pm & 2pm-5pm; Sun., 2pm-5pm
Place: High St.
Contact: ph. 62395

Fascinating Finds

Don't miss the Royal Museum and Gallery, with its Roman finds,
Anglo-Saxon jewelry and glass, the silver Canterbury Cross, and
old English procelain. The same building houses the Regimental
Museum of the Buffs, with displays of photos, weapons, and
trophies of the Royal East Kent Regiment.
Time: Mon.-Sat., 10am-5pm
Place: High St.
Contact: ph. 45247

Mother Church

Canterbury Cathedral, Britain's mother church, stands on the site
of St. Augustine's original church of the 6th century. Tall and regal,
the cathedral incorporates grand architecture, superb stained glass,
and ancient shrines; it awes the pilgrim and casual visitor alike.
The Trinity Chapel contains the site of Thomas a Becket's martyrdom and the tombs of Henry IV and Edward, the Black Prince.
Time: Mon.-Fri., 9:30am-5:30pm; Sat., 9:30am-3:15pm
Place: Palace St.
Contact: ph. 64212

Cardiff

Cardiff, the capital of Wales, is a lively seaport city with acres of
parkland and an acclaimed Civic Center. Only traces remain of
Cardiff's Roman founders and Norman conquerors, but there's
abundant evidence of its 19th-century prosperity. With its extravagant castle and excellent museums and galleries, Cardiff is a
must for the traveler interested in Wales.

National Museum

The National Museum of Wales is one of Britain's best museums.
Finds from all prehistoric periods are housed in the Archaeology
Department, with Bronze Age jewelry, Iron Age firedogs, and ear-
ly Christian relics. The Art Department has works by Renoir, Matisse,

and Turner. The outstanding Department of Industry is noted for steam engines, ship models, and the Mining Gallery, with an ingenious display of a working coal mine.
Time: Mon.-Sat., 10am-5pm; Sun., 2:30pm-5pm
Place: Museum Ave., Cathays Park
Contact: ph. 397951

New Museum
At the new Welsh Industrial and Maritime Museum, working exhibits portray industrial growth in Wales. There are collections of boats, cars, and trains, including a famous Penydarren locomotive.
Time: Mon.-Sat., 10am-5pm; Sun., 2:30pm-5pm
Place: Butte St.
Contact: ph. 481818

Cheltenham
At the edge of the Cotswolds, Cheltenham is a spa town of style and elegance, with many fine Georgian homes on tree-lined avenues. In 1715, a farmer discovered an alkaline spring in his field, and by 1738, the first spa was built. A visit by King George III in 1788 added royal respectability, and the rest, as they say, is history.

Pumproom
A masterpiece of Greek Revival architecture and the most impressive building in town, the Pittville Pumproom is the epitome of English elegance. The spa is used for concerts, receptions, and dances. It also houses the Cheltenham Gallery of Fashion and a history of the town from the 18th century to the present.
Time: April-Oct.: Tues.-Sun., 10:30am-5pm; Nov.-March: Tues.-Sat., 10:30am-5pm
Place: Pittville Park
Contact: ph. 521621

Composer's Birthplace
Gustav Holst's birthplace is now a museum honoring the innovative

musician. The museum contains Holst's piano, memorabilia, and a reference collection.
Time: Tues.-Sat., noon-5pm
Place: 4 Clarence Rd.
Contact: ph. 524846

Arts and Crafts Movement
Cheltenham's Art Gallery and Museum houses a collection on the British Arts and Crafts movement, along with 17th-century Dutch paintings, ceramics, folklife exhibits, and local archaeological finds.
Time: Mon.-Sat., 10:30am-5pm
Place: Clarence St.
Contact: ph. 37431

Medieval Church
The 12th century Church of St. Mary has many interesting Norman features and a beautiful 14th-century rose window.
Time: Mon.-Sat., 9am-5pm
Place: Well Walk
Contact: ph. 22878

Chester

No other city in Great Britain rivals Chester in its abundance of archaeological and architectural treasures. Founded in 70 AD as the Roman fortress of Deva, Chester is wealthy in Roman artifacts. Medieval walls built on Roman foundations still encircle the town center. Unique to Chester's old town are the Rows, a double tier of shops, each with its own covered walkway. Chester's preservation of its past has made it a popular tourist spot, so be prepared for crowds during the summer.

Annual Festival
Each June, Chester presents a two-week festival with a variety of free events and activities—from raft races on the River Dee to marching band contests.
Contact: Tourist Information, Town Hall Square, ph. 40144, ext. 2111

Roman Relics
Replicas of the Roman fortress Deva, dioramas, and a life-size model

of a Roman legionnaire are just a few of the exhibits at the Grosvenor Museum in Chester.
Time: Mon-Sat., 10:30am-5pm; Sun., 2:30pm-5pm
Place: 27 Grosvenor St.
Contact: ph. 21616

Wall Tours
Chester has the best-preserved medieval townwalls in Great Britain. More than two miles of wall, rising as high as 40 feet, completely enclose the town center. The tourist office offers free guided tours along the entire circuit; check at the Town Hall Square for dates and times.

Ancient Cathedral
The restored Chester Cathedral began as a shrine for the relics of St. Werburgh, a Mercian princess. The interior reveals something from every period and style, but the carved 14th-century choir stalls are the finest feature.
Time: daily, 8am-5:15pm
Place: St. Werburgh's St.
Contact: ph. 24756

Chichester
One of Britain's oldest towns, Chichester was a thriving settlement when the Romans arrived about 40 AD. The Saxons gave the city the name Cissa Ceaster in the 5th century, and the Normans made it an important cathedral town in 1091. Today, it's a town of Georgian and Victorian homes within medieval walls. On the western edge of town, archaeologists have uncovered Fishbourne Palace, the largest Roman building yet discovered in Great Britain.

Warehouse Museum
Set in an 18th-century warehouse, Chichester's District Museum presents displays on local archaeology, folklife, and geology.
Time: Tues.-Sat., 10am-5:30pm
Place: 29 Little London Rd.
Contact: ph. 784683

Roman Finds

The Guildhall Museum, a branch of the District Museum, is noted for its early English architecture. The medieval Greyfriar's Hall shows Roman finds from the West Sussex region.
Time: June-Sept.: Tues.-Sat., 1pm-5pm
Place: Priory Park
Contact: ph. 784683

Norman Cathedral

The soaring spire of Chichester Cathedral dominates the city and the Sussex countryside. Built between 1091 and 1199, the Cathedral possesses some of the finest medieval stone carving in Britain. Originally colored and bejeweled, the carvings depict the raising of Lazarus and Christ at Bethany. In contrast, the Cathedral also has contemporary features: Chagall's stained glass, Sutherland's paintings, and a beautiful John Piper tapestry.
Time: daily, 9am-5:30pm
Place: Market Cross
Contact: ph. 78729

Colchester

Colchester, England's oldest town, was the capital of the Belgie Kingdom when the Romans established their first colony there in 50 AD. Today, the foundations of Roman walls and temples stand together with Saxon fortifications, a Norman castle and churches, and 17th- and 18th-century homes.

Hollytrees

This Georgian mansion, dating from 1718, has a fine collection of antiquities discovered in and around Colchester.
Time: Mon.-Sat., 10am-1pm & 2pm-5pm
Place: High St.
Contact: ph. 712481

Ancient Abbey

Only the nave and parts of the west front remain from the 11th-century St. Botolph's Priory, England's first Augustinian abbey. The ruins, however, are dramatic, with huge columns supporting tiers

of massive arches, built mostly of bricks pilfered from the ruins of Roman Camulodinum.
Time: always open
Place: Priory St.

Pastoral Ways

The Colchester Museum of Social History offers a look at the lifestyles of the Essex countryside. Displays include crafts, costumes, and domestic items.
Time: Mon.-Sat., 10am-1pm & 2pm-5pm
Place: Trinity St.
Contact: ph. 712481

Natural History

Housed in the former All Saints Church, the Natural History Museum features finds from around Essex, with special reference to the Colchester area.
Time: Mon.-Sat., 10am-1pm & 2pm-5pm
Place: High St.
Contact: ph. 712481

Coventry

Thanks to German air raids, Coventry is a new city, with only a few reminders of a rich heritage. One of England's most important medieval towns, Coventry developed around a 7th-century convent, hence the name. No one knows for certain if Lady Godiva's famous ride occurred there, but she and her husband Leofric are buried in the ruins of the abbey they founded in the 11th century.

Modern Cathedral

On the night of November 14, 1940, a Nazi bombing raid demolished the 14th-century Coventry Cathedral. In 1962, the new Cathedral was consecrated just north of the old St. Michael's. The contemporary cathedral is filled with outstanding modern art. Best known are the immense Sutherland tapestry, Epstein's St.

Michael and the Devil, and the stained glass.
Time: daily, 8:30am-7pm
Place: Priory Row
Contact: ph. 27597

Medieval Gem

St. Mary's Guildhall, near the cathedral ruins, was built in 1345 for the Merchant's Guild. The restored hall has a medieval kitchen, a minstral's gallery, and a hall with portraits and Flemish tapestries.
Time: May-Oct.: Mon.-Sat., 10am-5pm; Sun., noon-5pm
Place: Bayley Lane
Contact: ph. 25555, ext. 2874

Art and Archaeology

The Herbert Art Gallery and Museum includes folk arts, archaeology, natural history, and design. After visiting the new Cathedral, the Sutherland studies for the *Life of Christ* tapestry will be of special interest.
Time: Mon.-Sat., 10am-6pm; Sun., 2pm-5pm
Place: Jordan Wells
Contact: ph. 25555, ext.2315

Crieff

Distillery Tours

Glenturret Distillery, Scotland's oldest, welcomes visitors for tours and tastings. There's a film on the history of Glenturret and whisky, and a museum.
Time: March-Oct.: Mon.-Fri., 10am-12:30pm & 1:30pm-4pm; July & Aug.: Mon.-Sat., 9:45am-4:30pm; Nov.-Feb.: Mon.-Fri., 2pm-4pm
Place: The Hosh (off A85)
Contact: ph. 07-642424

Crystal Tours

The Stuart Strathearn Factory opens its doors to visitors interested in watching craftsmen create crystal the traditional way. After view-

ing a film on Stuart crystal, guests are given demonstrations by master glass workers and a tour.
Time: Mon.-Sat., 9am-5pm
Place: Muthill Rd.
Contact: ph. 07-644004

Revived Art
Perthshire Paperweights Ltd. has revived the 19th-century European art of glass paperweight making. They produce limited editions and collectors' items based mainly on original Venetian designs.
Time: Mon.-Fri., 9am-12:30pm & 1pm-4pm
Place: Muthill Rd.
Contact: ph. 07-642409

Derby
Conquered by Romans, Saxons, and Danes, ill-fated Derby was also devasted by the Plague during the 16th and 17th centuries. The town recovered and prospered during the Industrial Revolution, but little remains of its past.

Industrial Derbyshire
Housed in a restored silk mill, the Derby Industrial Museum presents a large collection of airplane engines and an exhibit of aviation history. The gallery shows a multi-media "Introduction to Derbyshire Industries," which is surprisingly interesting.
Time: Tues.-Fri., 10am-5pm; Sat., 10am-4pm
Place: Full St.
Contact: ph. 31111, ext. 740

Porcelain Tour
The Royal Crown Derby Porcelain Company is open for tours by appointment. This old firm produces some of Great Britain's finest china and porcelain. A large collection of historic porcelain is displayed in the company museum.
Time: Mon.-Fri., 10am-noon & 2pm-4pm (by appointment)
Place: Osmaston Rd.
Contact: ph. 47051

Museum and Gallery

The Derby Museum and Art Gallery exhibits local folklife, antiquities, paintings, sculpture, and porcelain.
Time: Tues.-Sat., 10am-5pm
Place: The Strand
Contact: ph. 31111

Devizes

Collected around its ancient marketplace, Devizes sustains an aura of past prosperity as an important old cloth town. Wealthy in medieval buildings, Divizes has an abundance of picturesque lanes, old coaching inns, and ancient buildings.

Peerless Museum

The Devizes Museum is one of the richest repositories of English archaeology in the nation. Its holdings extend from models of nearby Stonehenge and Avebury Circle to priceless Bronze Age ornaments and weapons. In addition, there are Neolithic tools, Roman sculpture, and jewelry.
Time: Thurs., 11am-1pm & 2pm-5pm
Place: 31 Long St.
Contact: ph. 2765

Pygmy Pines

The Pygmy Pinetum—created in 1958 to establish a collection of dwarf conifers—covers four acres near Devizes. The largest such collection in the world, it has over 1,200 species growing in a formal, landscaped setting.
Time: Mon.-Fri., 8am-5pm
Place: Hillworth Rd.

Dorchester

Dorchester will evoke memories of fictional Casterbridge for Thomas Hardy fans. Though a busy commercial town today, it preserves enough old inns, shops, and homes for one to picture it as it was in Hardy's day.

Tolpuddle Martyrs
In 1834, Dorchester's Old Shire Hall was the scene of the trial of the Tolpuddle Martyrs, farm workers persecuted for forming a union. The building is now a memorial to the men who were transported in irons to Australia.
Time: May-Oct.: Mon.-Sat., 10am-noon & 2:30pm-4pm; Nov.-April: 10am-noon
Place: Crown Court
Contact: ph. 65211, ext. 210

Prehistoric Fortress
Maiden Castle, a complicated system of ramparts and ditches, is Britain's most impressive ancient hillfort. The huge oval was once the largest earthwork fortification in Europe. In use for over 2,000 years, beginning around 1800 BC, Maiden Castle incorporates palisades, Neolithic burials, earthworks, and the foundations of a Roman temple.
Time: always accessible
Place: half-mile southwest of town

Dufftown

Little Dufftown is the capital of Scotland's important malt whisky industry. The modern town was established in 1817 by James Duff, Earl of Fife, but the 6th-century St. Moluag Church is testimony to a more ancient habitation.

Town Museum
The Dufftown City Museum displays whisky-making apparatus, historical exhibits, and items from the 13th-century Mortlach Kirk.
Time: May-Sept.: daily, 9:30am-6:30pm
Place: Tower Square
Contact: ph. 73701

The Whisky Story
Founded in 1887 by Major William Grant, the Glenfiddich Distillery has a museum dedicated to Scotch whisky. You'll emerge an ex-

pert on the secrets of mashing, malting, fermenting, distilling, and bottling the liquor.
Time: May-Oct.: Mon.-Sat., 9:30am-4:30pm; Sun., noon-4:30pm; Nov.-April: Mon.-Fri. only
Place: A941 at north end of town
Contact: ph. 20373

Gratis Drams
At Glenlivet Distillery, you can see an exhibit of ancient artifacts used by Scotland's earliest distillers and tour the distillery. Following the tour, free drams are offered to all.
Time: April-Oct.: Mon.-Fri., 11am-4pm
Place: 11 miles southwest on B9136
Contact: ph. 08-073427

Dundee

Dundee is an active seaport on the north shore of the Firth of Tay. The city's beautiful location almost makes up for the unsightly factory sprawl.

Planetarium
Mills Observatory has a planetarium, astronomy and space exploration galleries, and a terrific refracting telescope.
Time: April-Sept.: Mon-Fri., 10am-5pm; Sat., 2pm-5pm; Oct.-March, Mon.-Fri., 3pm-10pm; Sat., 2pm-5pm
Place: Glams Rd.
Contact: ph. 67138

Scottish Wildlife
The Barrack Street Museum presents exhibits on Scottish natural history and wildlife of the Highlands, as well as a display on the Great Tay whale.
Time: Mon.-Sat., 10am-5:30pm
Place: Barrack St.
Contact: ph. 23141

Castle Museum
The 15th-century Broughty Castle houses a museum of weaponry

and armor, plus wildlife displays and a retrospective on Dundee's whaling industry.
Time: Mon.-Thurs. & Sat., 10am-1pm & 2pm-5:30pm
Place: Broughty Ferry
Contact: ph. 76121

Dunfermline

A thousand years ago, Dunfermline was Scotland's capital, but today the "auld grey town" is just a busy manufacturing city. Dunfermline's rich (but mostly lost) heritage is expressed in its ruined abbey and a few ancient buildings.

Carnegie Birthplace

The cottage in which industrialist-philanthropist Andrew Carnegie was born in 1835 has been transformed into the Carnegie Birthplace Museum. The memorial hall examines his life and the good works done by the trust created with his massive wealth.
Time: April-Oct.: Mon-Sat., 11am-5pm; Sun., 2pm-5pm; Nov.-March: daily, 2pm-5pm
Place: Moddie St. & Priory Lane
Contact: ph. 724302

Mansion Museum

Pittencrieff House Museum is set in a romantic glen beneath the ruined Malcomb Canmore Tower. The mansion has exhibits of Scottish history, costume, and culture. In 1902, Carnegie purchased the house and presented it to the city.
Time: May-Aug.: Mon. & Wed.-Sun., 11am-5pm
Place: Pittencrieff Park
Contact: ph. 722935

Edinburgh

A beautiful city, Scotland's capital is really two cities in one. The Old Town spreads from the ancient castle in a maze of medieval alleys and passageways, while the 18th-century "New Town" is a masterpiece of Georgian town planning, with broad avenues and elegant townhouses.

Great Museum

The Royal Scottish Museum has such diverse displays as decorative arts, geology, and technology. The old locomotives and ships are particularly interesting. Daily lectures and films supplement the exhibits.
Time: Mon.-Sat., 10am-5pm; Sun., 2pm-5pm
Place: Chambers St.
Contact: ph. 225-7534

Canongate

Dating from 1591, Canongate Tolbooth has an unusual turreted steeple and projecting clock. Highland costumes are on display, with explanations on how ancestry is traced through tartan plaids. Items from the Museum of Childhood are also on display.
Time: Mon.-Sat., 10am-5pm
Place: 163 Canongate
Contact: ph. 225-1131, ext. 6638

Art Treaures

The National Gallery of Scotland, opened in 1859, contains works by European masters from the 14th through 20th centuries. Just some of the greats represented are Titian, Van Gogh, Goya, Cezanne, Turner, and Velasquez.
Time: Mon.-Sat., 10am-5pm; Sun., 2pm-5pm
Place: The Mound
Contact: ph. 556-8921

Local History

Huntley House, a 16th-century aristocrat's mansion, is today the City Museum of Local History. Historical memorabilia is augmented by displays of pottery, glassware, and silver.
Time: June-Sept.: Mon.-Sat., 10am-6pm; Oct.-March: Mon.-Sat., 10am-5pm
Place: 142 Canongate
Contact: ph. 225-2424, ext.6689

Scottish Parliament

Parliament House was built in 1639 to house the Scottish Parlia-

ment, which met there until the Union of 1707. Today the Hall is the Supreme Law Court of Scotland.
Time: Mon.-Fri., 10am-4pm
Place: East George IV Bridge
Contact: ph. 225-2595

Portrait Gallery
The Scottish National Portrait Gallery contains paintings of individuals who have made contributions to national history, such as Robert Burns, Sir Walter Scott, Mary Queen of Scots, James I, and Ramsay MacDonald.
time: Mon.-Fri., 10am-noon & 2pm-4:40pm
Place: Queen St.
Contact: ph. 556-8921

Literary Giants
Lady Stair's House, an elegant townhouse dating from 1622, contains a museum of literary relics of Sir Walter Scott, Robert Burns, and Robert Louis Stevenson.
Time: Mon.-Sat., 10am-5pm
Place: Lawnmarket
Contact: ph. 225-2424, ext.6593

Free Concerts
During the summer there are free concerts, variety shows, dances, and a puppet theater at the Princes Street Gardens.
Contact: Tourist Information Bureau, 5 Waverly Bridge, ph. 226-6591

Modern Arts
Scotland's National Gallery of Modern Art has a large collection of 20th-century painting, sculpture, and graphic arts. Among the modern greats represented are Picasso, Magritte, Matisse, Dali, and Lichtenstein. The gallery of prints and lithos is also impressive.
Time: Mon.-Fri., 10am-12:30pm & 2pm-4:30pm
Place: Belford Rd.
Contact: ph. 556-8921

National Archives
The Register House is now the headquarters for the Scottish Record

Office and a repository for the National Archives of Scotland. The Historical and Legal Research rooms are open to the public, and there are changing exhibits of historical documents.
Time: Mon.-Fri., 9am-4:45pm
Place: Princes St.
Contact: ph. 556-6585

Municipal Art
Edinburgh's City Art Center houses a collection of paintings, sculpture, prints, and drawings by Scottish artists, dating from the 16th century to the present. They also present temporary exhibitions.
Time: Mon.-Sat., 10am-5pm
Place: 2 Market St.
Contact: ph. 225-2424, ext.6650

Exeter

Exeter was settled by the Dumnoni long before the Romans built a walled town there in the first century AD. Bits of those ramparts can be seen in Rougemont Castle and on West Street. During Elizabethan days, Drake, Raleigh, Frobisher, and other "Seadogs" met in the Ship Inn to lift a pint or two before sailing. In May of 1942, Nazi bombers flattened much of the city center, but restoration has guaranteed lots to see.

Ancient Hall
Exeter's Guildhall, in use since 1330, is the oldest Municipal Hall in the United Kingdom. Inside, there are displays of civic regalia, guild crests, portraits, and silver.
Time: Mon.-Sat., 10am-5:15pm
Place: High St.
Contact: ph. 72979

Grand Cathedral
The architectural glories of Exeter Cathedral's interior are unmatched in England. The stonework, woodwork, stained glass, and window tracery are breathtaking, and the roof is the longest uninterrupted stretch of Gothic vaulting in the world. The Cathedral's other treasures include the 14th-century Bishop's Throne, the Minstral

Gallery, and a medieval astrological clock which shows the earth at the center of the universe.
Time: Mon.-Sat., 8am-5:30pm
Place: Cathedral Close
Contact: ph. 32189

Regimental Souvenirs
Covering the history of the Devonshire Regiment from its foundation in 1685, the Regimental museum displays weapons, medals, and military memorabilia.
Time: Mon.-Fri., 9am-4:30pm
Place: Barracks Rd.
Contact: ph. 218178

Tuckers Hall
The guildhall of the Incorporation of Weavers, Fullers, and Shearmen has been occupied by the guild since 1471. The hall has an oak barrel roof and outstanding carved paneling. Items discovered when a false ceiling was removed are on display.
Time: June-Sept.: Tues., Thurs., & Fri., 10:30am-12:30pm; Oct.-May: Fri. only
Place: Fore St.
Contact: ph. 36244

Glasgow

Scotland's most populous city has always played the ugly sibling to fair Edinburgh. Still, Glasgow has many pleasant surprises for the visitor who takes the time to explore. Medieval Glasgow grew up around the Cathedral, but the town's architectural glory is Victorian. Today, the city is acquiring a reputation as a cultural center and has some of Scotland's best museums, galleries, and schools.

Award Winner
The Burrell Collection, Glasgow's newest museum, has over 8,000 pieces: Asian jades and ivories; Middle Eastern carpets; ancient

artifacts from Greece and Italy; medieval and European art; and stained glass and tapestries.
Time: Mon.-Sat., 10am-5pm; Sun., 2pm-5pm; guided lecture tours at 11am & 2pm
Place: Pollock County Park
Contact: ph. 649-7151

Palatial Hall
The City Chambers is a neo-Renaissance structure opened in 1888 by Queen Victoria. The opulent lobby, stairways, and chambers seem more suited to a Venetian palace than a Scottish city hall.
Time: guided tours Mon.-Wed. & Fri., 10:30am & 2:30pm
Place: George St.
Contact: ph. 221-9600

Manor and Park
With 400 acres of lawns, woods, and gardens, the Pollock County Park has something to suit any visitor. There are demonstration gardens, a jogging trail, agricultural exhibits, and a mansion with a collection of European art and furnishings.
Time: Park: daily, 7am-7pm; House: Mon.-Sat., 10am-5pm; Sun., 2pm-5pm
Place: Pollockshaw Rd.
Contact: Park: ph. 632-9299; House: ph. 632-0274

Gothic Perfection
Glasgow Cathedral, Scotland's finest Gothic structure, was the only Scottish cathedral spared by Protestant rioters during the Reformation. The Lower Church dates from the 6th century and contains the tomb of Glasgow's patron saint, Mungo. Most of the church dates from the 13th and 14th centuries.
Time: Mon.-Sat., 10am-7pm; Sun., 1pm-6pm
Place: Cathedral Square & Castle St.
Contact: ph. 552-0220

Victorian Necropolis
You'll find a senstional graveyard behind the cathedral, with tombs of Glasgow's rich and famous.
Time: daylight hours
Place: Cathedral Square

Oldest House

Just across the square from the cathedral, Provand's Lordship, built in 1471, is Glasgow's oldest standing house. It now exhibits period furnishings and decor.
Time: Mon.-Sat., 10am-5pm; Sun., 2pm-5pm
Place: 3 Castle St.
Contact: ph. 552-8819

Getting Around

Glasgow's Museum of Transport portrays the development of land and sea transportation from horse-drawn vehicles to ocean liners. Vintage bikes, cars, locomotives, and trams are displayed, along with the Subway Gallery, a reconstruction of a Glasgow underground station.
Time: Mon.-Sat., 10am-5pm; Sun., 2pm-5pm
Place: 25 Albert Drive
Contact: ph. 423-8000

Fine Art

The Hunterian Art Gallery presents a major collection of 17th- and 18th-century paintings from France, Italy, and the United Kingdom.
Time: Mon.-Fri., 10am-12:30pm & 1:30pm-5pm; Sat., 9:30am-1pm
Place: Hillhead St.
Contact: ph. 339-8855, ext. 7431

Award Winner

The award-winning Hunterian Museum contains exhibits on geology, anthropology, coins, and history.
Time: Mon.-Fri., 10am-5pm; Sat., 9:30am-1pm
Place: University Ave.
Contact: ph. 339-8855, ext. 221

Botanic Gardens

The Glasgow Botanic Gardens covers 40 acres along the River Kelvin. There's an herb garden, annuals, and the Kibble Palace, one of Britain's largest glasshouses. The greenhouses maintain a

colorful pageant year-round with orchids, begonias, and semi-tropical plants.
Time: Gardens: daily, 7am-sunset; Greenhouses: Mon.-Sat.,
1pm-4:45pm
Place: Great Western Rd.
Contact: ph. 334-2422

Military Memorabilia
Three centuries of military history are explored at the Royal Highland Fusiliers Museum.
Time: Mon.-Fri., 10am-5pm
Place: 518 Sauchiehall St.
Contact: ph. 332-0961

History for Kids
Haggs Castle, built in 1585, is now a museum designed for children. Time exploration—especially the 400-year castle's history—is the main theme. Children can participate in activities of the past, such as spinning, weaving, and butter-making, and the gardens recreate the household plots of the 16th and 17th centuries.
Time: Mon.-Sat., 10am-5pm; Sun., 2pm-5pm
Place: 100 St. Andrew Drive
Contact: ph. 427-2725

Zoo and Park
Linn Park covers more than 200 acres of woodlands in south Glasgow. Along with nature trails, flower gardens, and a ruined castle, there's an enjoyable little zoo with collections of highland animals and British ponies.
Time: daily, 7am-sunset
Place: Cathcart
Contact: ph. 637-1147

People's Palace
Variety is the order of the day at the People's Palace Museum, which presents a record of Glasgow's history and social life. Exhibits in-

clude everything from music hall entertainment to the Tobacco Lords.
Time: Mon.-Sat., 10am-5pm; Sun., 2pm-5pm
Place: Glasgow Green
Contact: ph. 554-0223

City Landmark
Melding Scottish Baronial and Art Nouveau styles of architecture, Charles Rennie Macintosh created Glasgow's most famous building, the School of Art. Don't miss the free tour of this masterpiece.
Time: Mon.-Fri., 10am-noon & 2pm-4pm
Place: 167 Renfrew St.
Contact: ph. 332-9797

Museum-Gallery
Glasgow's Art Gallery and Museum has one of Britain's best art collections. Old Masters, French Impressionists, and pre-Raphaelites are all well-represented, and there are galleries of pottery, sculpture, natural history, and European weaponry.
Time: Mon.-Sat., 10am-5pm; Sun., 2pm-5pm
Place: Kelvingrove Park
Contact: ph. 334-1134

Gloucester

Already well-established when the Romans built their great fortress of Colonia Glevum here in the first century AD, Gloucester has figured in many important events in English history. Still standing on its Roman street plan, Gloucester is worth a visit, if only to see its sublime cathedral.

Historic Cathedral
Begun in 1089, Gloucester Cathedral achieved its present Gothic Perpendicular form in the 14th century. The cathedral's major attractions are the tomb of Edward II, England's earliest fan vaulting, and the spectacular East Window—at 72 feet high, the largest stained glass window in Britain. Gloucester Cathedral is full of historic

monuments, including the tomb of Robert of Normandy, the eldest son of William the Conqueror.
Time: Mon.-Sat., 7:30am-6pm
Place: Northgate St.
Contact: ph. 28095

Folk Museum

A group of Tudor and Jacobean half-timbered houses now hosts a charming Folk Museum devoted to Gloucestershire. Exhibits illustrate domestic life, rural trades, and handicrafts. Best of all is the delightful Double Gloucester cheese dairy.
Time: Mon.-Sat., 10am-5pm
Place: 99-103 Westgate St.
Contact: ph. 26467

Museum and Gallery

Local archaeology, emphasizing Roman mosaics and sculpture, is the focus of Gloucester's City Museum and Art Gallery. You'll also find an aquarium, 18th-century furniture, paintings by Gainsborough and Turner, and more.
Time: Mon.-Sat., 10am-5pm
Place: Brunswick Rd.
Contact: ph. 24131

Guildford

Guildford is an old Saxon town with many interesting buildings along cobbled High Street. The emblem of this lively town near London is its fine old guildhall with a projecting clock.

House Gallery

Built in 1660, Guildford House Gallery has exhibitions that change monthly and include material from children's art to fine paintings and craftwork from ceramics to quilts.
Time: Mon.-Sat., 10:30pm-4:30pm
Place: High St.
Contact ph. 503406, ext. 3531

Abbot's Hospital

The Hospital of the Blessed Trinity, founded in 1619, is a splended

Tudor building with a magnificent gatehouse. Inside, there are exhibits of antiques and memorabilia.
Time: May-Sept.: Sat., 11am-4pm
Place: High St.
Contact: ph. 62670

Guildford Museum
Local history and Surrey archaeology form the core of the Guildford Museum collections. Finds include Roman and Saxon items from local digs, along with ecclesiastic articles from Chertsey Abbey. The Industrial Gallery covers glass-making and wrought iron work. Another gallery features the life and works of Lewis Caroll.
Time: Mon.-Sat., 11am-5pm
Place: Castle Arch, Quarry St.
Contact: ph. 503497, ext. 3540

Halifax

This West Yorkshire city was one of northern England's great textile towns, and it has preserved a number of buildings from its heyday in the 18th century.

Cloth Hall
Piece Hall, built in 1779, is perhaps the finest cloth hall in Europe. After recent use as a food market, it has been restored and converted into a museum and gallery. The hall houses craft and antique booths and holds local art exhibits and entertainment programs.
Time: Mon.-Sat., 8am-6pm; Sun., 10am-5pm
Place: Gibbet Rd.
Contact: ph. 68725

Mansion Museum
The Bankfield Museum is set in a park overlooking Halifax and contains costumes and textiles from around the world. There are also local history displays, including a model guillotine, toys, and the Royal Dragoon Guards Museum.
Time: Mon.-Sat., 10am-5pm; Sun., 2:30pm-5pm
Place: Boothtown Rd.
Contact: ph. 54823

Hastings

Although much of this port town reflects a Victorian face, there's still a warren of close-built lanes with huddled houses and cottages. A large section of Saxon Hastings has disappeared under the sea.

Fishermen's Museum

This former fishermen's church is now a museum devoted to the local fishing industry. The principal exhibit is the Hastings Sailing Lugger, designed with a flat bottom to allow winching up the beach.
Time: April-Sept.: Mon.-Thurs., Sat., & Sun., 10:30am-noon & 2pm-6pm
Place: Rock a Nore Rd.
Contact: ph. 424787

Museum and Gallery

The Hastings Museum and Art Gallery houses collections of local history, archaeology, Sussex iron work, and pottery. But the real highlight is Dunbar Hall, a replica of an Indian palace built for an exhibition in 1888 and now a gallery for Oriental art.
Time: Mon.-Sat., 10am-1pm & 2pm-5pm; Sun., 3pm-5pm
Place: Cambridge Rd.
Contact: ph. 435952

Hull

Britain's third-largest port is a somewhat dreary industrial center, typical of northern England. Nevertheless, Hull does have some interesting historic attractions.

Dockology

The Town Docks Museum has displays on shipping, fishing, whales, and whaling, plus an exhibit called "Hull and the Humber."
Time: Mon.-Sat., 10am-5pm; Sun., 1:30pm-4:30pm
Place: Queen Victoria Square
Contact: ph. 222737

Abolitionist's House

William Wilberforce, Britain's leading abolitionist, was born in this mansion in 1759. As a member of Parliament for 45 years, he

devoted his career to banning the slave trade. The Slave Room has mementoes of his campaign.
Time: Mon.-Sat., 10am-5pm; Sun., 1:30pm-4:30pm
Place: 25 High St.
Contact: ph. 222737

Cars and Carts
The Transport and Archaeology Museum contains Roman and Saxon finds from the Humberside area, along with an exhibit on road transportation through the ages.
Time: Mon.-Sat., 10am-5pm; Sun., 1:30pm-4:30pm
Place: High St. 36

Kirkhill

Unique Enterprise
Once a fortress of the Lovat Clan, Moniack Castle is now headquarters for a novel Scottish undertaking—the Highland Winery. This pioneering vineyard produces a variety of wines, including mead.
Time: Mon.-Sat., 10am-5pm
Place: Moniack Castle Rd.
Contact: ph. 04-638-3283

Leicester

Below Leicester's rows of brick buildings lies an ancient heritage that's just being rediscovered. Established during the Bronze Age, Leicester later became the Roman town of Ratae. Among the Roman relics found are Britain's largest Roman bath and many mosaic pavements. Sadly, most of Leicester's medieval streets have been bulldozed for commercial development.

Roman Ratae
Mosaics and a 75-foot section of fortifications at the Jewery Wall Museum are reminders of Leicester's past as the Roman colony

of Ratae. Inside, you'll find Roman relics and the remains of a public bath.
Time: Mon.-Thurs. & Sat., 10am-5:30pm; Sun., 2pm-5:30pm
Place: St. Nicholas Circle
Contact: ph. 554100

British Costume
English clothing from 1769 to 1925 and reconstructions of shops of the 1920's are on display at the Wygston House Museum of Costume.
Time: Mon.-Thurs. & Sat., 10am-5:30pm; Sun., 2pm-5:30pm
Place: Applegate
Contact: ph. 554100

Medieval Hall
Leicester's 14th-century guildhall is a museum piece in its own right. Its principal attractions are the half-timbered Great Hall, the Mayor's parlor, the old jail, and the library.
Time: Mon.-Thurs. & Sat., 10am-5:30pm; Sun., 2pm-5:30pm
Place: Guildhall Lane

Industrial Revolution
The city's industrial past is displayed at the Leicester Museum of Technology. Exhibits include an antique steam shovel, textile machinery, land transportation devices, and ingenious engines.
Time: Mon.-Thurs. & Sat., 10am-5:30pm; Sun., 2pm-5:30pm
Place: Corporation Rd.
Contact: ph. 661330

Letchworth

Utopian Town
Built in 1903, Letchworth was the world's first "Garden City." Displays in the Garden City Museum (in the offices of architects Parker and Unwin) explain the concept and development of this planned community, a vision of writer Ebenezer Howard.
Time: Mon.-Fri., 2pm-4:30pm; Sat., 10am-4pm
Place: 296 Norton Way South
Contact: ph. 3149

Museum and Gallery
The Letchworth Museum and Gallery presents archaeolgical material from North Herfordshire, including Iron Age and Roman finds, plus natural history exhibits and art shows.
Time: Mon.-Sat., 10am-5pm
Place: Broadway
Contact: ph. 5647

Liverpool

If you choose to take a nostalgic trip and "ferry 'cross the Mersey," be prepared to deal with the poverty that grips Britain's largest export port. Although a cheerful stroll down Penny Lane is possible, much of Liverpool has a depressing pall of gloom over it.

Blue Coat Chambers
A Queen Anne building in the heart of Liverpool houses the Blue Coat Chambers Gallery. With a garden courtyard and cobblestone quadrangle, this 18th-century school now holds artists' studios, galleries, and a concert hall.
Time: Mon.-Sat., 10am-5pm
Place: School Lane
Contact: ph. 709-5297

Outstanding Variety
You could spend a full day exploring the entertaining Merseyside County Museum. Displays include a vivarium, aquarium, vintage vehicles, African and Mediterranean antiquities, maritime history (with superb models of the port), time and space galleries, and a planetarium.
Time: Mon.-Sat., 10am-5pm; Sun., 2pm-5pm
Place: William Brown St.
Contact: ph. 207-0001

Fine Arts
The Walker Art Gallery is one of Britain's finest provincial art museums. Besides a gallery of British art with works by Hogarth

Constable, and Turner, the Walker is known for its valuable Italian and Flemish Old Masters.
Time: Mon.-Sat., 10am-5pm; Sun., 2pm-5pm
Place: William Brown St.
Contact: ph. 227-5234, ext. 2064

Church of Superlatives

Begun in 1904, but not completed until 1978, Liverpool's Anglican Cathedral is the largest Anglican church in the world. This neo-Gothic monument has the highest Gothic arches ever built (107 feet), the highest and heaviest bells (219 feet high, 31 tons), and the biggest organ (10,000 stops) in the world. One of its stained glass windows took 18,000 square feet of glass to construct.
Time: daily, 8:30am-6pm
Place: St. James Mount
Contact: ph. 709-6271

London

Great Britain may not be a great power any longer, and London long ago ceased to be an Imperial capital, but it is still a city of vitality, variety, and cosmopolitan fascination. Packed with historical associations, monuments, and memories, London is Europe's largest capital city.

The heart of the metropolis is the tiny City of London, barely one mile square and no larger than the old Roman town of Londinium. But that is only offical London; the great city, sprawling over 620 square miles, is really made up of dozens of villages and neighborhoods, each with its own character. London is actually the sum total of Camden and Kensington, Paddington and Chelsea, Holborn and Hampstead, and dozens of neighborhoods woven into the fabric of this fascinating capital.

Children's World

The Bethnal Green Museum of Childhood, opened in 1875, exhibits old toys, model soldiers, and antique dollhouses. However,

the museum is not devoted exclusively to kids. The upper galleries contain clothing, furniture, and Art Nouveau art.
Time: Mon.-Thurs. & Sat., 10am-6pm; Sun., 2:30pm-6pm
Place: Cambridge Heath Rd., E2
Contact: ph. 980-2415

Classic Furnishings
Situated in an interesting set of almshouse buildings, the Geffrye Museum pays tribute to the woodworkers of the past. The collection is distributed throughout a series of period rooms, ranging from the Elizabethan era to the 1930's.
Time: Tues.-Sat., 10am-5pm
Place: Kingsland Rd, E2
Contact: ph. 739-8368

Political History
The development of British democracy is portrayed in the National Museum of Labor History. A visual history from the 18th to 20th centuries is explored in two sections: Autocracy to Democracy, and the Growth of Socialism.
Time: Tues.-Sat., 9:30am-5pm; Sun., 2:30pm-5:30pm
Place: Limehouse Hall, Commercial Rd., E14
Contact: ph. 515-3229

Science and History
Essex County geology, biology, archaeology, and local history are displayed at the stately Passmore Edwards Museum.
Time: Mon.-Wed. & Fri., 10am-6pm; Thurs., 10am-8pm; Sat., 10am-1pm & 2pm-5pm
Place: Romford Rd., E15
Contact: ph. 519-4296

Walthamstow Village
The Vestry House Museum shows items of local historical significance. Artifacts from the Stone Age onward are displayed, including a Bremer Car, the first British automobile with an internal combustion engine.
Time: Mon.-Fri., 10am-5:30pm; Sat., 10am-5pm
Place: Vestry Rd., E17
Contact: ph. 527-5544, ext.4391

William Morris Gallery

The Water House, home to William Morris, now exhibits the artist's designs, furnishings, pre-Raphaelite paintings, and Rodin sculpture.

Time: Tues.-Sat., 10am-1pm & 2pm-5pm
Place: Lloyd Park, Forest Rd., E17
Contact: ph. 527-5544, ext. 4390

War and Remembrance

Established in 1920 in what had been the notorious Bedlam Asylum, the Imperial War Museum covers wars involving Commonwealth countries since 1914. The vast collection is a miscellany of weapons, vehicles, models, posters, photos, and films—all a poignant reminder of Britain's sacrifices during the 20th century.

Time: Mon.-Sat., 10am-5:50pm; Sun., 2pm-5:50pm
Place: Lambeth Rd., SE1
Contact: ph. 735-8922

International Stamps

Britain's National Postal Museum contains the world's most comprehensive assemblage of postage stamps. The collection includes nearly every stamp issued since 1878, plus the archives of the Thomas de la Rue Co., which furnished stamps to 150 countries for a century. Original drawings and proofsheets of every British stamp issued since 1840 are also displayed.

Time: Mon.-Fri., 10am-4:30pm
Place: King Edward St., EC1
Contact: ph. 606-3769

A History of Service

The Museum of the Order of St. John traces the history of two organizations founded by the Order—the St. John Ambulance Brigade and the St. John Association. The collections include medical instruments, memorabilia, and books.

Time: Fri. & Sat., 10am-6pm; guided tours at 11am & 2:30pm
Place: St. John's Lane, EC1
Contact: ph. 253-6644

Ancient Hall

Rebuilt in 1411, 1666, and after WWII bomb damage, London's

historic Guildhall has been the center for civic ceremonies for centuries and the setting for many famous trials. There's a magnificent vaulted crypt, the Guild Library, and a Clock Museum with timepieces illustrating 500 years of clockmaking.
Time: Mon.-Sat., 10am-5pm; (also Sun., 2pm-5pm from May-Sept.)
Place: Basinghall St., EC2
Contact: ph. 606-3030

Londonology
The Museum of London, one of the city's most entertaining museums, is devoted entirely to London and its people. Everything on view portrays some aspect of the 2,000-year history of London. The real showstopper is the Lord Mayor's Ceremonial Coach.
Time: Tue-Sat., 10am-6pm; Sun., 2pm-6pm
Place: 150 London Wall, EC2
Contact: ph. 600-3699, ext. 240

High Finance
The London Stock Exchange, the world's second-largest, is the center of Britain's commercial finance. Reconstruction in the 1960's created the modern trading floor, which can be viewed from the public gallery. Guides describe the transactions, and an explanatory film is presented eight times daily.
Time: Mon.-Fri., 9:45am-3:15pm
Place: 8 Throgmorton St., EC2
Contact: ph. 588-2355

Telecom Showcase
The past, present, and future of Britain's telecommunications industry is explored at the Telecom Technology Showcase. Exhibits demonstrate 200 years of telecommunications progress.
Time: Mon.-Thurs., 10:30am-4:30pm
Place: 135 Queen Victoria St., EC4
Contact: ph. 248-7444

Middle Temple
Originally the site of the Knights Templar complex, the Middle Temple is a superb Tudor structure built during the reign of Elizabeth I. The hall features medieval paneling, a double hammerbeam roof, and stained glass windows. Other treasures include a table made

from timbers of the *Golden Hind* (the ship in which Drake circum-navigated the globe) and a huge table carved from a single oak from Windsor Forest. Shakespeare's play *Twelfth Night* was first presented in the Great Hall in 1601.
Time: Mon.-Sat., 10am-noon & 3pm-4:30pm
Place: Temple Ave.
Contact: ph. 353-4355

Temple Church
Consecrated in 1185, the Middle Temple Church is the finest of Britain's five surviving Round Churches. It contains the best collection of knightly effigies in the country.
Time: Sept.-June: Mon.-Fri., 9:30am-4pm
Place: Inner Temple Lane

Antique Brewery
Whitbread's Beer was first brewed at this location in 1749, and many of the 18th-century buildings are now open for tourists.
Time: Mon.-Fri., 10am-5pm
Place: Chiswell St., EC2

Bishop's Palace
In use for nearly 800 years, Lambeth Palace is the London residence of the Archbishop of Canterbury. Much of the present building is 15th and 16th century, but the crypts date from 1197. There's an extensive collection of portraits and a fine gatehouse.
Time: by appointment only
Place: Lambeth Palace Rd., SE1
Contact: ph. 928-8282

Villa Collections
Set on windy, historic Blackheath, Rangers House is a gracious 18th-century mansion. Today it houses Jacobean and Stuart portraits and Old Masters. Rangers House also hosts chamber concerts, poetry readings, and temporary exhibits.
Time: Mon.-Sat., 10am-5pm
Place: Chesterfield Walk, SE3
Contact: ph. 853-0035

London Marvel
Londoners describe the new Thames Barrier as the "Eighth Wonder of the World." The ⅓-mile barrier, built to protect the city from catastrophic flooding, is the world's largest moveable flood barrier. The exhibition center has displays describing the extraordinary construction project.
Time: Mon.-Sat., 10:30am-5pm
Place: Eastmoor St., SE7
Contact: ph. 854-1373

Old London
The Cuming Museum displays Roman and medieval finds from the area south of London Bridge, along with items from the community through the ages. There's a great exhibit on the family dairy which operated in the neighborhood for nearly two centuries, plus local pottery and Dickens memorabilia.
Time: Mon.-Fri., 10am-5:30pm; Sat., 10am-5pm
Place: 155 Walworth Rd., SE17
Contact: ph. 703-3324, ext. 32

Famous Gallery
Tate Gallery houses the national collection of British paintings and sculpture from the 19th and 20th centuries. Works by Blake, Turner, Constable, and Hogarth, plus French post-Impressionists and the International Abstract school, are well-represented. The Tate presents free lectures and films on various art topics.
Time: Mon.-Sat., 10am-5:30pm; Sun., 2pm-5:30pm
Place: Millbank, SW1
Contact: ph. 821-1313 or 821-7128

Militaria
The National Army Museum exhibits the history of the British and Colonial Armies from 1485 onward.
Time: Mon.-Sat., 10am-5pm; Sun., 2pm-5pm
Place: Royal Hospital Rd., SW3
Contact: ph. 730-0717

Big Guns
The Royal Artillery Museum contains a selection of artillery pieces

from a 15th-century bombard to WWII Howitzers. Small arms and machine guns are also on display.
Time: Mon.-Fri., noon-4pm; Sat. & Sun., 1pm-4pm
Place: Repository Rd., SE18

Townsend Gem

Designed by C. H. Townsend, London's Horniman Museum is a marvelous Art Nouveau building. The collections include musical instruments, natural history exhibits, dolls, and religious articles. Frequent lectures and concerts are given, along with a variety of special exhibits.
Time: Mon.-Sat., 10:30am-6pm; Sun., 2pm-6pm
Place: London Rd., SE23
Contact: ph. 693-5254

Geological Heritage

The intriguing and entertaining Geological Museum's exhibits include "The Story of the Earth" (the largest earth science exhibit in the world), British fossils, minerals of the world, the Gemstone Collection, and much more. There are also frequent lectures and films.
Time: Mon.-Sat., 10am-6pm; Sun., 2:30pm-6pm
Place: Exhibition Rd., SW7
Contact: ph. 589-3444

Science and Industry

The London Science Museum traces the development of science and industry in Great Britain over the centuries. The extensive collection (more than you can possibly see in one day) includes textile machinery, early locomotives, antique cars, nuclear energy, astronomy, the history of medicine, printing, and computers. And don't miss the National Aeronautical Gallery, with Britain's first jet.
Time: Mon.-Sat., 10am-6pm; Sun., 2:30pm-6pm
Place: Exhibition Rd., SW7
Contact: ph. 589-3456, ext. 632

Victoria and Albert

Possibly the largest museum of applied art in the world, the Victoria and Albert displays everything from Venetian glass to high-

button shoes. Special treasures include Chinese art and sculpture by Donatelo.
Time: Mon.-Sat., 10am-5:30pm; Sun., 2:30pm-5:30pm
Place: Cromwell Rd., SW7
Contact: ph. 589-6371, ext. 411

Natural History

The pink- and blue-tiled facade of the British Museum of Natural History is a fitting introduction to this popular institution. Devoted to the evolution of life, it houses a permanent collection and also produces special exhibitions. Displays cover British natural history, the origin of species, meteorites, and a lifesize model of a blue whale.
Time: Mon.-Sat., 10am-6pm; Sun., 2:30pm-6pm
Place: Cromwell Rd., SW7
Contact: ph. 589-6323

Primitive Peoples

Embracing the cultures of pre-industrial societies, the Museum of Mankind houses engrossing displays on the people of Asia, Africa, the Pacific basin, and the Americas.
Time: Mon.-Sat., 10am-5pm; Sun., 2:30pm-6pm
Place: 6 Burlington Gardens, W1
Contact: ph. 437-2224, ext. 43

Beautiful Variety

Hertford House has paintings by Rubens, Rembrandt, Hals, and many others. There's also furniture by master craftsmen, Sevres porcelain, Limoges enamels, and a collection of armor.
Time: Mon.-Sat., 10am-5pm; Sun., 2pm-5pm
Place: Manchester Square, W1
Contact: ph. 935-0687

Hogarth House

William Hogarth lived in this charming 17th-century house from 1749-1764. Personal mementoes, drawings, and engravings of the artist are on view.
Time: Mon.-Sat., 11am-6pm
Place: Hogarth Lane, Great West Rd., W4
Contact: ph. 994-6757

Rothschild Mansion

The Gunnersbury Park Museum, formerly Rothschild Mansion, is home to the Borough of Ealing Museum. On display are local archaeological finds, costumes, old Rothschild coaches, and the original Victorian kitchens. There are frequent craft shows and demonstrations on weekends.
Time: March-Oct.: Mon.-Fri., 1pm-5pm; Sat. & Sun., 2pm-6pm.
Nov.-Feb.: Mon.-Fri., 1pm-4pm; Sat. & Sun., 2pm-4pm
Place: Popes Lane, W3
Contact: ph. 992-1612

Commonwealth Institute

Unmistakable with its extraordinary copper roof, the Commonwealth Institute is a permanent exhibition about peoples and countries of the Commonwealth. Opened in 1962, it has displays on each nation and a library, cinema, and art gallery.
Time: Mon.-Sat., 10am-5:30pm; Sun., 2pm-5pm
Place: Kensington High St., W8
Contact: ph. 603-4535

Victorian Fantasy

A simple exterior belies the exotic interior of Leighton House, where Lord Fredrick Leighton created a Moorish fantasy in the 1870's. The walls of the amazing Arab Hall are clad in rare Islamic tiles and gilt decoration. Galleries in the house show modern and Victorian art.
Time: Mon.-Sat., 10am-5pm
Place: 12 Holland Park Rd., W14
Contact: ph. 602-3316

Drury Lane

Drury Lane, as the Theatre Royal is known, is London's most beautiful theater. The delightful interior has a domed entrance, an ornate rotunda, and a Grand Salon.
Time: free tours by appointment only
Place: Catherine St., WC2
Contact: ph. 836-8108

British Museum

Founded in 1753, the British Museum houses the world's greatest

collection of international antiquities. The museum is far too vast to be seen in just one visit: ancient Greek, Roman, and Oriental art, prehistoric Britain, coins, medals, prints, drawings, and much, much more. By law, the famed British Library receives one copy of every book published in the United Kingdom, and it has attracted scholars for years (most notably Karl Marx, who wrote *Das Kapital* there). The spectacular hall, with its massive dome and windows, can be visited only with a guide. The Library Gallery, devoted to priceless books and documents, displays such treasures as the Magna Carta, a Guttenburg bible, first editions of Shakespeare's plays, da Vinci sketches, and the Lindisfarne Gospels.
Time: Mon.-Sat., 10am-5pm; Sun., 2:30pm-6pm
Place: Great Russell St., WCl
Contact: ph. 636-1555

British Crafts
Contemporary British crafts, jewelry, furniture, prints, and books are shown at the British Crafts Centre.
Time: Mon.-Fri., 10am-5:30pm; Sat., 11am-5pm
Place: 43 Earlham St., WC2
Contact: ph. 836-6993

Archival Museum
The Public Record Office contains British government records dating back to the Norman conquest. Among the treasures, you'll find the Domesday Book of 1086, the log of *H.M.S. Victory,* Shakespeare's will, Guy Fawkes' confession, and royal letters.
Time: Mon.-Fri., 1pm-4pm
Place: Chancery Lane, WC2
Contact: ph. 405-3488, ext. 475

National Gallery
One of the world's great galleries, the National Gallery has works by Titian, Rubens, Van Gogh, Rembrandt, da Vinci, Renoir, Monet, and many more. There are lectures and tours daily, along with special exhibits and programs.
Time: Mon.-Sat., 10am-6pm; Sun., 2pm-6pm
Place: Trafalgar Square, WC2
Contact: ph. 839-3321

Portrait Gallery
The National Portrait Gallery has Britain's collection of portraits of eminent citizens, protrayed through paintings, busts, photos, and cartoons. Special exhibitions on historical themes are held throughout the year.
Time: Mon.-Fri., 10am-5pm; Sat., 10am-6pm; Sun., 2pm-6pm
Place: St. Martins Place, WC2
Contact: ph. 930-1552

Unique Museum
Nothing has changed at Sir John Soane's House since his death in 1837. On request of the famous architect, this block of houses has been maintained as a museum for his collection of paintings, sculpture, fossils, clocks, and Egyptian sarcophagi.
Time: Tues.-Sat., 10am-5pm
Place: 12 Lincoln's Inn Fields, WC2
Contact: ph. 405-2107

Keats House
The Regency House, where John Keats lived, is now a museum housing the author's manuscripts, letters, and memorabilia.
Time: Mon.-Sat., 10am-1pm & 2pm-6pm; Sun., 2pm-5pm
Place: Keats Grove, NW3
Contact: ph. 435-2062

Air Force Museum
Great Britain's Royal Air Force Museum incorporates WWI hangers and modern facilities. The museum is devoted to the RAF and its role during WWII. Aircraft on display include a Sopwith Camel, a Spitfire, a Lancaster bomber, a Harrier jump-jet, and many more.
Time: Mon.-Sat., 10am-6pm; Sun., 2pm-6pm
Place: Aerodrome Rd., NW9
Contact: ph. 205-2266, ext. 38

Jewish Heritage
London's Jewish Museum houses items from Jewish communities

in Great Britain and Europe. The Venetian Ark and Torah decorations are especially noteworthy.
Time: Mon.-Thurs., 12:30pm-3pm; Sun., 10:30am-12:45pm
Place: Adolph Tuck Hall, Tavistock Square, WC1
Contact: ph. 387-3081

Oldest Synagogue
The Spanish and Portuguese Synagogue, built in the 1700's, is Britain's oldest standing synagogue. The interior is richly decorated with woodwork and Dutch chandeliers.
Time: Fri. & Sun., 10am-noon
Place: Bevis Marks, EC2

Lord Mayor's Procession
On the second Saturday in November, the new Lord Mayor of London rides from the old Guildhall to the Royal Law Courts in a three-ton carriage, accompanied by armored guards and colorful floats.
Contact: City Public Relations Office, Guildhall, London, EC2, ph. 606-3030

Diamond Tours
The London Diamond Centre offers free tours through their exhibition covering diamonds from the mine to the finished gem. There's also a free film. (Sorry, no samples.)
Time: Mon.-Fri., 9:30am-5:30pm
Place: 10 Hanover St.
Contact: ph. 629-5511

Manchester

Manchester is a no-nonsense industrial city, where old neighborhoods have been replaced with hideous tower blocks. Still, Manchester is an old city, and there's much to see and do.

Fashion Statement
The world of fashion from the 16th century to the present is reviewed at the Manchester Gallery of English Costume. Exhibits of ever-

changing style don't overlook essential accessories, such as shoes, hats, and underwear.
Time: Tues.-Fri., 10am-6pm
Place: Platt Fields, Rushholme
Contact: ph. 224-5217

Gothic Extravaganza
Manchester's neo-Gothic city hall looks more like a Bavarian castle than a municipal building. Outside, it's all turrets and carvings; inside, it's regal, with a hammerbeam roof and murals by Ford Maddox Brown.
Time: guided tours: Mon.-Fri., 10am & 2:30pm
Place: Albert Square

Renowned Library
The John Rylands Library, housed in a Victorian Gothic hall, merged with the University Library in 1972 to become one of the world's best research libraries, with over three million volumes. Bibliophiles will be interested in the Petrarch Manuscripts, early Biblical fragments, and writings on silk, skins, and stone.
Time: Mon.-Fri., 10am-5:30pm; Sat., 10am-1pm
Place: Deansgate
Contact: ph. 834-5343

Science and Industry
The Greater Manchester Museum of Science and Industry contains steam engines, computers, electrical exhibits, locomotives, and a restored 1830's train station.
Time: daily, 10:30am-5pm
Place: Liverpool Rd.
Contact: ph. 832-2244

Municipal Gallery
Manchester's City Art Gallery, set in an outstanding Greek Revival building, has works by Turner, Constable, and Gainsborough, along with enamels, glass, and sculpture.
Time: Mon.-Sat., 10am-6pm
Place: Mosley St.
Contact: ph. 236-9422

Something for Everyone
A ramble through the staid Manchester Museum will reveal exhibits from Egyptian tombs to Roman coins and a natural history collection with eight million specimens.
Time: Mon.-Sat., 10am-5pm
Place: Oxford Rd.
Contact: ph. 273-3333

Celebrated Gallery
Whitworth Gallery has a world-class collection of British and European watercolors by Turner, Van Gogh, Cezanne, and Picasso. There are also Japanese prints, Renaissance drawings, and tapestries.
Time: Mon.-Sat., 10am-5pm
Place: Whitworth Park
Contact: ph. 273-4865

Modern Arts
The Gallery of Modern Art is devoted to contemporary paintings, sculpture, and decorative arts. Loan exhibits periodically replace the permanent collection.
Time: Mon.-Sat., 10am-6pm
Place: Princess St.
Contact: ph. 236-9422

Marypark

A Wee Dram
Sample one of Scotland's finest malt whiskies at the Glen Farcias Distillery. While you're there, visit the museum and exhibition center to learn more about the product.
Time: Mon.-Fri., 9am-4:30pm
Place: one mile west of Marypark
Contact: ph. 08-072257

Morcombe Lake

Cookie Tours
If you've developed a sweet tooth for those delectable English

biscuits, you'll enjoy a tour of Moore's Dorset Biscuits Factory. Established as a cottage industry on a local farm, More's still produces tasty Dorset shortbread and ginger biscuits.
Time: Mon.-Fri., 9am-5pm
Place: A35
Contact: ph. 789-253

Newark-on-Trent

The Council for British Archaeology voted Newark-on-Trent one of the 50 best towns in the nation. The honor derives from the town's marvelous medieval homes, inns, shops, and churches, along with the impressive Newark Castle.

Folklife
The Millgate Museum of Social and Folklife houses a collection reflecting the domestic and commercial life of Nottinghamshire. There are also workshops for local crafts.
Time: Mon.-Fri., 9am-noon & 1pm-5pm
Place: Millgate
Contact: ph. 79403

Georgian Hall
The Newark Town Hall is one of England's finest Georgian municipal halls. A collection of 17th- and 18th-century documents, paintings, and civic regalia are on display.
Time: Mon.-Fri., 10am-noon & 2pm-4pm
Place: Market Place
Contact: ph. 700200

Medieval Church
Quaint St. Mary Magdalene Church has some amazing medieval sculpture—gargoyles, knights, fools, and foliage—plus a Norman crypt and a beautiful rood screen.
Time: Mon.-Sat., 9:30am-4pm
Place: Market Place
Contact: ph. 702358

Newcastle-upon-Tyne

Newcastle began as a minor Roman fort at the end of Hadrian's Wall. Today, it's a dreary industrial city. This drab town, however, does have some fine museums and Roman relics, but there's little else to entice the traveler.

Antiquities
Newcastle University's Museum of Antiquities specializes in Roman remains, with an ingenious representation of Hadrian's Wall.
Time: Mon.-Sat., 10am-5pm
Place: University Quadrangle
Contact: ph. 328511

British Arts
Set in an unusual neo-Renaissance building, Laing Art Gallery has pre-Raphaelite works, porcelain, silver, and rare glass.
Time: Mon.-Fri., 10am-5pm; Sat., 10am-4pm; Sun., 2:30pm-5pm
Place: Higham Place
Contact: ph. 327734

Science and Engineering
The Museum of Science and Engineering emphasizes industrial development in northeastern England. There are historical displays (like the first hydraulic engine) and a Maritime Gallery.
Time: Mon.-Fri., 10am-5:30pm; Sat., 10am-4:30pm
Place: West Blanford Street
Contact: ph. 326789

Crafts Center
Geordie artisans create and display their wares at Newcastle's old Blackfriars Monastery.
Time: Mon.-Sat., 10am-5pm
Place: Monk Street
Contact: ph. 615367

North Wootton

Mendip Vineyard
Wootton Vineyard, in the Mendip foothills, is planted with vines

introduced from Alsace and the Rhineland. Visitors are welcome to tour the vineyards and buildings of this bold enterprise.
Time: Mon.-Sat., 10am-1pm & 2pm-5pm
Place: North Townhouse Road
Contact: ph. 07-498-9359

Norwich

With its twisting, cobbled lanes, magnificent cathedral and castle, and hundreds of medieval buildings, Norwich is a great place to wander and explore. How can you resist a town that boasts "a church for every Sunday and a pub for every other day of the year"?

Religious Art
St. Peter Hingate Church, one of Norwich's 32 medieval churches, is now a museum for ecclesiastical art. The stained glass, fine roof, and art collection make this 15th-century church worth a visit.
Time: Mon.-Fri., 10am-5pm
Place: Princess Street
Contact: ph. 611277, ext. 296

Military Memorabilia
Medals, weapons, uniforms, and trophies amassed by the Royal Norfolk Regiment over the centuries are on display at the Regimental Museum.
Time: Mon.-Fri., 9am-noon & 2pm-4pm
Place: Brittania Road
Contact: ph. 28455

Nottingham

Robin Hood and his merry men would be hard pressed to find their way around Nottingham today. Although the hero's old stomping ground was founded in the 5th century, it is now a product of the Industrial Revolution, with factories, warehouses, and offices. But it's still possible to discover a few medieval holdovers, especially Nottingham's celebrated old pubs.

Brewhouse Yard

As the name implies, the Brewhouse Yard Museum, once a brewery, now portrays daily life in old Nottingham in a row of 17th-century buildings. Ancient cellars, carved from the rock below the city, are also open, with exhibits describing their uses through the ages.
Time: Mon.-Sat., 10am-noon & 1pm-5pm
Place: Castle Boulevard
Contact: ph. 411881, ext. 67

Canal Museum

The Canal Museum depicts the history of the River Trent from the Ice Age through the 20th century. Exhibits include boats, artifacts, and navigational devices.
Time: April-Sept.: Wed.-Sat., 10am-noon & 1pm-6pm; Sun., 1pm-5pm. Oct.-March: Wed., Thurs., & Sat., 10am-noon & 1pm-5pm; Sun., 1pm-5pm
Place: Canal Street
Contact: ph. 598835

Science at Work

A restored flour mill, once belonging to the miller and mathematician George Green, now houses a museum with displays of Green's scientific contributions.
Time: Wed.-Sat., 10am-noon & 1pm-5pm
Place: Belvoir Hill
Contact: ph. 503635

Goose Fair

Long before Robin Hood camped in Sherwood Forest, Nottingham was celebrating the annual Goose Fair. Originally a market for the goose trade, the yearly event is now a fair with games, rides, and events for children of all ages.
Time: first Thursday in October
Contact: Information Office, 18 Milton Street, ph. 40661

Fashions and Textiles

Costumes from 1730 to 1960 are shown in furnished period rooms at the Museum of Costume and Textiles. Other galleries contain

rare tapestries, embroideries, and displays of lace. Be sure to peek at "200 Years of Underwear"—it's quite revealing.
Time: daily, 10am-5pm
Place: 43 Castlegate
Contact: ph. 411881

Historic Hall
Built in 1580 for the High Sheriff of Nottingham, Wallaton Hall now houses the Natural History Museum. Set in a large park, the mansion is all towers, balustrades, and friezes. The stable block displays Nottingham's industrial history and explores the textile, tobacco, and pharmaceutical industries.
Time: April-Sept.: Mon.-Sat., 10am-6pm; Sun., 2pm-6pm. Oct.-March: Thurs. & Sat., 10am-4:30pm; Sun., 1:30pm-4:30pm
Place: Wallaton Park
Contact: ph. 281333

Oban

Backed by a ring of hills and slung around a sheltered harbor, Oban is one of Scotland's leading seaside resorts, as well as a bustling port. Ferries depart Oban's docks for islands all over Scotland.

Whiskey Tour
You can tour the distillery and have a free dram of another great malt whiskey at the friendly Oban Distillery.
Time: March-Oct.: Mon.-Fri., 10am-noon & 2pm-4pm
Place: George Street
Contact: ph. 63551

Oxford

Oxford is a jewel in the crown of Britain's civic treasures. Even though the "sweet city with her dreaming spires" is being surrounded by industry and tacky housing, the core of Oxford remains intact. All of the colleges have historic and architectural merit and are set in park-like grounds. The first students came to Oxford in the 12th century, but the earliest colleges weren't established until 1249. Rebuilding during the 18th century destroyed many ancient buildings, but Oxford remains a beautiful town, guaranteed to inspire.

Historic Museum
The Ashmolean Museum is Britain's oldest public museum, founded in 1683. Devoted mostly to archaeology and art, the fine arts collection is truly superb. There are also displays of silver, porcelain, and applied arts.
Time: Tues.-Sat., 10am-4pm; Sun., 2pm-4pm
Place: Beaumont Street
Contact: ph. 512651

Great Library
Bodleian Library, one of the world's oldest and finest, receives a copy of every book published in Britain. Founded in 1602, the library's exhibits include Shelly memorabilia, Shakespeare manuscripts, ancient books, and illuminated manuscripts.
Time: Mon.-Fri., 9am-5pm; Sat., 9am-12:30pm
Place: Broad Street
Contact: ph. 244675

History of Science
Oxford's Museum of the History of Science houses the best collections of early astronomical and mathematical instruments in the world. Particularly noteworthy are the Islamic astrolabes, primitive microscopes, cameras, and medical machinery.
Time: Mon.-Sat., 8:30am-5pm; Sun., 10am-noon & 2:30pm-4pm
Place: Broad Street
Contact: ph. 243997

Oldest Garden
The Oxford University Botanic Garden, founded in 1621, is the oldest garden of its type in Britain. The diverse collections include tropical plants, roses, and economic gardens.
Time: Mon.-Sat., 8:30am-5pm; Sun., 10am-noon & 2pm-4:30pm
Place: High Street or Rose Lane
Contact: ph. 242737

Modern Art
Housed in a converted brewery, the Museum of Modern Art

presents 20th-century art, plus lectures, films, and seminars.
Time: Tues.-Sat., 10am-5pm; Sun., 2pm-5pm
Place: Pembroke Street
Contact: ph. 722733

Prehistoric Collections
Over a million items crowd the Pitt Rivers Museum, one of Britain's oldest archaeological museums. Displays include Stone and Bronze Age finds, plus artifacts contributed by British explorers.
Time: Mon.-Sat., 2pm-4pm
Place: South Parks Road
Contact: ph. 512541

Rothes

Distillery Tours
Established in 1840, the Glen Grant Distillery produces a superb single malt whisky. Visitors can observe distillation methods and sample the product.
Time: Mon.-Fri., 10am-4pm
Contact: ph. 03-403494

Shrewsbury

Standing within a great loop of the River Severn, Shrewsbury is a wonderful medieval town, crammed with old houses and shops on narrow lanes and dominated by its haughty Norman castle.

Townhouse Museum
The elegant home of Lord Robert Clive now displays china and porcelain produced locally, plus costumes, industrial archaeology, and the Museum of the Queen's Dragoon Guards.
Time: Mon.-Sat., 10am-5pm
Contact: ph. 61196

Culinary Center
Radbrooke Culinary Museum is a turn-of-the-century kitchen and

pantry, with old cookbooks and equipment.
Time: Mon.-Fri., by appointment
Place: Radbrooke Road
Contact: ph. 52686

Swansea

This once ugly seaport is revitalizing its rundown districts. Founded by Vikings in the 10th century, Swansea developed as a thriving port through the Middle Ages, and, by the 19th century, it was a leading coal and copper town. Today, many of the city's scarred areas have become parkland, and Swansea wins the "Wales in Bloom" award year after year.

Seafaring Days

The Swansea Maritime and Industrial Museum, on the redeveloped seafront, has displays relating to the Port of Swansea, its industry, and its environment. Exhibits include old steam locomotives and antique boats, and there's even a working woolen mill.
Time: daily, 10:30am-5:30pm
Place: South Dock
Contact: ph. 50351

Pots and Paintings

European and British porcelain and pottery are displayed, along with French and British paintings, at the Glynn Vivian Gallery and Museum.
Time: Mon.-Fri., 10:30am-5:30pm
Place: Alexandra Road
Contact: ph. 55006

Twickenham

Baroque Octagon

Designed in 1719, the Orleans House Gallery is a unique Baroque octagon in a gorgeous Thames River setting near London. Much of the original house, where exiled King Louis Phillipe of France resided from 1830-48, was demolished, but the octagon was

preserved. A gallery shows art exhibits throughout the year.
Time: Tues.-Sat., 1pm-5:30pm; Sun., 2pm-5:30pm
Place: Riverside, Richmond Road
Contact: ph. 892-0221

Palladian Villa
Built in 1724 for a mistress of King George II, Marble Hill House
is a splendid example of English Palladian architecture, with love-
ly views of the Thames. Marble Hill now houses Georgian fur-
nishings and paintings by Hogarth, Reynolds, and Wilson.
Time: Mon.-Thurs., Sat., & Sun., 10am-5pm
Place: Richmond Road
Contact: ph. 892-5115

Warwick

Warwick's streets are lined with old gabled houses, beautiful
chapels, and Elizabethan gems. Standing guard above them all is
the Warwick Castle, set majestically along the River Avon.

Shire Museum
The Warwickshire Museum displays the geology, ecology, and
history of the shire. It's noted for the Sheldon tapestry map, fine
habitat exhibits, and a giant, fossilized pleisaur.
Time: Mon.-Sat., 10:30am-5:30pm
Place: Market Place
Contact: ph. 493431, ext. 2500

St. John's House
Now a branch of the county museum, St. John's House stands on
the site of a medieval hospice. Inside, you'll find domestic scenes,
a Victorian schoolroom, costumes, old musical instruments, and
mementoes of the Royal Warwickshire Regiment.
Time: Tues.-Sat., 10am-12:30pm & 1:30pm-5:30pm
Place: Coten End
Contact: ph. 493431, ext. 2021

Willenhall

Unique Exhibit

Willenhall Library houses England's only museum devoted entirely to the locksmith's trade. Locks from all over the world are on display, with ancient and modern examples, minatures, and monster padlocks.

Time: Mon., Tues., and Thurs.-Sat., 9:30am-4:30pm
Place: Walsall Street
Contact: ph. 21244, ext. 3115

Winchester

Graceful Winchester mirrors England's long history in its treasure of medieval buildings and its great cathedral. An important town in Roman times, Winchester became the capital of the Kingdom of Wessex. William the Conqueror ignored London and made Winchester his seat of government. The heart of the city remains ancient High Street—narrow, steep, and rich in history.

Visions of Camelot

High on the west wall of Winchester Castle's Great Hall hangs the legendary Round Table of King Arthur. William the Conqueror built the first fortress on this site, but Henry III enlarged and remodelled it in 1235. All that remains today is the Great Hall, with its imposing marble columns and fabled relic, where Sir Walter Raleigh was condemned to death and where Judge Jeffreys held the bloody Assize trial in 1685.

Time: Mon.-Fri., 10am-5pm; Sat. & Sun., 2pm-5pm
Place: Castle Street
Contact: ph. 54411, ext. 366

Militaria

Serle House, a Baroque mansion with a beautiful garden, now houses the Royal Hampshire Regiment Museum. Displays include weapons, maps, and other paraphernalia.

Time: Mon.-Fri., 10am-noon & 2pm-4pm
Place: Southgate Street
Contact: ph. 61781, ext. 261

York

York is one of Britain's most important and interesting cities. The heart of the old walled city is a maze of lanes lined with ancient houses leaning crookedly against each other. At the center of this web, York Minster, England's largest cathedral, dominates York's old Viking streets. The best way to discover this town is on foot. Despite the hordes of tourists, you'll enjoy York's boundless charm.

Wall Walks

A footpath extends along the top of York's medieval wall, providing a unique perspective on the great city. During the summer, the tourist office sponsors free tours beginning in Exhibition Square. The office also hosts tours on topics like medieval stained glass and Roman York.

Contact: Tourist Information Office, Exhibition Square, ph. 21756

Railway History

The National Railway Museum illustrates the history and development of British railroading, from horse-drawn rolling stock to modern locomotives.

Time: Mon.-Sat., 10am-6pm; Sun., 2:30pm-6pm
Place: Leeman Street
Contact: ph. 21261

Summer Festival

During the month of June, historic York celebrates itself with concerts, plays, lectures, fairs, and outdoor shows around town.
Contact: York Festival Office, One Museum Street, ph. 26421

Marvelous Minster

York Minster, England's largest cathedral, contains Britain's greatest concentration of medieval stained glass. Built from 1220-1472, it replaced a wooden church that had stood there for 500 years. The East Window has the largest area of stained glass, but the Five Sisters Window has the oldest glass. The Minster's finest feature is the west facade, with the glorious Rose Window, commemorating the end of the War of the Roses.

Time: Mon.-Sat., 7am-6pm

Greece

Greece

Argos

Modern Argos, a town of low whitewashed houses and noisy traffic, lies over the ancient city of the Argonauts. The contemporary town and historic ruins are dominated by a well-preserved Venetian Citadel.

Amphitheater and Baths
Erected in the 4th century BC, the Amphitheater of Argos could seat 20,000 spectators, making it one of Greece's largest theaters. Set in a steep hillside, the odeum was once paved with blue marble and used for naval combat. Below the amphitheater are ruins of 2nd-century AD Roman baths.
Time: Mon.-Sat., 8:30am-4pm; Sun., 10am-3pm
Place: Theater Street

Arkanes

Two connecting villages, Epano Arkanes and Kato Arkanes, make up this small town in the hilly wine country of Crete. Minoan remains abound in this region of olive groves and vineyards.

Minoan Settlement
The small town of Arkanes, about ten miles south of Iraklion Crete, is noted for its excavation of a late Minoan settlement. Ar-

chaeologists have exposed a temple, palace, and necropolis. Finds from the tombs and palace have been placed in Iraklion's Museo Arkhaiologiko, but the site itself is fascinating, especially the eerie necropolis.
Time: daily, 9am-sunset
Place: Founi Hill Road (two miles from town)

Arta

Arta bears witness to its medieval splendor with monuments, squares, and fabulous old churches. The town is also known for its ancient stone bridge over the Arahthos and its ruined theater, which dates from Corinthian colonization 2,500 years ago.

Byzantine Shrine
In Arta, a town of many impressive churches, the most imposing religious monument is the 13th-century Panagia Parigoritissa Church. From the exterior, the church looks like a multi-storied palace with five cupolas. The dome inside is covered by an extraordinary mosaic rondel of Christ. A gallery allows close-up views of the mosaics and a perspective on the unusual architecture.
Time: Mon.-Fri., 8:30am-12:30pm & 4pm-6pm
Place: Skoupha Street
Contact: ph. 27580

Despot's Castle
With its tall, irregular walls and 18 towers, Despot Michael II's fortress is as threatening today as it was in the 13th century. The walls surround the remains of Michael's Byzantine castle.
Time: daily, 9am-5pm
Place: Northend
Contact: ph. 27413

Athens

Athens is a cacophonous city, utterly unlike any other European capital. Beyond its colorful confusion, smelly traffic, and haphazard architecture, Athens has a heart and soul all its own. Only 150 years ago, Athens was a shabby town with just 10,000 inhabitants. During a thousand years of Byzantine and Ottoman rule, Athens had withered in the Mediterranean sun. But in 1834, it became the capital of the new kingdom of Bavarian King Otto, and the golden age of Athens' renaissance is still evident in the dignified architecture imported by Otto's German designers.

Today, swamped by immigration from the countryside and the islands, Athens' population has risen to four million. Though it's difficult to discern 3,000 years of history beneath the modern urban sprawl, the persistant tourist can discover tiny Byzantine chapels down dusty side streets, explore timeless classical temples, or imagine the ancient glory of Athens on the Acropolis.

Ancient Greece

The National Museum of Archaeology houses priceless artifacts from archaic, classical, and Hellenistic Greece. The exhibits include the Golden Mask of Agamemnon, a statue of Poseidon (fittingly recovered from the sea), a sensational collection of vases, the Stathatos jewelry collection, and thousands of ancient relics.
Time: free on Sunday, 9am-2pm
Place: One Tositsa Street
Contact: ph. 821-7717

Changing of the Guard

Don't miss the colorful changing of the guard at the Tomb of the Unknown Soldier on the Syntagma Square. The ceremony at the somber monument is provided by kilted mountain troops of an elite honor guard.
Time: Sundays, 11am; weekdays, 6pm
Place: Syntagma Square

The Acropolis

Greece's foremost tourist attraction, the Acropolis rises majestically above the Plains of Attica. With traces of habitation as far back as the Neolithic Age, the ancient sanctuary reached its height of splendor in the 5th century BC, during the Golden Age of Pericles. Today, four buildings from that age remain standing—the Parthenon, the Temple of Nike, the Propylae, and the Erechtheion. Together, these buildings are an incomparable creation of the Classical Era.
Time: free on Sunday, 10am-3:45pm
Contact: ph. 321-0219

Attic Sculpture
The Acropolis Museum, incorporated into the Acropolis complex, contains finds from the site along with ancient Korai statuary, noted for its intricacy. Large sections of the Parthenon frieze provide a vivid impression of life during Athen's Golden Age.
Time: free on Sunday, 11am-3pm
Place: Acropolis 16
Contact: ph. 323-6665

Folk Arts
Athens' Museum of Greek Popular Arts is housed in the Turkish Tzesdaraki Mosque. The collection includes handicrafts and folk arts from throughout Greece, plus a rare exhibit of Coptic costumes, icons, and jewelry.
Time: Tues.-Sat., 9am-3pm
Place: 17 Kidathineon Street & Monastiraki Square
Contact: ph. 321-3018

Greek Weaponry
Swords, uniforms, flags, and model ships dating back as far as 8000 BC can be found in the Athens War Museum. Actual combat aircraft are displayed in the courtyard.
Time: Tues.-Sat., 9am-2pm
Place: Vassilissis Sofias Ave. 24 & Rizari Street
Contact: ph. 729-0543

Fine Arts
The National Gallery and Soutzos Museum of Art exhibit works by Greek artists of the 19th and 20th centuries (including four works by El Greco), along with European art from the Renaissance through the 20th century.
Time: Tues.-Sat., 9am-3pm
Place: Vassilios Konstantinou Avenue 60
Contact: ph. 721-1010

Jewish Heritage
Greece's Sephardic Jewish community is memorialized in the Beth Shalom Jewish Museum, which displays an old Greek synagogue

and Judaica from Greece, Turkey, and Asia Minor.
Time: Sun., Mon., & Wed., 10am-1pm
Place: Milindori 8
Contact: ph. 324-2875

Royal Digs

Documents, artworks, and other exhibits relating to King Otto and
his reign are on display in the Museum of the City of Athens, housed
in the King's first Athenian home.
Time: Mon.-Fri., 9am-1:30pm
Place: Paparigopoulu Street 7
Contact: ph. 323-0168

Eclectic Collections

The Benaki Museum houses an assortment of icons, ceramics, il-
luminated manuscripts, jewelry, Egyptian artifacts, Islamic art, and
traditional handicrafts. Be sure to see the materials relating to the
Greek struggle for independence in the 19th century, with memen-
toes of Lord Byron.
Time: free Sunday, 8:30am-2pm
Place: Koumbari Street 7
Contact: ph. 361-1617

Byzantium Endures

The Byzantine Museum contains a collection of icons, vestments,
ecclesiastic art, and sculpture. Reconstructed Byzantine chapels,
with rare frescoes and mosaics, provide a picture of the architecture of Byzantium.
Time: free on Sunday, 9am-3pm
Place: Vassilissis Sofias Avenue 22
Contact: ph. 721-1027

Chios (Khios)

Chios is wealthy, thanks to the shipping dynasties based there and
the rare mastic trees growing on the rugged island. Only five miles
from the Turkish mainland, Chios has had a brutal history, often
subject to conquest, occupation, and, in 1822, a massacre of its
populace. The town has an old quarter behind the walls of an an-

cient Byzantine fortress and a charming modern district extending in a semi-circle around the busy harbor.

Stately Library

Beside the Chios Cathedral stands the renovated Korais Library. The athenaeum, named for the Chios-born scholar Adamantio Korais, has priceless books, manuscripts, engravings, and paintings.
Time: Mon.-Fri., 8am-1:30pm; Sat., 8am-noon
Place: Platia Vounakis
Contact: ph. 26555

Glorious Convent

Six miles west of town, the Convent of Nea Moni, founded about 1045, is emblazoned with mosaics and frescoes depicting the life of Christ. At the gateway, a funeral chapel contains the neatly stacked bones of thousands of islanders massacred by Turks in 1822.
Time: daily, 7am-1pm
Place: Karyes Road

Corinth

New Corinth is a lackluster town on the Gulf of Corinth. Its primary attraction is its proximity to the famous ancient city.

Ancient Ruins

With foundations dating to 800 BC and fortifications developed during Byzantine, Turkish, and Venetian occupations, the ruins of Akrokorinthos command a mountain redoubt above the remains of ancient Corinth. Among the rocks is the ancient ruin of the Aphrodite Temple, where countless prostitute-priestesses shared their affections with worshippers.
Time: daily, sunrise-sunset
Contact: ph. 23282

Delfi

When the ancient ruins of Delfi were excavated at the turn of the century, the village was demolished and a new one was built along the mountainside. Despite swarms of tourists, Delfi has retained its charm, with steep stairways and lovely panoramas of the sacred valley and the Gulf of Itea.

Temple of Athena
Providing unforgettable views of the Giona Mountains, the Sanctuary of Athena Pronaia was established around 500 BC. Surrounding the temple are remains of priestly dwellings, and nearby is the marble Rotunda of Tholos, one of Delfi's most impressive monuments.
Time: always accessible
Place: Arakhova Road

Edessa

A handsome town near Yugoslavia, Edessa overlooks a deep gorge where streams cascade to the valley floor. Beneath the falls, there's a grotto full of stalactites, and beyond the falls there's a site where ancient Edessa stood.

Festival of Flowers
Each May, Edessa hosts the Anthesteria, a flower festival with concerts, folk dancing, and events emphasizing Greek-Macedonian culture.
Contact: Tourist Police, Leoforos Filippou 31, ph. 23355

Gurnia

Minoan Town
Located in eastern Crete, Gurnia is the only Minoan town to have been excavated in its entirety. The town dates from 1600 BC but was devastated by an earthquake around 1475 BC. From the hilltop palace, there's an excellent view of the ruined city.
Time: daily, 9am-6pm
Place: 12 miles southeast of Agios Nikolas

Iraklion (Herakleion)

Iraklion is probably the least attractive city on Crete, but it makes an ideal base for visiting Minoan sites in the region.

Outstanding Icons
The Cathedral of Agios Minos features icons by the Cretan master

Michael Damaskinos, who was El Greco's tutor.
Time: Mon.-Sat., 9:30am-1pm
Place: Agin Ekaterinas Square

Venetian Walls
The old town of Iraklion is encircled by massive Venetian town walls. A walk atop the walls brings you to the Martinengo Bastion, where a simple cross marks the tomb of the Cretan writer Nikos Kazantzakis. Because of his "heretical" beliefs, the author of *Zorba the Greek* was denied burial by the Greek Orthodox Chruch and interred in the town wall. His tomb bears the epitaph: "I hope for nothing, I fear nothing, I am free."

Kalambaka

Nestled below steep cliffs, Kalambaka is a picturesque town of narrow, quiet streets. It's become popular with European tourists because of its proximity to the eerily beautiful Meteora region.

Ancient Basilica
Kalambaka's premier attraction is the 10th-century Byzantine Mitropolis Church. Remains of the mosaic pavements are found in the apse, and the soot-covered frescoes date from the 15th century.
Time: Mon.-Sat., 9am-noon & 5pm-8pm
Place: Vlakhava Street
Contact: ph. 22109

Kos

Despite throngs of tourists, Kos has retained a charm that other Dodecanese Island capitals have lost. Kos is a pleasant garden town encircled by low hills and dotted with historic spots.

Crusader Castle
The mighty Hospitallers of Rhodes Castle guards Kos' harbor. Built with "borrowed" building materials—Greek capitals and Roman

pediments and columns—it's separated from the city by a deep moat and entered by a splendid bridge.
Time: free Sunday, 10am-2pm
Place: Mandraki Harbor

Aegean Antiquities
The Kos Archaeological Museum features a 2nd-century mosaic depicting Hippocrates and Asklepios, along with vases and classical statuary.
Time: free Sunday, 10am-2pm
Place: Stephanou Kazouli
Contact: ph. 28724

Megalopolis

Modern Megalopolis is a dusty town whose only attraction is the nearby ruined city.

Arkadian Ruins
The valley below Megalopolis holds ruins of the administrative center of the Arkadian Confederation. Along with a theater seating 20,000, there are the remains of the Thersileion Assembly Hall, which had room for 16,000 representatives.
Time: Mon.-Sat., 9am-3:30pm

Methoni

Methoni is a real gem. This medieval town has a majestic waterfront castle and lighthouse, lovely beaches, and a maze of colorful streets.

Venetian Citadel
Methoni's fortress is a beautifully engineered citadel, incorporating Byzantine, Turkish, and Venetian bastions. Inside the gates, there's a minaret, a Turkish bath, and ancient crypts.
Time: Mon.-Sat., 9am-6pm; Sun., 10am-5pm
Place: Harbor

Missolongi (Mesolongion)

Only poets or dedicated admirers of Lord Byron will want to visit this unappealing city on the Ionian Coast.

Poet's Heart

During Greece's 19th-century War of Liberation, Lord Byron came to Missolongi to fight the Turks, but he died of malaria in 1824. Today, the poet and other war heroes are memorialized in the Iroon Heroes Park. Along with statues, tombs, and busts of the fallen, there's a tomb containing Lord Byron's heart.
Time: daylight hours
Place: Iroon Park

Liberation Museum

There is a collection of memorabilia relating to Missolongi's role in the 1821-26 War of Liberation at the Municipal Museum in the Dimarkhion Hall.
Time: Mon.-Fri., 10am-1pm
Place: Damaskinou
Contact: ph. 22555

Mykonos

This popular island town remains a picturesque place, but be prepared for high prices, tacky souvenir shops, and cheek-to-cheek crowds from May to October.

Unforgettable Church

Overlooking the azure sea, the blindingly white Paraportiani Church consists of four separate chapels vaulted by a tall dome and surmounted by gables.
Time: daily, 9am-5pm
Place: Mitropoleos Georgouli

Fun Folklore

Next door to the Paraportiani Church, the Mykonos Museum of Popular Arts and Folklore includes Cycladic handicrafts, ship

models, artworks, furniture, and statuary.
Time: Mon.-Sat., 4:30pm-8:30pm; Sun., 6:30pm-8:30pm
Place: Paraportiani
Contact: ph. 22235

Patras

Patras, Greece's third-largest city, is dominated by its ancient acropolis and old fortress. The hard edges of this bustling port are smoothed by arcaded streets and lovely old plazas trimmed with neo-classical buildings.

Grand Carnival
Patras is the place to be each February, during the exciting Carnival. The week-long extravaganza includes chariot races, street dances, and concerts. Costumed revelers parade through the streets on the final Sunday of the festival, tossing chocolates and candy to the crowds.
Time: changing weeks in February
Contact: National Tourist Organization, Iroon Polytekniou, ph. 420304

Roman Theater
Located near the Agora ruins, Patras Roman Odeon has many beautiful mosaics and carvings. In the summer, dances and plays are held there.
Time: Mon.-Sat., 9:30am-5pm
Place: Aigio Georgiu Street

Byzantine Fortress
Built by the Byzantines in the 7th century on ruins of an ancient Temple of Zeus, and rebuilt by the Crusaders in the 13th century, the Patras Kastro offers superb views of the Gulf of Patras and the countryside.
Time: always open
Place: Akropolis

Piraeus

Piraeus has been Athens' port since antiquity. Lively, crowded, and colorful, it merits a visit on your way to or from the islands.

Accessible Artifacts
The Piraeus Archaeological Museum houses a variety of objects from Classical, Hellenistic, and Roman periods, all recovered in the vicinity of this ancient port.
Time: free on Sunday, 10am-2pm
Place: 31 Harliaou Trikoupi
Contact: ph. 452-1598

Maritime History
Lovers of things nautical will enjoy the Piraeus Naval Museum. This exhibition provides a view of Greek maritime history from ancient times to the present.
Time: Mon.-Sat., 9:30am-3pm; Sun., 10am-2pm
Place: Freatida Street
Contact: ph. 451-6822

Rethymnon

Rethymnon is an ancient port rich in medieval atmosphere. The old quarter of narrow alleys has Venetian palazzi, an old citadel, mosques, minarets, and time-worn Turkish houses.

Venetian Stronghold
Ramparts of the Fortressa Frurio overlook Rethymnon. Built between 1573 and 1585, the citadel stands on a rocky hill, providing a panorama of the city and the sea. Although the outer walls have survived the centuries, Turkish and German bombardment destroyed the interior palace and cathedral.
Time: daily, 9am-7:30pm

Sunion

Temple of Poseidon
Situated on a crag 40 miles southeast of Athens, the Temple of

Poseidon never fails to impress, with splendid views of the sea god's marine domain.
Time: free Sunday, 9am-sunset
Place: Cape Sunion
Contact: ph. 0292-39363

Thasos

Historic Town
Thasos, the main town on the island of the same name, is dotted with ancient ruins. The old harbor, acropolis, town walls, agora, and fortifications are all worth a visit. The ruins date from the 6th century BC (the agora) to 400 AD (the Christian basilica). For information about the various sites (all free), see the Tourist Office.
Contact: Greek National Tourist Office, Limenaria, ph. 21500

Venerable Artifacts
Valuable finds from island excavations are on display at the Thasos Arkhaiologiko Museo. The exhibition is donimated by an enormous marble Kourous sculpture. Don't miss the lovely Aphrodite on a dolphin or the ivory lion.
Time: Sunday, 9am-3pm
Place: Agora

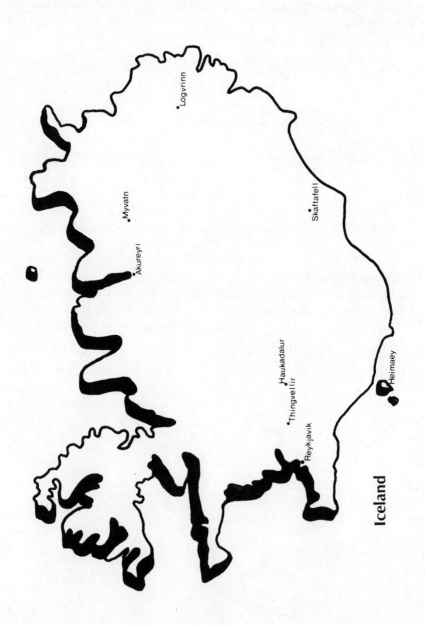

Iceland

Iceland

Akureyri

Encircled by snowcapped mountains, Iceland's second city lies at the head of the Eyjafjordur. Because of its sheltered harbor, Akureyri has become North Iceland's center of trade and transport. With only 13,000 inhabitants, Akureyri is a small town, but there's no shortage of activities or civic events.

Botanical Gardens
Akureyri's Municipal Botanical Gardens are the northern-most botanic gardens in the world. The horticultural park has more than 450 varieties of Icelandic plants. The views of Akureyri and the Eyjafjord from the gardens are breathtaking.
Time: daily, 8am-8pm
Place: Eyrarlandvegur

Folk Museum
The City Museum houses a variety of objects collected locally. The emphasis is on handicrafts, the fishing industry, implements of everyday life, and local history.
Time: June 15-Sept. 15: daily, 1:30pm-5pm
Place: Athalstraeti 58
Contact: ph. 25000

Children's Festival

The children of Akureyri celebrate the holiday of Bolludagur each February by banging on pots and barrels until they are bribed with *bollur* (cakes) to stop. Everyone gets into the act by dressing in costumes and parading through town.

Time: Monday before Shrove Tuesday in February

Haukadalur

Great Geysir

Iceland's hot springs often spout incredible geysers. At Haukadalur, the Great Geysir can shoot water 200 feet, but it's dormant most of the time these days. One of its neighboring geysers, Strokkur, spouts every few minutes.

Heimaey Island

Summer Festival

The first weekend in August, a festival attracts most of the island's population to Herjolsdalur. The merrymaking includes dancing, eating, singing, and drinking for three days.

Contact: Icelandic Tourist Bureau, ph. 25855

Reykjavik

Built on rolling hills that slope down to steel-blue Faxa Bay, Iceland's capital is the northern-most metropolis in the world and the cleanest and frendliest capital in Europe. By heating exclusively from geothermal springs, the city is virtually free of pollution.

But as modern as Reykjavik is, reminders abound that it's the capital of a nation that lives by fishing and farming. Wherever you go in town, you can spot the masts of the fishing fleet bobbing up and down in the harbor. Cows and sheep still graze on fields near the new stadium. And on a hill at the edge of the city, there's River Farm, a group of traditional turf and wood buildings that show how the city's farmers lived not long ago.

National Museum

The National Museum and Art Gallery exhibit artifacts from the

Viking period and objects illustrating the island's cultural history.
Time: May-Sept.: daily, 1:30pm-4pm; Oct.-April: Tues., Thurs., Sat.,
& Sun., 1:30pm-4pm
Place: Sudurgata
Contact: ph. 13264

Turf Houses

Arbaejarsafn, an open-air museum centered around a farm dating
from the mid-1400's, is a good example of Icelandic agricultural
construction. There are also 19th-century buildings from Reykjavik
and an authentic turf-roofed church from northern Iceland.
Time: Tue.-Sun., 1:30pm-6pm
Place: Arbaer Hill
Contact: ph. 84412

Supernatural Art

The home of Iceland's first well-known painter, Asgrimur Jonsson,
has become a gallery for his fanciful watercolors and oils. Folklore,
fairytales, and stunning landscapes are on display.
Time: May-August: Sun.-Fri., 1:30pm-4pm; Sept.-April: Tues. &
Thurs., 1:30pm-4pm
Place: Bergstradastraeti 74
Contact: ph. 13644

Panorama

From the tower of Hallgrims Church, the view of the mountains,
fjords, rooftops, harbors, and parks can't be beat. The incomplete
church has a Calder statue of Leif Eriksson, a gift from the American
people to Iceland.
Time: Mon.-Fri., 10am-noon; Sat., 1pm-5pm
Place: Skolavordustigur

Scandanavian Culture

There is always something happening at the Nordic House, a
cultural link between Iceland and the other Nordic countries. The
exhibitions include photography, art from the cultures of the North
Atlantic, textile displays, and more.
Time: Mon.-Fri., 9am-7pm; Sat. & Sun., 2pm-7pm
Place: Hringbraut

City Gallery

Reykjavik's municipal art gallery, Kjarvalsstadir, honors Johann Kjarval, one of Iceland's most famous artists. The display halls are divided between exhibitions of Kjarval's work and shows of native and foreign art.
Time: Tue.-Sun., 2pm-10pm
Place: Miklatuni
Contact: ph. 26131

Handicraft Center

In Iceland's Handicraft Center, you will find a selection of traditional Nordic crafts. The highlight is the renowned woolen ware, with demonstrations of spinning and weaving techniques. Other unique specialties are lava ceramics, Viking ship models, and jewelry.
Time: Mon.-Fri., 9am-4pm
Place: Hafnarstraeti 3
Contact: ph. 21890

Sculpture Garden

Sculptures by Asmundur Sveinsson are displayed in and around the Sveinsson Museum. The former home and studio of the artist are interesting sites on their own.
Time: June-August: Tue.-Sun., 10am-5pm. Gardens open at all times.
Place: Sigtun
Contact: ph. 32155

Fireworks Display

New Year's Eve is celebrated in Reykjavik with merrymaking, bonfires, and a fireworks extravaganza. The revelers keep warm by imbibing the potent local liquor, *brennivin*; you should do the same. For a complete list of festivals and events, check with the tourist office.
Contact: Iceland Tourist Bureau, Reykjanesbraut 6, ph. 25855 or 10044

Mystical Sculptures

The Einar Jonsson Museum displays sculpture by Iceland's leading sculptor. Jonsson's work, grounded in Icelandic mysticism, reflects

the harsh, challenging environment of the country.
Time: May-August: Tues.-Sun., 1:30pm-4pm
Place: Eriksgata

Nationwide

National Park
The Skaftafell National Park, at the foot of the vast Vatnajokull
glacier, has waterfalls, mountains, cliffs, caves, wild rivers, and very
few tourists.

Ancient Parliament
The Thingvellir, a national shrine and holy place, is where the
world's first parliament met in 930 AD. At the Logberg cliff, speakers
stood to address the representatives below. The striking scene, set
amidst steep cliffs, is awe-inspiring.

Natural Wonderland
The Lake Myvatn region of Northern Iceland is famous for its
bizarre, lunar-like environment. In the same region, you will find
Dettifoss (Europe's highest waterfall), the Asbyrgi earth formations,
Vaglaskogur (the country's largest birch forest), the Jokulsa Canyon
National Park, and mountains, volcanic pools, and caves.

Ireland

Ireland

Athlone

In the heart of Ireland, Athlone is a busy river port on the tip of Lough Ree. The narrow lake has many fascinating islands with ruined churches and retreats. Athlone's historic character is apparent in its oldest district along the east bank of the River Shannon.

Ruined Town

Clonmacnoise, one of Ireland's most interesting sacred sites, was founded in 546 by Saint Ciaran. Plundered more than 50 times, it was finally abandoned in 1647. Today, the remains include a 10th-century basilica, eight ruined churches, and an eerie cemetary.
Time: daily, 9am-5:30pm
Place: five miles southwest of Athlone
Contact: ph. 2866

Cashel

Cashel is dominated by a huge granite outcrop known as the Rock of Cashel. The imposing monolith, crowned by magnificent ruins, was once the seat of the Kings of Munster, who ruled for 700 years. The pleasant town below the Rock has many 18th-century homes, shops, and churches.

Rare Manuscripts

Adjoining the Cathedral of St. John, Cashel's Diocesan Library houses a superb collection of books, manuscripts, and incunabula. The library represents one of the greatest accruals of 16th- and 17th-century books in Ireland.
Time: Mon.-Fri., 10am-noon & 2pm-4pm
Place: John Street
Contact: ph. 613333

Cavan

Crystal Tours

Visitors are invited to watch crystal being mixed, blown, and cut by hand at Cavan Crystal Ltd. The guided tour covers the entire process of traditional crystal-making.
Place: Dublin Road
Contact: ph. 31942

Clonmel

Clonmel lies on the bank of the River Suir in the famous county Tipperary. Known throughout Ireland as a center of horse-breeding and cider-making, Clonmel is a friendly, historic town.

Civic Museum

Clonmel's modern town hall houses the Municipal Museum, Library, and Art Gallery. Displays include artifacts from Clonmel's history, mementoes of native Laurence Sterne (author of *Tristan Shandy*), local art, and corporation regalia.
Time: Mon.-Fri., 9am-4:30pm
Place: Parnell Street
Contact: ph. 22960

Ancient Church

Restored in 1886, the Franciscan Friary is only a remnant of the great abbey built there in 1269. The original choir, tower, and font

have survived intact. Arrive early to catch the stained glass in the St. Francis Chapel at its best.
Time: Mon.-Sat., 8am-6pm
Place: Abbey Street

Cork

Cork, a dynamic port with 135,000 residents, is the Republic's second-largest city. Established in the 6th century, Cork received its municipal charter in 1185. Cork is an inviting place to stroll, with most sights in walking distance of the old Marsh section of town.

Irish Arts
The Crawford School of Art presents 19th- and 20th-century Irish paintings and sculpture, along with local glass, silver, and Rodin bronzes.
Time: Mon.-Fri., 10am-5pm; Sat., 9am-1pm
Place: Emmet Place
Contact: ph. 965033

University College
Reminiscent of Oxford's collegiate architecture, Cork's University College occupies a quadrangle overlooking the Lee Valley. The University's real gem is the Honan Chapel, an Irish-Romanesque structure with a glorious interior. Inside, you'll find modern stained glass, tabernacle enamels, embroidered vestments, and the Canticle Mosaic.
Time: Mon.-Sat., 9am-3pm
Place: College Road

Cork Museum
Ensconced in Fitzgerald Park, the Cork Public Museum presents the archaeology and history of ancient Cork. There are also exhibits of local lace and glass and regional commerce.
Time: Mon.-Fri., 9:30am-5pm; Sat., 9:30am-12:30pm
Place: Mardyke Walk
Contact: ph. 20679 or 23251

Estate Park

Owned by University College, the Fota Island Wildlife Park and Aboretum covers 800 acres of gardens, experimental farms, forests, and zoological parks. The aboretum has an amazing variety of plants from around the world.
Time: April-Oct.: Mon.-Sat., 10am-6pm; Sun., 11am-6pm
Place: Carrigtwohill (eight miles east of Cork)
Contact: ph. 812678

Contemporary Arts

Cork's Art Society maintains a gallery for shows by Ireland's newest popular artists.
Time: Tue.-Sat., 11am-6pm
Place: 16 Lavitt's Quay
Contact: ph. 505749

Dublin

Dublin is a sad and splendid place. A city of broad avenues and elegant houses, ancient churches and soaring spires, it's also a city of dreary, rundown neighborhoods and tacky suburbs. Dublin is one part Gaelic village, one part Georgian London, and one part modern metropolis.

The recorded history of the city begins with a settlement in the 2nd century AD. After Vikings had built up the town in 840, Dublin began to develop as an important city. Architecturally, Dublin reached its zenith during the 18th century, with an Anglo-Irish aristocratic town renewal.

Dublin today is a friendly and walkable city, with monuments, museums, churches, stately buildings, and secluded parks, all in the city center.

Walking Tour

A terrific way to get acquainted with historic Dublin is to use the city's Tourist Trail. This posted walking tour through the center of town focuses on landmarks of cultural and historic interest. The tour booklet (available at the City Tourist Office) describes each location along the route.
Contact: Dublin Tourist Information Office, 14 O'Connell Street, ph. 747733

Bountiful Brew

Guinness Brewery, founded in 1759, is the largest brewery in Europe. Until alteration and modernization is completed, there are no public tours, but visitors are welcome for an entertaining audio-visual show. After the presentation, guests may sample a glass or two of the dusky brew.
Time: Mon.-Fri., 10am-2pm
Place: St. James Street
Contact: ph. 689786

Priceless Collections

The Chester Beatty Library and Gallery is a gem of an attraction in Dublin's Ballsbridge district. Prize features include Islamic art and manuscripts, Oriental art and books, Biblical papyri (with the world's oldest known New Testament), fine jewelry, and illuminated manuscripts.
Time: Tue.-Fri., 10am-1pm & 2:30pm-5:30pm; Sat., 2pm-5pm
Place: 20 Shrewsbury Road
Contact: ph. 692386

Irish Parliament

In 1921, the Parliament of the new Irish Free State chose the Leinster House as its meeting place. Today, both the Dail Eireann and Seanad Eireann—the two houses of Parliament—meet here. When the Dail is in session, it's possible to observe the proceedings from the visitors' gallery. Leinster House also can be toured when Parliament isn't in session. Apply for tickets in the Superintendent's Office at the main gate.
Place: 20 Kildare Street
Contact: ph. 789911

Joyce Fest

June 16th is a great day to be in Dublin, when James Joyce fans from around the world descend on the city to celebrate the author and Bloomsday. Leopold Bloom's trail through Dublin is recreated, while readings of *Ulysses* and other events are held throughout the city. Contact Dublin Tourist Office for a schedule of events.

National Museum

The Irish Museum illustrates the history of humans in Ireland, from

prehistoric times through the Middle Ages, with Bronze Age ornaments, reconstructed grave sites, early Christian art, and much more.
Time: Tue.-Sat., 10am-5pm; Sun., 2pm-5pm
Place: Kildare Street
Contact: ph. 765521

National Library
Bibliophiles shouldn't miss Ireland's National Library. The Department of Printed Books alone maintains over one million volumes. There's also a unique collection of Irish periodicals and a large selection of old prints.
Time: Mon.-Fri., 10am-10pm; Sat., 10am-1pm
Place: Kildare Street

National Gallery
Ireland's National Gallery presents European painting from the 14th through 20th centuries, including Italian Renaissance works, the Dutch and Flemish schools, French Impressionists, major English works, and Irish painting. The Irish National Portrait Gallery, housed in the same building, displays portraits of figures who have influenced Irish history.
Time: Mon.-Fri., 10am-5pm; Sat., 10am-1pm; Sun., 2pm-5pm
Place: Merion Square
Contact: ph. 765521

Natural History
Specimens of native mammals, fish, insects, and birds are just some of what you'll find at the Natural History Museum. There's everything from stuffed elephants to embalmed squid in this amusing old museum.
Time: Tue.-Sat., 10am-5pm; Sun., 2pm-5pm
Place: Merion Street

Botanic Gardens
Founded in 1795, the National Botanic Gardens now extend over 50 acres along the River Tolka. The gardens feature 19th-century

glasshouses and palm, orchid, and camelia houses.
Time: Summer: Mon.-Sat., 9am-6pm; Sun., 11am-6pm; Winter:
Mon.-Sat., 10am-4:30pm; Sun., 11am-4:30pm
Place: Botanic Road, Glasnevin

Old Dublin
Dublin's Civic Museum is housed in a fine 18th-century mansion.
Its collections include antiques and articles relating to local history.
Time: Tue.-Sat., 10am-6pm; Sun., 11am-2pm
Place: South William Street

Modern Art
Dublin's Municipal Gallery of Modern Art has a distinctive collec-
tion of works by Renoir, Degas, Monet, Picasso, and Manet, among
others. The Stained Glass Gallery shows superb examples of Irish
glass.
Time: Tue.-Sat., 10am-6pm; Sun., 11am-2pm
Place: Parnell Square
Contact: ph. 741903

St. Patrick's Cathedral
Consecrated in 1192, St. Patrick's Cathedral underwent extensive
alteration during the 13th century. Jonathan Swift, author of
Gulliver's Travels, served as Dean there for 32 years, and he and
his wife Stella are interred near the southwest entryway. The best-
preserved portion of the ancient church is the choir, with colorful
banners, helmets, and swords displayed over the stalls.
Time: Mon.-Fri., 9am-5pm; Sun., 10am-4pm
Place: Patrick Street
Contact: ph. 754817

Ennis

New Museum
An old parish church has been renovated to house the De Valera
Library and Museum, with exhibits relating to the careers of Eamon
De Valera and Daniel O'Connell.
Time: Mon.-Fri., 10am-5pm
Place: Harmony Row
Contact: ph. 21366

Ancient Friary
Hidden among the winding lanes of old Ennis is the ancient Franciscan Friary founded by Donough O'Brien, King of Thomond. One thousand monks and students once lived at this monastery.
Time: daily, 7am-sunset
Place: Church Street

Enniscorthy

This picturesque County Wexford town grew up around its ancient castle, which guarded the River Slaney. A revolt by townspeople in 1798 inspired an ill-fated uprising against English occupation. In a battle at Vinegar Hill, 10,000 rebels, armed only with pikes, were slaughtered by British artillery.

Summer Festival
The first week of July, the County Wexford Strawberry Fair sponsors a week of concerts, dances, sporting events, and, of course, mass consumption of strawberries.
Contact: Tourist Information Office, Abbey Square, ph. 2341

Castle Museum
Wexford County Museum, housed in a fortress built in 1290, contains relics of local battles, objects from ships wrecked off the Wexford coast, and folklife exhibits. The castle is also known as the temporary home of the poet Edmund Spenser.
Time: Tue.-Sat., 10am-5pm
Place: Castle Hill

Galway

Galway is full of old houses, pleasant squares, and waterfront views. The Renaissance facades of many homes testify to Galway's long trading ties with continental Europe. Today the town of 30,000 is the cultural center of Ireland's Gaelic west coast.

Lynch's Castle
The wealth of Galway's old Lynch family (the folks who gave us the term "lynching") is evident in their 16th-century town castle,

which now houses a bank. The exterior is festooned with medallions, gargoyles, and escutcheons. The restored interior has lovely windows and an exhibition on the town's history.
Time: Mon.-Fri., 10am-3pm
Place: Shop Street
Contact: ph. 63081

Kenmare

Druid's Circle
Nearly 4,000 years ago, immigrants from the continent landed on the Kenmare Estuary and built a ceremonial site overlooking the river. Archaeologists suggest that this Druid's Circle was used for human sacrifice.
Time: always open
Place: The Shrubberies

Lovely Lace
Kenmare has a long history as a lace and textile center. The Convent of Poor Clares is known throughout Ireland for its outstanding point lace. Contemporary and antique lace is exhibited at the school.
Time: Mon.-Fri., 10am-12:30pm & 1:30pm-4pm
Place: Church Street
Contact: ph. 41233

Killarney

National Park
Killarney's famous Lake District encompasses Ireland's largest national park. The Boune-Vincent National Park and the 11,500-acre Muckross Estate form the nucleus of the wooded lakeland. Within the park, there are the Muckross Gardens, the Muckross Manor, and a ruined abbey.
Time: April-June, Sept., & Oct.: daily, 8am-7pm; July & August: daily, 9am-9pm
Place: Muckross Road
Contact: ph. 31633

Kilkenny

Kilkenny has been called "The Pearl of South Ireland," and there's hardly a more attractive town in the region. Snuggled at the base of the Slieveardagh Hills along the banks of the River Nore, Kilkenny is a well-preserved old town with narrow lanes and medieval buildings.

Design Center

Butler Castle dominates the High Town District above the River Nore. The Castle's stables and outbuildings have been transformed into the Kilkenny Design Workshop Centre, which produces and displays jewelry, pottery, textiles, and furnishings.
Time: Mon.-Sat., 10am-5pm
Place: Castle Road Parade
Contact: ph. 22118

Brewery Tour

Smithwicks Brewery has been producing a tasty local beer for over 200 years. Visitors are invited to tour the facility and sample the product.
Time: Mon.-Sat., 3pm-4pm
Place: Parliament Street

Alms House

Built in 1581 as a refuge for outlawed Catholics, Shree's Almshouse today serves as Kilkenny's Municipal Tourist Office. The almshouse is one of the few surviving Tudor buildings in Ireland.
Time: Mon.-Fri., 9:30am-5pm
Place: Rose Inn Street
Contact: ph. 21755

Arts Week

Kilkenny makes a pleasant venue for the summer Arts Week. Daily concerts, readings, plays, and art shows highlight this enjoyable festival.
Time: last week in August
Contact: Kilkenny Arts Week, Butler House, Patrick Street

Medieval Cathedral

St. Canice's Cathedral is one of Ireland's best-preserved medieval

churches. Built in 1252 in the Decorated Style, the most notable features of the exterior are quatrefoil clerestory windows, battlement parapets, and a 100-foot tower which pre-dates the Cathedral. The interior contains many monuments and tombs, and the library maintains rare books and manuscripts.
Time: daily, 9am-5pm
Place: Church Lane

Town Hall
The Tholsel, or Town Hall, was constructed as a commercial exchange in 1761. The exterior is distinguished by a peculiar cupola and tower, known locally as "the lighthouse." On the upper floor, there's a preserved assembly hall and an exhibit of documents relating to Kilkenny's long history.
Time: Mon.-Fri., 9am-4:30pm
Place: High Street

Killorglin

Celtic Festival
Every August, thousands of Irish converge on the town of Killorglin for three days of non-stop merrymaking. Dating to pagan times, the annual Puck Fair begins on Gathering Day, when townsmen capture a wild goat (a puck) to reign over the festivities from a platform in the town square. The streets are crowded with clowns, bands, parades, and inebriates.
Time: August 10-12

Limerick

Limerick, a thousand-year old river port, is Ireland's third-largest city. Often a bleak place, Limerick's attraction rests in its ancient castle, city walls, old churches, and Georgian buildings.

Norman Castle
King John's Castle, on the banks of the River Shannon, was constructed for the Norman king around 1210. Surviving features in-

clude the castle's gate, sentry towers, curtain walls, and corner towers.
Time: May-Sept.: Mon.-Sat., 9:30am-6pm
Place: Castle Street
Contact: ph. 47522

Museum and Gallery
Limerick's People's Park Museum and adjacent Art Gallery house local antiquities and archaeological finds, along with contemporary art by Irish and British artists.
Time: Mon.-Fri., 10am-6pm; Sat., 10am-1pm
Place: Perry Square
Contact: ph. 314668

Irish Artifacts
At the National Institute for Higher Education, the Hunt Collection displays Irish artifacts and early Christian relics, with many Bronze and Iron Age finds uncovered at nearby Lough Gur.
Time: Mon.-Fri., 9:30am-5:30pm
Place: Dublin Road

Prehistoric Ireland
Lough Gur, about nine miles south of Limerick, is rich in Neolithic and Bronze Age archaeological sites. Finds here indicate continuous settlement in the area since at least 3000 BC. The area around Lough Gur abounds in stone circles, cairns, huts, and forts.
Time: always accessible
Place: Bluff Road (just before Holycross)

New Ross

Kennedy Park
Opened in 1968 near the Kennedy ancestral home south of New Ross, the John F. Kennedy Memorial Park covers nearly 500 acres and has an arboretum and forest garden.
Time: April-Sept.: daily, 10am-6:30pm; Oct.-March: daily, 10am-5pm
Place: five miles south on L159A
Contact: ph. 21433

Sligo

Lying on lovely Sligo Bay, Sligo is a genial town with ancient ruins, old buildings, friendly pubs, and surrounding scenery.

Yeats Remembered

Sligo County Library and Museum has historical exhibits, folklife displays, and an extensive collection of memorabilia commemorating poet William Butler Yeats, born in Sligo. Yeats is buried north of town in the Drumcliffe Churchyard. His epitaph reads, "Cast a cold eye on life, on death. Horseman, pass by."
Time: Library: Tue.-Sat., 10am-5pm
Place: Stephen Street
Contact: ph. 2212

Megalithic Cemetary

Carrowmore is the site of Ireland's greatest collection of megalithic tombs. It's thought that there were once hundreds of burial chambers there among the dolmen, stone circles, and stone forts.
Time: always open
Place: Church Hill Road, two miles southwest of town

Dominican Friary

Established in the 13th century, Sligo Abbey today is represented by the original nave, south transept, and a 15th-century cloister. In the nave, you'll find the curious O'Crainan tomb and an altar with floral carvings.
Time: Mon.-Sat., 9:30am-6pm
Place: Lower Abbey Street

Waterford

Waterford's first residents were Danes, who settled on the bay at the mouth of the River Suir in 850. The original Viking town has all but disappeared, save for bits of old walls. Today, Waterford is a prosperous city of 30,000, known for Europe's largest crystal factory.

Renowned Glass

During the 18th century, Waterford produced some of Europe's

finest glassware, but by the 1850's Britain had crippled the industry with onerous export duties. In 1947, the company was revived and, though it now employs 3,000, it can't meet the demand for Waterford crystal. You can observe the entire process of crystal-making—from selecting raw ingredients to blowing and cutting—on the free guided tours.
Time: Mon.-Fri., 10:15am, 11am, 11:45am, 1:45pm, 2:30pm, & 3pm (call first for a reservation)
Place: Cork Road
Contact: ph. 73311

Municipal Hall

Waterford's City Hall displays historic Waterford crystal, royal commendations, and a flag from the Irish Brigade, which fought in the Union Army during the U. S. Civil War.
Time: Mon.-Fri., 9am-4:30pm
Place: The Mall
Contact: ph. 75788

Italy

Italy

Agrigento

The Sicilian city of Agrigento is set high above the Valley of the Temples, where honey-colored columns evoke an ancient Hellenistic glory. During the 5th and 6th centuries BC, the affluent Greek colony of Akragas flourished there.

Greco-Roman Archaeology

Before visiting the Valley of the Temples, stop by the Museo Archeologico Nazionale for an orientation. The museum has relics from Akragas, colossal telamon figures, and artifacts from digs throughout Sicily, along with maps and photos of the Valley of the Temples.
Time: Tues.-Sat., 9am-2pm; Sun., 9am-1pm
Place: Via Passeggiata Archeologica
Contact: ph. 29008

Ancient Akragas

The ancient Greek city of the Zona Archeologica once supported twice the population of modern Agrigento. Hundreds of ruined temples and secular buildings in the valley represent a fraction of the great outpost that once thrived there. The Temple of Concord, built about 500 BC, is the best-preserved and noblest Doric temple in Sicily. Ironically, it owes its good condition to early Christians, who transformed the temple into a church. Other temples

to Juno, Jupiter, and Hercules are in various states of decay, but all warrant close inspection.
Time: daily, 9am till dusk

Medieval Agrigento

Most visitors head directly for the classical ruins and ignore the city's engaging medieval quarter, where the highlight is the Santo Spirito Convent, with its dilapidated cloister and lovely old chapel. Founded in the 13th century, the church has some beautiful stucco work and an interesting ceiling.
Time: Tues.-Sat., 9am-noon & 1:45pm-6pm
Place: Via Santo Spirito

Ancona

On the slopes of a rocky promontory, Ancona is the ancient capital of the Marches and a flourishing port. Although damaged during World War II and by a 1972 earthquake, Ancona sustains glimpses of its past grandeur as a Roman town and an independent maritime republic during the Middle Ages.

Renaissance Treasures

Housed in the 16th-century Palazzo Bosdari, the Pinacoteca Communale boasts a wealth of Renaissance masterpieces. The collection features works by Guercino, Titian, Crevelli, and del Sarto. The museum also has Fauvist, Cubist, and Futurist works, as well as contemporary paintings, sculpture, and graphics by regional artists.
Time: Tues.-Sat., 9am-7pm; Sun., 9am-1pm
Place: Via Pizzeiolli 17
Contact: ph. 56342

Aosta

Aosta, founded in 25 BC, combines Roman and medieval remains with a spectacular alpine setting. The town makes a good base for exploring the Valle d'Aosta's secluded valleys, deep forests, and remote hamlets.

Gran Paridiso
The Gran Paradiso National Park became Italy's first national park in 1922. Within the park, the valleys are wooded up to 7,000 feet, and the alpine meadows are dazzling in early summer, covered in blossoms and butterflies. Once near extinction, ibex now roam Gran Paradiso in the thousands, along with chamois, fox, and golden eagles.
Contact: Ufficio Regionale de Turismo, Piazza Narbonne, ph. 35654

Roman Aosta
The Roman Arco di Augusto stands sentinal at the ancient eastern wall of Aosta. Pass through the arch and down the Via San Anselmo and you'll reach the Pretorian Gate. But the most impressive Roman ruin is the amphitheather beside a stretch of the original Roman road off the Via Potre Pretoriane.

Aquileia
Founded as a Roman garrison in 200 BC, Aquileia prospered as an inland port until it was eclipsed by Venice in the early Middle Ages. This old town now boasts a number of Roman relics and early Christian monuments.

Ancient Basilica
Sequestered in a piney woodland, Aquileia's ancient Basilica was constructed in the 10th century on the foundations of a 4th-century sanctuary. The Basilica has some remarkable mosaic floors and frescoes.
Time: Tues.-Sat., 9am-noon & 3pm-7pm; Sun., 9am-1pm
Place: Piazza Capitalo

Paleo-Christian Museum
The collection of the little Museo Paleocristiano is limited, but it has some extraordinary 5th-century mosaic pavements and stone reliefs worth seeing.
Time: Tues.-Sat., 9am-2pm; Sun., 9am-1pm
Place: Piazza Pirano
Contact: ph. 92131

Roman Ruins
Excavations near the Basilica have unearthed remains of Roman Aquileia. The cypress-shaded ancient forum has been partially restored, and other buildings are now being uncovered.
Time: 8am-sunset
Place: Via Sacra

Arezzo

The Tuscan town of Arezzo is built in terraces up a gently sloping hill crowned by an ancient citadel. Mostly medieval in appearance, the upper city is crowded by winding lanes, fortified towers, and tranquil piazzi. Arezzo has avoided the over-commercialization of other old Italian cities and has kept its ancient charm.

Tuscan Arts
Housed in the elegant Palazzo Brui, Arezzo's Museo Statale d'Arte Medioevale e Moderna traces the development of Tuscan art from the 13th to 19th century. Along with fine paintings, there are medieval ivories, bronzes, glass, weapons, and coins.
Time: Tues.-Sat., 9am-2pm; Sun., 9am-1pm
Place: Via San Lorentino
Contact: ph. 23868

Renaissance Man
Designed and decorated by its owner in 1540, the Casa del Vasari was home to Giorgio Vasari: writer, painter, architect, sculptor—the epitome of the Renaissance man. His richly-ornamented villa is cheered by playful *trompe l'oeil*.
Time: Tues.-Sat., 9am-2pm; Sun., 9am-1pm
Place: Via Settembre 55
Contact: ph. 20295

Archaeological Heritage
The Museo Archeologico Mecenate, lodged in a monastery adjoining a ruined Roman amphitheater, displays Etruscan and Roman artifacts discovered in Arezzo. It has bronze statuettes, urns, and a collection of vases decorated with ancient gods and goddesses.
Time: Tues.-Sat., 9am-2pm; Sun., 9am-1pm
Place: Via Margaritone 10
Contact: ph. 20882

Gothic Cathedral

Arezzo's Gothic Duomo, begun in 1277, lacks the grand exterior of most Tuscan cathedrals, but it's redeemed by its interior. The nave is lit by stained glass by Guillaume de Marcellat, a monk who worked with Michelangelo at the Vatican. There are also terracottas, frescoes of Mary Magdalan, and some elaborate tombs.
Time: daily, 8am-noon & 2pm-5pm
Place: Piazza del Duomo

Medieval Joust

The Piazza Grande makes a great setting for Arezzo's annual Giostra del Saracino. Knights on horseback attack the effigy of a Saracen king with medieval lances. Other events, such as street dances, feasts, and processions, round out the festival, which celebrates Arezzo's glory as a free city in the early Middle Ages.
Time: first Sunday in Sept.
Contact: Turismo, Piazza Risorgimento 116, ph. 23952

Ascoli Piceno

Ascoli is a picturesque city with twisting old streets and limestone palazzi. The heart of the city is the Piazza de Popolo, surrounded by superb Gothic and Renaissance buildings.

Municipal Gallery

Ascoli's municipal art collection hangs in the Pinacoteca Civica in the Palazzo Communale. Unfortunately, the indiscriminate display detracts from the museum's treasures, and it takes some time to sort through the lesser works to discover pieces by Titian, Van Dyck, Reni, and Bellato.
Time: daily, 9am-1pm
Place: Piazza Arringo
Contact: ph. 64346

Summer Carnival

Each August, Ascoli presents the Marches' most colorful event, the Quintana Festival. Townspeople in medieval costumes participate in torchlight processions, armed horsemen joust in the Piazza

Popolo, and street parties go on all night long.
Time: first Sunday in August
Contact: Turismo, Corso Manzini 229, ph. 51115

Cathedral Treasure

Ascoli's massive 15th-century Duomo would be unexceptional were it not for Crivelli's masterful *Madonna and the Saints*. Rich in detail, the altarpiece is boldly colored and set in an intricately carved frame.
Time: daily, 9am-7pm
Place: Piazzo Arringo

Assisi

Though overrun daily by hordes of tourists, Assisi has preserved an atmosphere of medieval serenity. Dominated by the Basilica of Saint Francis, Assisi's lanes are lined by picturesque homes little-changed since the Middle Ages.

San Francesco

Assisi's principal attraction is the Basilica of St. Francis, founded in 1228, just two years after the Saint's demise. In the dark, beautiful lower church, you'll find frescoes by Giotto, Cimabue, and Martini, and the tomb of St. Francis. The upper basilica, in stark contrast to the mysterious lower church, is brightly lit and has frescoes by Giotto and Ciambue, although these have suffered greatly with age.
Time: daily, 6am-7pm
Place: Piazza Inferiore di San Francesco
Contact: ph. 812238

Umbrian Arts

The Pinacoteca Communale has a small collection of paintings, sculpture, and ceramics, all housed in the old Palazzo di Priori.
Time: Tues.-Sat., 9am-12:30pm & 3pm-6pm
Place: Piazza del Commune
Contact: ph. 812219

Bari

Capital of Apulia, Bari is really two cities—a labyrinthine old town above the harbor, and a new town of broad boulevards and elegant shopping districts. Colonized by the Greeks and Byzantines, Bari prospered until it came under Spanish domination during the 16th century. Today, Bari is an important port and industrial center.

Provincial Museum
Beginning with the 11th century, the Pinacoteca Provinciale's collection includes some rare Byzantine works, outstanding pieces by Titian and Bellini, icons, and 19th-century Italian paintings.
Time: Tues.-Sat., 9am-1pm & 4pm-7pm; Sun. 9am-1pm
Place: Via Spalato 19
Contact: ph. 334445

Santa's Own Church
Bari's San Nicola Church is a monument to the patron saint of children, Saint Nicholas, a Turkish Bishop who has been transformed into Santa Claus. The 12th-century Romanesque church is rich in Byzantine decor, but its real treasures are the Bishop's Throne (supported by comic figures who struggle to hold the throne upright), and the crypt of San Nicola.
Time: daily, 9am-6pm
Place: Piazza San Nicola
Contact: ph. 211169

Barletta

This uninspiring seaport is of interest only for its museum, Renaissance churches, and unusual ancient monuments.

Museum and Gallery
The Museo Civico is worth a visit on two counts. In the foyer there's an amazing statue of the Holy Roman Emperor Fredrick II. This statue—the only known likeness of the Emperor—was discovered in a ruined castle. Adjoining the museum is its other attraction, the Pinacoteca de Nittis. Giuseppi de Nittis was a successful artist who was befriended by Degas in Paris during the 1870's. Under his influence, de Nittis utilized Impressionist techniques, produc-

ing a colorful, unique style. The collection chronicles de Nittis' career and includes the contents of his local studio.
Time: Tues.-Sun., 9am-1pm
Place: Via Cavor 8
Contact: ph. 33005

Byzantine Colossus

Outside of the San Spolcro Church, there's an ancient bronze statue known as the Barletta Colosso, thought to represent the Byzantine Emperor Valentinianus. The herculean statue holds a stone globe and a cross, thought to symbolize temporal and spiritual powers. After you ponder the colossus, check out the enamels in the 12th-century San Sepolcro Church.
Place: Corso Vittorio Emmanuele

Bologna

Bologna has an illustrious history. Sacked by barbarians at the breakup of Rome, Bologna did not revive until the 11th century. Today, the capital of Emilia-Romagna echoes its medieval grandeur in monuments, palaces, and its great university, which is Europe's oldest, founded in 1076.

Antique Emilia

What makes the Museo Civico Archeologico so special is its collection of Etruscan finds from regional digs. There are also Egyptian antiquities and Roman artifacts and art.
Time: Tues.-Sat., 9am-2pm; Sun., 9am-12:30pm
Place: Via dell'Acrchigimnascio 2
Contact: ph. 221896

Renaissance Palace

The 16th-century Palazzo Salem is one of Bologna's loveliest old mansions. The finest decoration is found in the Salone d'Onore, adorned with friezes illustrating the founding of Rome. There are also antique furnishings from various eras.
Time: Mon.-Fri. by appointment
Place: Via Zamboni 20
Contact: ph. 268974

Bolzano

For centuries, Bolzano has been a gateway between northern and southern Europe. In its mountian setting, Bolzano is a garden city where modern boutiques occupy medieval arcades. Capital of the Alto-Adige since 1918, Bolzano's heritage is more Tyrolian than Italian.

Medieval Castle

Dating from the early 13th century, Schloss Runkelstein (or Castle Roncolo, as it's known in Italian) is one of the finest castles in alpine Italy. Inside, there are some interesting 15th-century frescoes and antiques.
Time: March-Nov.: Tues.-Sun., 10am-noon & 3pm-7pm
Place: Via Sant'Antonio
Contact: ph. 2608

Parish Treasure

Many of Bolzano's old churches are decorated with medieval frescoes and woodwork. The Parrocchiale Church at Gries under Monte Gucina contains an altarpiece created by the Austrian master Michael Pacher in 1475.
Time: Mon.-Fri., 9:30am-noon
Place: Via Knoller

Brescia

Although badly damaged during World War II, Brescia has restored many of its buildings and piazzi. Three centuries of political domination by the Doges left Brecia with a distictly Venetian flavor. Even though it's now a busy commercial center, Brescia has plenty to attract the traveler.

Roman Brixia

The Museo Civico Romano has been built amidst Brescia's impressive Roman ruins. It is best known for the bronze Winged Victory, uncovered in 1826. This Augustan-era statue is one of the most important pieces of Roman sculpture discovered to date. There are also collections of Roman coins, glass, and other statuary. The surrounding Capitoline temple, built in 73 AD, has three chambers:

the right has a mosaic pavement and funerary reliefs; the central cella has the best mosaics; and there are numerous Roman inscriptions in the left hall.
Time: Tues.-Sun., 9am-noon & 2pm-5pm
Place: Via dei Musei 57
Contact: ph. 46031

Renaissance Art
The Pinacoteca Tosio Martinengo is rich in Renaissance and Baroque art. Hidden treasures of the museum are the two small paintings by Raphael and a splendid piece by Lotto. While Brescia's Museo Civico dell'Eta Critiana undergoes restoration, many of its works are displayed at the Pinacoteca.
Time: Tues.-Sun., 9am-noon & 2:30pm-5:30pm
Place: Via Martinengo da Barco
Contact: ph. 91473

Titian Altar
All of Brescia's churches have fine examples of Renaissance and Baroque art, but the Santi Nazaro e Celso has a wonderful Titian altarpiece. Though poorly lit, it is intensely moving.
Time: daily, 9am-6pm
Place: Corso Giacomo Matteotti

Bressanone

Culturally and architecturally Tyrolian, Bressanone became part of Italy in 1918. The town was once a famous gateway for medieval travelers.

Palace Museum
Bressanone's Museo Diocesano is a museum and an art gallery. The former Prince-Bishop's palace is entered by a bridge over the castle moat, the museum has some unusual alpine woodcarvings, regional paintings, and assorted historical items.
Time: Tues.-Sat., 10am-5pm
Place: Piazzo dei Vescovi

Baroque Cathedral
The 13th-century Duomo was modified in the 18th-century and

given a sumptuous interior. The original cloister has fascinating *biblia pauperum* frescoes on three sides. These "poor man's bibles" once adorned churches throughout the region.
Time: daily, 9am-noon & 2pm-4pm
Place: Piazza de Duomo

Capua

Today Capua is a sleepy town, but during the Roman era it was much more important. There isn't much there to indicate a distinguished history, but it was at Capua that Hannibal camped during the Carthagenian Wars, and it was at Capua that Spartacus defied Rome and led a slave revolt.

Ancient Heritage

Capua's Museo Campano contains Greek and Roman archaeological finds, along with a fine medieval section. There are busts which once adorned a triumphal arch and a gallery of Renaissance paintings. Don't miss the bizarre statues in the basement.
Time: Tues.-Sat., 9am-2pm; Sun., 9am-1pm
Place: Via Roma
Contact: ph. 971402

Castello

Castello, a gentrified suburb of Florence, is best known for its three Medici villas.

Medici Villa

Originally a castle, Villa Medici della Petraia was converted into a villa for Cardinal Ferdinando Medici. The mansion has lovely gardens overlooking the Tuscan countryside, and in the main garden there's a fountain with a bronze Venus by Giavonni Bologna. The villa also has frescoes glorifying the Medici family.
Time: Tues.-Sun., 9am-6:30pm
Place: Via dell Petraia
Contact: ph. 451208

Catania

Destroyed several times by eruptions of Mount Etna and seriously damaged during World War II, Catania retains few of its ancient monuments. Sicily's second city and a major seaport is crisscrossed by broad boulevards and dotted by Baroque buildings.

Castle Museum
Gloomy and forbidding, Catania's 13th-century Castello Ursino serves as the Museo Civico. The castle's rambling collections include Greek and Roman sculpture, medieval and Renaissance paintings, and a variety of Sicilian Baroque works.
Time: Tues.-Sun., 9am-1:15pm
Place: Piazza Federico di Svevia
Contact: ph. 583035

Memorial garden
The Giardino Bellini was created in memory of composer Vincenzo Bellini, who was born in Catania. The park is filled with tropical plants and flowers and is famed for floral configurations commemorating Bellini's compositions.
Time: daily, 6:30am-9pm
Place: Via Etnea

Chieti

Italian Antiquities
Chieti's Museo Archeologico Nazionale degli Abruzzi has an excellent collection of Roman and pre-Roman antiquities recovered in the region, including the enigamtic *Gueriero di Capestrano*, dating from the 6th century BC.
Time: Tues.-Sun., 9am-1pm & 3pm-6pm
Place: Via della Villa Communale 3
Contact: ph. 64175

Chiusi

Standing on a Tuscan hilltop amidst rich vineyards and olive groves, Chiusi is a peaceful town and was one of the 12 cities of the Etruscan Federation.

Etruscan Patrimony
The Museo Nazionale Etrusco investigates Etruscan civilization in central Italy. The displays include many peculiar cinerary urns, such as the anthropomorphic jars found only in Chiusi.
Time: Tues.-Sat., 8:30am-2pm; Sun., 9am-1pm
Place: Via dei Longobardi 2

Fermo

Overlooking the Adriatic, Fermo today presents a predominantly medieval countenance. Its steep streets are flanked by towers, ancient churches, and palazzi.

City Gallery
The Pinacoteca Civica houses a small but tantalizing collection of medieval and Renaissance paintings, including an early Rubens and works by del Fiore and da Bologna.
Time: Tues.-Sun., 8:30am-12:30pm
Place: Piazza del Popolo
Contact: ph. 371167

Majestic Cathedral
Fermo's Duomo has fascinating remains from its earlier incarnations—a 5th-century mosaic floor, Byzantine icons, Roman sarcophagi, and monuments. St. Thomas a Becket's chausable, made in 1116, is kept in the sacristy, while in the crypt there's a 4th-century sarcophagus with scenes of St. Peter's life. The Duomo's marble facade frames a beautiful 14th-century rose window.
Time: daily, 9am-6pm
Place: Piazza del Duomo

Florence (Firenze)

Although Florence can trace its ancestry to the Etruscans, its most exciting period came with the Renaissance, when it became the artistic capital of Europe. Florence was home to the most celebrated men in the history of art—Giotto and Cimabue, Donattelo and the della Robbias, da Vinci and Michelangelo, Botticelli and Ghiberti.

Today, Florence endures as a center of art and beauty, and much of its appeal lies in the combination of its heritage and its exuberant streetlife. But try to visit Florence in spring or fall to avoid the crush of tourists and the oppressive heat of summer.

NOTE: At present, many of the city-administered museums offer free admission on the first and third Saturday and the second and fourth Sunday of the month. However, this has changed before and will probably change again, so check with the Office of Monuments (ph. 23440) or the tourist office (ph. 216544) for the latest information.

Renaissance Palace

Palazzo Medici, home to Florence's first family for over a century, is famed for its richly decorated family chapel. There, the *Procession of the Magi* by Gozzoli provides a vivid picture of 15th-century Florentine life; many of the figures are Medici family members and their friends.
Time: Mon., Tues., & Thurs.-Sat., 9am-1pm & 2pm-5pm; Sun., 9am-noon
Place: Via Cavour 1
Contact: ph. 2760

Peerless Sculpture

The forbidding 14th-century Bargello, which once served as a prison, today houses Renaissance sculpture. The grim exterior hides an elegant courtyard and galleries with works by giants of art history, including Michelangelo's befuddled *Bacchus*, his earliest free-standing figure.
Time: free on alternate Sat. & Sun., 9am-1pm
Place: Via del Proconsolo 4

Renowned Collections

The Galleria degli Uffizi contains the finest assemblage of Florentine Renaissance art in the world, along with sculpture and Flemish painting. The walls are hung with an amazing number of world-famous works: Botticelli's *Venus*, Raphael's *Madonna*, Lippi's *Coronation of the Virgin*, and da Vinci's *Adoration of the Magi*.
Time: Sun., 9am-1pm
Place: Piazzale degli Uffizi 6
Contact: ph. 218341

Medici Chapel

Cappelle Medicee contains the mausoleum of the Medici princes and the astonishing tombs by Michelangelo. Opposite the altar is Michelangelo's poignant *Madonna and Child*. In a basement room, drawings and studies by Michelangelo and his students were discovered in the 1970's.
Time: Sun., 9am-1pm
Place: Piazza Madonna degli Aldobrandini

Medici Library

Michelangelo also designed the Bibliotecca Laureziana, on a cloister of Chiesa San Lorenzo. A magnificent staircase leads to the library, which houses nearly 10,000 old manuscripts.
Time: Tues.-Sat., 9am-7pm; Sun., 9am-1pm
Place: Piazza San Lorenzo

Fabulous Michelangelos

Most visitors brave the crowds at the Galleria dell'Academia to see some of Michelangelo's most spectacular works. His *David* is probably the best-known statue in the world. The four unfinished *Slaves*, intended for the tomb of Pope Julius II, are displayed against a backdrop of 16th-century tapestries.
Time: free on alternate Sat. & Sun., 9am-2pm
Place: Via Ricasoli 60
Contact: ph. 214375

Ancient Palace

The Palazzo Vecchio originally was used by the Signoria, Florence's government. In 1540, the Medici moved in and gave the fortress a palatial make-over, with works by Michelangelo, Donatello, and Giambologna. In front of the palace are Donatello's *Judith* and a copy of Michelangelo's *David*.
Time: Sun., 9am-1pm
Place: Piazza della Signoria

Genoa

Genoa, Italy's greatest seaport, is a vibrant city, charged with maritime activity and a cosmopolitan atmosphere. Genoa's narrow medieval alleyways, called *carrugi*, twist and turn as they climb the city's hills, until they open suddenly onto grand boulevards with elegant palazzi and buildings.

Palace Galleries
Genoa's Palazzo Reale has a lovely courtyard garden opening out to the Gulf of Genova. The frescoed galleries shimmer with light and magnificent art.
Time: Tues., Thurs., & Sun., 9am-1pm
Place: Via Balbi 10
Contact: ph. 206881

Merchant's Palace
Hidden in a small square by the port, the Palazzo Spinola provides a glimpse of the lifestyle of Genoa's former merchant princes. Crowded with original furnishings and decor, the palace also serves as the National Gallery of Art, with works by Ribera, Van Dyck, Van Cleeve, and others.
Time: Tues.-Sun., 9:30am-1:30pm
Place: Piazza Pellicceria
Contact: ph. 294661

Iesi

Surrounded by 14th-century walls, the medieval heart of Iesi is a maze of slender lanes lined with ancient homes and shops.

Rococo Gallery
The Pinacoteca Communale, an opulent rococo gallery, has a number of beautiful works by Lorenzo Lotto, who lived in Iesi briefly.
Time: Tues.-Sat., 9:30am-12:30pm & 4pm-7pm; Sun., 10am-1pm
Place: Via XV Settembre
Contact: ph. 58659

Milan

Like ripples on a gigantic pond, Milan spreads in ever-growing rings. In the outer orbit, vast tracts of concrete and industry sprawl. But the heart of old Milan has an exciting mix of ancient and modern.

It's there, in the grandiose Galleria Vittorio Emanuele, that sophisticated Milanese window-shop and cafe-sit. And it's there you'll find Milan's greatest monument, the lavish Duomo.

Municipal History
The Museo della Cere Citta di Milano presents exhibits of the city from its days as an Etruscan outpost to the present.
Time: Tues.-Sun., 9:30am-12:30pm & 2:30pm-5:30pm
Place: Via Sant'Andrea 6
Contact: ph. 272495

Medieval Castle
One of Italy's finest museums is housed in the Castello Sforzesco, a fortress built during the 15th century. The art galleries contain works by Bellini, Donatello, da Vinci, and many other masters, and the sculpture galleries include Roman, Gothic, and Renaissance statues. The most celebrated treasure is Michelangelo's last work, the *Rondanini Pieta*.
Time: Tues.-Sun., 9:30am-noon & 2:30pm-5:30pm
Place: Piazza Castello
Contact: ph. 026236

Ancient Church
Founded by St. Ambrose in 386, Sant'Ambrogio Basilica has been rebuilt and restored many times. However, it's still seminally important to the development of Romanesque architecture throughout Italy. Inside the Basilica, there's a fabulous gold and silver high altar, a 12th-century pulpit, and a rare, 11th-century mosaic.
Time: Mon.-Sat., 8am-5pm
Place: Piazza Sant'Ambrogio

Ecclesiastic Museum
The small Museo di Sant'Ambrogio, to the left of the Basilica, has a collection of vestments, religious paintings, sculpture, and records of Sant'Ambrogio.
Time: Wed.-Fri., 10am-noon & 3pm-5pm; Tues., Sat., & Sun., 3pm-5pm
Place: Piazza Sant'Ambrogio 15
Contact: ph. 872059

Modern Arts
Milan's Civica Galleria d'Arte Moderna has an engaging collection of 19th- and 20th-century art. The 19th-century collection focuses on the Romantic and Neo-Classical schools, while the Grassi Gallery includes works by French and Italian Impressionists and 20th-century artists. There's also a gallery dedicated to Marino Marini, the famed Italian sculptor and painter.
Time: Wed.-Mon., 9:30am-noon & 2:30pm-5:30pm
Place: Via Palestro 16
Contact: ph. 702819

Modena

Historic Library
Modena's grand Palazzo dei Musei houses the Biblioteca Estense, one of Italy's wealthiest repositories of old books and manuscripts. Among the 600,000 volumes is an early copy of Dante's *Divine Comedy* and a 1,200-page illustrated Bible from the 15th century.
Time: Tues.-Sat., 9am-2pm
Place: Via Emilia
Contact: ph. 222145

Montefalco

Perched above the olive groves and vineyards of Umbria, Montefalco has managed to sustain a rich, medieval atmosphere.

Tower Panorama
A climb to the top of Montefalco's Torre Communale will help you understand why the little town is called the "Balcony of Umbria." The vista encompasses Spoleto, Trevi, Assisi, and Perugia.
Time: Mon.-Sat., 8am-1pm & 2pm-5pm
Place: Piazza del Comune 15

Franciscan Museum
The San Francesco Church, now an art museum, contains frescoes by Florentine and Umbrian artists dating from the 14th and 15th

centuries, including a brilliant cycle of the life of St. Thomas.
Time: Mon.-Sat., 9am-noon & 3:30pm-6pm; Sun., 9am-noon
Place: Via della Ringhiera Umbria
Contact: ph. 79146

Monte Oliveto

Hidden Abbey
Romantically isolated in the hills of Tuscany, the immense Monte
Oliveto Maggiore Abbey is nearly concealed by a circle of cypress
trees. The Abbey, founded in 1315, is best known for its frescoes
depicting the life of St. Benedict, and the church has choir stalls
with delicate wooden mosaics.
Time: daily, 9am-12:30pm and 3pm-7pm
Place: two miles east of Buonoconvento

Naples (Napoli)

The legendary beauty of Naples—its magnificent bay, azure skies,
and romantic charms—has been lauded by travelers for centuries.
Unfortunately, that enchanting city has sunk beneath the pollution and squalor of Italy's most densely-populated metropolis.

Nevertheless, the resolute visitor can glimpse the splendor that
was once Naples: majestic monuments, museums, and archaeological treasures are all over the city. Above all, Naples is
a vibrant, dramatic city—chaotic, noisy, and exciting!

Royal Palace
The Palazzo Reale was built in 1600 and then redone in rococo
style during the 18th century. From the courtyard, a magnificent
marble staircase leads to suites and a theater. The Sala Diplomatica
is adorned with priceless tapestries, and other apartments display
paintings, antiques, and porcelain.
Time: Sun., 9am-1pm
Place: Piazza de Plebiscito
Contact: ph. 417010

Ancient Castle
The Castel Nuovo, built in 1279 for Charles of Anjou and altered

by Spanish rulers, remains surrounded by deep moats. The triumphal arch at the entrance is richly ornamented.
Time: daily, 9am-6pm
Place: Piazza del Municipo

Villa Museum
With spectacular views of the Bay of Naples, the Villa Floridiana houses an outstanding museum of the ceramic arts, with porcelains, ivories, enamels, and Neapolitan paintings. The villa also has an aviary, greenhouses, gardens, and a temple.
Time: Sun., 9am-1pm
Place: Via Cimarvia 77
Contact: ph. 377315

Historic Theater
Teatro San Carlo is Italy's most celebrated opera house, after La Scala in Milano. Built by Charles of Bourbon in the early 18th century, it was rebuilt in 1816 in neo-classical style.
Time: Sun., 9am-noon
Place: Piazza del Plebiscito

Narni

Governor's Palace
The Palazzo del Podesta incorporates three medieval buildings behind a 13th-century facade. This former Governor's Palace displays medieval sculpture and paintings, and the highlight is Ghirlandaio's *Coronation of the Virgin* in the Sala del Consiglio.
Time: Mon.-Fri., 9:30am-5pm
Place: Piazza dei Priori
Contact: ph. 715171

Church Museum
The 12th-century San Domenico Church has been converted to a museum dedicated to sacred art, with frescoes, reliquaries, and decorative pieces.
Time: Mon.-Fri., 9:30am-5pm
Place: Piazza XIII Giugno

Parma

Duchess' Mementoes
The Museo Glauco Lombardi is devoted to French Empress Marie-Louise, the Duchess of Parma. Many of her possessions, gifts from Napoleon, furnishings, and royal portraits are displayed, along with a gallery of French paintings.
Time: Tues.-Sat., 9am-noon & 4pm-6pm
Place: Via Garibaldi 15
Contact: ph. 33727

National Gallery
Situated in the large, gloomy Palazzo della Pilotta, the Galleria Nazionale presents one of northern Italy's finest collections. The great artists represented include Holbein, da Vinci, Van Dyck, and El Greco.
Time: Sun., 9am-1pm
Place: Piazza Marconi
Contact: ph. 33309

Palatine Library
Also located in the Palazzo della Pilotta, the Biblioteca Palatina preserves thousands of rare books and incunabula. It also has a small museum commemorating the inventor of Bodoni type, Giambattista Bodoni.
Time: Mon.-Sat., 9am-noon
Place: Piazza Marconi

Pavia

As the capital of the Lombard Kingdom from 572 to 774, and as an independent city-state in the 12th and 13th centuries, Pavia rivalled Milan in importance. Medieval towers and Romanesque churches give the city a rich flavor of the Middle Ages.

Medieval Castle
Pavia's Museo Civici is set in the Castello Viscontio, built in 1360. The courtyard is marred by crumbling walls and overgrown gardens, but this impressive castle still preserves a hint of its past grandeur.

The museum houses an archaeological section, a sculpture gallery, and medieval art.
Time: Tues.-Sun., 10am-noon & 3pm-5pm
Place: Piazza Castello
Contact: ph. 33853

Saint's Tomb
The famed Church of San Pietro in Ciel d'Oro, consecrated in 1132, shelters the magnificent tomb of St. Augustine. This elaborate marble monument is busy with delicate carved figures; its base alone is crowded with saints and apostles under scenes from Augustine's life.
Time: Mon.-Sat., 9:30am-noon & 3pm-5pm
Place: off Viale Matteotti

University Gardens
The University of Pavia, founded in 1361, is one of Europe's oldest centers of learning. Its Botanical Gardens, begun in 1558, covers eight acres and specializes in roses.
Time: Sun., 9am-noon & 3pm-7pm
Place: Via Epifanio 14

Pescasseroli

National Park
Located in the central Apennines, the Abruzzo National Park is one of Italy's most interesting conservation areas. The mountains are richly forested in beech, maple, and black pine, but the park is best known for its large population of brown bears and for the rare Apennine wolf, which survives only in the park.
Contact: Ufficio di Zona del Parco, ph. 91955

Rome

Rome has enticed and enthralled travelers for 30 centuries. In no other European city are legend and history so tangible for the visitor. Around every corner, down every alley, there's a reminder of the glory and the splendor that was—and is—Rome.

Rome is like the mosaics of its great old churches, inlaid with the color and patina of history. There are ancient Roman remains in modern subway stations, ancient travertine arches under 19th-century apartments, and pagan temples adopted by Christian churches. Rome abounds in statues, squares, ruins, parks, museums, and palaces—a surprise down every street, up every stairway.

Renaissance Gem

Villa Farnesina is decorated with radiant Renaissance frescoes and paintings. The decor includes whimsical works by Raphael and *The Marriage of Roxanne and Alexander* by Il Sodoma.
Time: Mon.-Sat., 9am-1pm
Place: Via della Lungara
Contact: ph. 650831

Perfect Antiquity

The Pantheon, originally a temple to all the gods of Rome, is the best-preserved ancient Roman building in the city. Erected in 27 BC by Marcus Agrippa, this circular hall beneath a vast dome is a marvel of ancient architecture. Its powerful arches are fixed in walls 20-feet thick to accommodate the incredible dome, which remained the largest in the world until modern times. The Pantheon was saved from demolition by Pope Boniface, who converted it to a church commemorating Rome's Christian martyrs in 608. In later years, it was used for many ignoble purposes, including a fish market which existed there until 1847.
Time: Tues.-Sat., 9am-1pm & 2pm-6pm
Place: Piazza della Rotunda

Palatial Gallery

The Palazzo Corsini is home to part of the Galleria Nazionale d'Arte Antica collection, with works by Van Dyck, Rubens, Brueghel, and many schools of Italian painting.
Time: Sun., 9am-1pm
Place: Via della Lungara 10
Contact: ph. 6542323

Ancient Church

Santa Maria Sopra Minerva, next to the Pantheon, was founded in the 8th century on the site of a Roman temple of Minerva. Inside it contains beautiful chapels, and Michelangelo's statue *Christ*

Bearing the Cross is in the chancel. St. Catherine, who died in the neighboring convent, is buried beneath the altar.
Time: daily, 7:30am-12:30pm & 2:30pm-5pm
Place: Piazza della Minerva

Etruscan Art
The Museo Nazionale di Villa Guilia houses Etruscan art treasures, with materials from all of the great cities.
Time: Sun., 9am-1pm
Place: Viale della Belli Arti
Contact: ph. 360-1951

Roman Baths
The Baths of Diocletian once covered 30 acres, with galleries, concert halls, libraries, and baths that could accommodate up to 3,000 people. Abandoned in the 6th century, the baths decayed until Pope Pius IV commissioned Michelangelo to convert them into a Basilica of Santa Maria Degli Angeli. The church still provides a good impression of the original baths.
Time: Tues.-Sun., 8am-noon & 2:30pm-6pm
Place: Via delle Terme di Diocleziano

Vatican Collections
The museums that comprise the Vatican Museum testify to the diversity of the great institution: the Pinacoteca, the Museo Pio Cristiano, the Museo Gregoriano, the Collections of Greek and Roman Antiquities, the Gallery of Maps, the Museo Missionario-Etnologico, the Lapidary Gallery, the Museo Etrusco, the Museo Egizo, the Collezione D'Arte Religiosa Moderna, and the Museo Pio-Clementine. Obviously, there's too much to see in one visit, so it's best to plan ahead. Some savvy visitors head for the Sistine Chapel when the doors open, so they can experience the finest achievement in Western art in peace.
Time: free last Sunday each month, 9am-2pm
Place: Viale Vaticano
Contact: ph. 066982

St. Peter's Basilica
The first Saint Peter's was built by Emperor Constantine between 320 and 330 AD. By the 15th century, it was overflowing with tombs,

altars, and liturgical furnishings that spanned a millenium, and it was in very poor condition. The present Basilica is the result of a reconstruction project that covered 176 years, the reign of 22 popes, and the direction of 10 architects, including Bramante, Michelangelo, and Bernini. When you visit this spectacular sanctuary—the largest in all of Christendom—plan to spend an entire day. A good way to absorb the enormity of St. Peter's is to take the free guided tours offered each afternoon at 3:15 by Capuchin monks, who have a life-long knowledge of the Basilica. The tour meets on the porch.
Place: Piazza San Pietro

Rare Mosaics
Santa Maria Maggiore, one of Rome's four great Basilicas, was built in 432 AD. Remodelling has altered the Basilica substantially, but 28 original mosaics have survived, depicting Old Testament scenes in naturalistic detail. There are also monumental tombs, jeweled altars, and a ceiling decorated with the first gold to come from South America.
Time: daily, 7:30am-12:30pm and 2pm-6pm
Place: Piazza di Santa Maria Maggiore

Siena

Siena, the most perfectly preserved medieval city in Italy, has zealously guarded its heritage and culture. The Piazza del Campo, Siena's historic heart, is the loveliest square in the country. Rich in art, monuments, and medieval atmosphere, Siena provides an excellent experience of Old World Europe.

Brilliant Cathedral
Siena's Duomo is a masterpiece of Tuscan architecture. The multicolored marble facade is adorned with carvings and ornaments. The interior is equally eye-catching, with black and white marble walls, mosaic floors, and a soaring cupola. Donatello contributed the bronze statue of St. John, the altar has statues by Michelangelo, and there are two fine works by Bernini in the Chapel of the Virgin.
Time: daily, 9am-6pm
Place: Piazza del Duomo

Renaissance Sculpture

Inside the dim San Giovanni Baptistry, you'll discover statues and reliefs by Tuscany's leading Renaissance sculptors—Donatello, Ghiberti, and della Quercia. The highlight is Donatello's *Feast of Herod*.

Time: daily, 9:30am-5pm
Place: Piazza san Giovanni

Trento

Enveloped by mountain slopes and alpine meadows, this ancient Roman town has long been the meeting place of northern and southern Europe. The cobbled streets of old Trento are lined with Renaissance palaces and medieval monuments.

Grand Castle

Trento's best free attraction is the Castello del Buon Consiglio, once home to the city's Prince-Bishops. Actually a complex of old palaces and towers incorporated into one citadel, it now houses a fine museum collection. Throughout the castle, there are wonderful furnished loggia, galleries, and salons.

Time: April-Sept.: Tues.-Sun., 9am-noon & 2pm-6pm; Oct.-March: Tues.-Sun., 9am-noon & 2pm-4pm
Place: Via Bernardo Clesio 5
Contact: ph. 21324

Varallo

Sacro Monte

The peaceful town of Varallo is dominated by the bizarre Sacro Monte complex. This vast manifestation of religious devotion was planned by Bernadino Carini, a monk who had been the gatekeeper of the Holy Sepulchre in Jerusalem during the 15th century. His original plan was to turn the hills above Varallo into a reconstruction of Jerusalem's holy places. Today, the sanctuary has 43 chapels, each presenting scenes from the life of Jesus. These astonishingly realistic depictions incorporate life-size statues with glass eyes and real hair, set before frescoed walls. Although there

are stylistic relationships among the chapels, each is unique in execution.
Time: Mon.-Sat., 9am-noon & 2pm-6pm
Place: Via Sacro Monte
Contact: ph. 51424

Varese

Baroque Sanctuary
Varese is a genial, modern resort north of Milan, but its greatest attraction is the pilgrimage chapels at Santa Maria del Sacro Monte. Lining a steep path nearly 3,000-feet up the mountain, 14 chapels represent the "Stations of the Cross." There are magnificent views of Varese and Lago Varese along the way.
Time: daily, 9am-5pm
Place: Santa Maria del Monte
Contact: ph. 225593

Venice

Despite mobs of tourists and messy floods, Venice can be the most romantic city in Europe. The time you visit is of small consequence—Venice is equally lovely under summer skies or in the melancholy mists of winter.

Venice is wed to the sea, built on 117 islands, threaded by 150 canals, and linked by 400 bridges. From the 9th to 15th centuries, Venice flourished as her commercial and political hegemony spread throughout the Adriatic, Mediterranean, and the Aegean. Ironically, the maritime republic's decline coincided with its zenith in the arts. But even as the fortunes of the city ebbed, Venetian artists began a revolutionary flirtation with color and light, preserving Venice's grandeur on canvas.

Today, Venice is a museum city living on tourism, and its sublime location is now a threat to its very survival. The national government continues to create schemes to save her from the sea, but Venice is threatened everyday with inundation and ruin.

Palace Collection
The 16th-century Palazzo Querini-Stampalia has important works by Bellini, Tiepolo, Vecchio, and Schiavone.
Time: Sun., 10am-3pm
Place: Campiello Querini
Contact: ph. 25235

Palatial Art
Few tourists visit the Palazzo Labia, with its superb Tiepolo frescoes. Used mostly for official functions and concerts, the grand palace is adorned with floor-to-ceiling frescoes by one of Italy's greatest artists. Visits are free, but call first to insure access.
Time: Mon.-Fri., 3pm-5pm
Place: Campo San Geremia
Contact: ph. 716666

Venetian Glass
For centuries, famed Venetian glass has been produced in the shops on the island of Murano in the lagoon. Murano's canals are lined by colorful houses, glass shops, and glassware studios. Many companies invite visitors to tour their workshops and galleries, but the best exhibits are found in the Museo dell'Arte Vetraria, which has the finest collection of Venetian glass in the world.
Time: Sun., 9am-12:30pm
Place: Fondamenta Giustinian
Contact: ph. 739586

Sublime San Marco
The Basilica of San Marco is Venice's best known—and most unforgettable—monument. Beginning as a private chapel for the Doges in 1063, it soon became the focal point of Venice. The interior is a dazzling fantasy of Byzantine, Renaissance, and Baroque decor, every inch embellished with mosaics, marble, gold, and gems. The experience of Saint Mark's was intended to be totally seductive, and it is!
Time: Mon.-Sat., 9:30am-5:30pm; Sun., 2:30pm-5:30pm
Place: Piazza san Marco

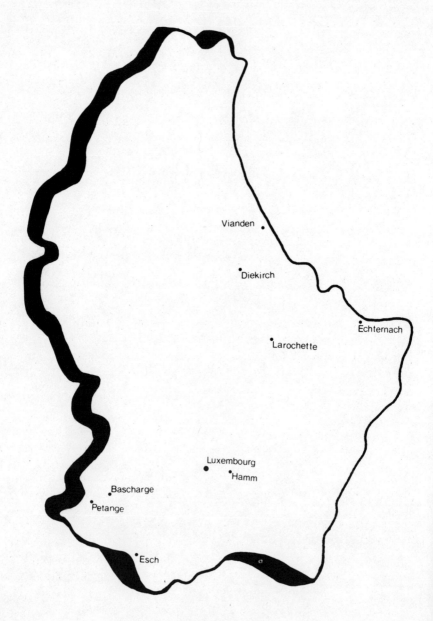

Luxembourg

Luxembourg

Bascharge

An agreeable commercial and industrial town, Bascharge is well-known for its ambrosial brews.

Brewery Tour
Brewing is an ancient and noble tradition in Luxembourg. The Brewery Brasserie Nationale, whose motto is "Pure Malt and Hops," provides an interesting tour of their facilities, with a free beer at the finish.
Contact: ph. 5-090-1121 for an appointment

Diekirch

Diekirch, situated at the western boundry of the German-Luxembourg Nature Park, is rich in natural attractions, Roman and early Christian antiquities, cultural events, and monuments.

Diekirch's Regional Museum
Diekirch's museum has two marvelous mosaics discovered in a Roman villa under the local esplanade. Other Gallo-Roman and medieval ruins in the collection make this a worthwhile visit.
Time: Tues.-Sat., 10am-noon & 2pm-6pm
Place: Place Guillaume
Contact: ph. 803023

Echternach

Echternach's old houses, narrow lanes, and medieval ramparts have helped the town retain a wonderful Old World atmosphere. Situated within the German-Luxembourg Nature Park, Echternach lies in a region known as "Little Switzerland" for its magnificent scenery.

Unique Processional

Echternach is known throughout Europe for its unique religious dancing procession, which attracts pilgrims and spectators from around the world. As an act of thanksgiving for the end of the Plague, villagers began an annual dancing procession as penance to St. Willibord, who got credit for their survival.
Time: Whit Tuesday in June, 9am-1pm
Contact: Sundicate d'Initiative, ph. 72230

Ancient Basilica

The Basilica of St. Willibord contains a magnificent sarcophagus housing the saint's remains, and the church vaults have frescoes dating to 1100. Don't miss the modern stained glass and 13th-century windows that miraculously survived two world wars.

Esch-sur-Alzette

Resistance Museum

This lovely town on the French frontier has a small but moving museum to the local resistance of Nazi aggression during World War II. To visit the museum, apply at the Tourist Office in the Hotel de Ville (ph. 547383).

Hamm

U. S. Cemetery

The military cemetery at Hamm is the final resting place for 5,100 American soldiers of the Third Army, along with General George Patton. Most of the men fell during the Battle of the Bulge. Ironically, just down the road a German cemetery contains the graves of 11,000 troops who fell during the same battle.
Contact: National Tourist Office, Place de la Gare, ph. 481199

Larochette

Dual Ruins

The quaint village of Larochette is dominated by the ruins of two feudal castles. The tourist office can provide walking-tour maps through the countryside, leading up to the castles.
Contact: Syndicat d'Initiative, Place de la Gare, ph. 87676

Luxembourg City

This 2,000-year old capital of the Grand Duchy must be Europe's best travel secret. Dotted with romantic squares, churches, and ancient citadels, Luxembourg has the whimsical air of a city conjured up by some medieval Disney. Surprisingly, few tourists visit this charming anachronism, leaving the city uncrowded and delightful.

National Museum

Situated in Luxembourg's old quarter, the State Museum includes the Museum of Natural History—with divisions of zoology, mineralogy, and paleontology—and the Museum of Art and History, which houses collections of art, archeology, and folklore.
Time: Tues.-Sun., 10am-noon & 2pm-6pm
Place: Marche aux Poissons
Contact: ph. 27565

Rare Stamps

If you're stuck on stamps, you'll enjoy Luxembourg's Post, Telegraph, and Telephone Museum. The displays include some rare Luxembourg stamps, which should make a devoted philatelist drool.
Time: Tues., Thurs., & Sat., 10am-noon & 2pm-5pm
Place: rue de Reims 19
Contact: ph. 22809

Free Concerts

Every summer, free concerts are held in the Place d'Armes, Luxembourg's public square in the Old City. It's a joy to linger under

the trees of this beautiful square anytime—and a sheer delight with music.
Contact: Office Nationale du Tourisme, Place d'Armes

Mersch

Mersch is located at the threshold of the Valley of the Seven Castles, the geographic center of Luxembourg. Graced with beautiful scenery, feudal castles, and Roman ruins, Mersch makes an ideal travel destination.

Roman Museum
Remains of a Roman villa, mosaics, sculpture, and frescoes are the principal features of Mersch's Musee Romain.
Time: Mon.-Fri., 10am-5pm
Place: la rue des Romains
Contact: ph. 32523

Petange

Roman Fortress
Petange lies at the foot of the historic Roman fortifications of Tetelberg. Dating from the first century BC, the fort is surrounded by nearly three kilometers of ramparts.
Contact: Syndicat d'Initiative, Hotel de Ville, ph. 501251

Vianden

One of the Grand Duchy's most beautiful towns, Vianden can trace its roots to the early 9th century. The Old Town quarter, still encircled by medieval ramparts and watch towers, is dominated by a massive feudal castle.

Hydropower
Outside Vianden, you can visit Europe's most powerful hydroelectric pumping station. Even if you have no interest in hydropower,

it's worth a detour for the gorgeous scenery.
Time: Mon.-Sat., 10am-5pm
Place: Mt. Nikolas
Contact: ph. 84257

Nationwide

Natural Park
The German-Luxembourg Natural Park stretches from the Grand Duchy to West Germany. There are hundreds of kilometers of hiking trails through countryside with incomparable scenery.
Contact: Office Nationale du Tourisme, Findel Airport, Luxembourg City, ph. 487993

Walking Paths
Luxembourg has the most extensive network of marked walking and hiking trails in the world. Besides the national network of trails, the Youth Hostel Association maintains its own system of inter-hostel paths.
Contact: Federation Luxembourgeoise des Marches Populaire, Rue de Rollingergrund 176, Luxembourg City, ph. 449302
Also: Luxembourg Youth Hostel Association, Place d'Armes 18, Luxembourg City, ph. 25588

The Netherlands

The Netherlands

Aalsmeer

Located a few miles from Amsterdam's Schiphol Airport, Aalsmeer is the hub of Netherland's floral industry. Besides the immense Bloemenveiling flower auction, you'll find acres of hot houses, fields, and floral nurseries.

Flowers Galore

Even if you can't get to the Netherlands for the spring flower season, you can still get a peek at Holland's floral industry by visiting the colossal Aalsmeer flower auction, the world's largest flower market—over eight million flowers are sold there daily. Visitors are welcome.
Time: Mon.-Fri., 7am-10am
Place: Legmeerdijk 313

Floating Parade

On the first Saturday of September, Aalsmeer is the departure site for the grandest floral parade in Europe. Elaborately decorated floats travel to Amsterdam and back by canal. The floats are on display in the Aalsmeer auction hall on the Friday before the parade.
Place: Legmeerdijk 313

Alkmaar

Although most visitors crowd the town on Fridays to see the old-fashioned cheese market, Alkmaar is worth a trip on its own merit. This picturesque city is rich in gabled houses and ornate buildings.

Cheese Market

Alkmaar holds one of the few remaining traditional cheese markets in the Netherlands. At the weekly auction, cheeses are sold to bidders clapping hands and shouting prices, while white-suited porters, each sporting a red, yellow, or blue straw hat, carry sleds stacked with cheeseballs to the weigh house. It's worth the short trip from Amsterdam to see this 400-year old tradition, even if it is staged primarily for tourists.
Time: April 20-Sept. 21: Fri., 9:30am-11:30am
Place: Waagplein

Amsterdam

Every European capital has its own special charm, but none compares with Amsterdam's appeal. Intriguing and inviting, Amsterdam has Europe's largest intact old city center and as diverse a variety of attractions as any city in the world. The heart of the city, with miles of tree-lined canals and elegant mansions, looks virtually the same today as in Rembrandt's time, 300 years ago. But the center of Amsterdam isn't merely the world's largest open-air museum—it's a vibrant, exciting place, where old buildings house modern shops, cafes, galleries, and even brothels.

Diamond Cutting Tours

Amsterdam has been associated with diamond cutting and polishing since the early 16th century, and today the city is home to a dozen diamond cutting centers, which all provide tours. One of the friendliest and most informative tours is at the Holshuijsen-Stoeltie Factory.
Time: May-Sept.: daily, 9am-5pm; Oct.-April: Mon.-Fri., 9am-5pm.
Place: Wagenstraat 13
Contact: ph. 237601

Punch and Judy Show

Every summer, free puppet shows are staged in Dam Square. The performances are in Dutch, but there's really no language barrier to the merriment.

Time: Wed. & Sat., 2pm-4pm
Place: Dam Square
Contact: ph. 266444

Free Maps

Be sure to pick up a free city map and transit plan from the VVV tourist office.

Time: May 1-Sept. 30: Mon.-Sun., 8:45am-11pm; Oct. 1-April 30: Mon.-Sat., 9am-7pm
Place: Stationplein 10
Contact: ph. 266444 or 221016

Free Beer

Don't miss the tour offered by Heineken, one of the world's best beers—and best tours. You will be guided through each area of the brewery and then invited for free samples in the beerhall.

Time: June-Aug.: Mon.-Fri., 9am & 11am; Sept.-May: Mon.-Fri., 10am
Place: Stadhouderskade 78
Contact: ph. 709111

Bakery Museum

The traveler with a sweet tooth will find the combined Dutch Bakers and Confectioners Historical Museum a real treat. The displays of utensils and bakery apparatus, along with a reconstructed 18th-century confectioner's shop, make for a fascinating visit.

Time: Wed. only, 10am-4pm
Place: Wibautstraat 220
Contact: ph. 153344

A Walk on the Wildside

No visit to Amsterdam is complete without a stroll through the famed Red Light District. The medieval city center is home to a wide-open sex-for-sale neighborhood, where the "ladies of the night" sit in neon-lit windows at street level, advertising their wares.

Place: between OZ Achterburgwal & OZ Voorburgwal

Venerable Synagogue

The Portuguese Synagogue was the focal point for the Jews who fled to Amsterdam from Portugal and Spain at the time of the Inquisition. The interior has remained unchanged since the temple's construction in 1675, and services are held by candlelight.
Time: Mon.-Fri., 10am-4pm; Sun., 10am-1pm
Place: Visserplein 3
Contact: ph. 245351

Tranquil Refuge

Founded in 1345 as a religious retreat, the Begijnhof is a sactuary for today's weary tourist. This patch of 18th-century Amsterdam is now a home for the elderly, but the courtyard is open to visitors. The Begijnhof also houses the pleasant English Church and Amsterdam's oldest standing house.
Place: entrance on Spui

Walking Tour

If you aren't fortunate enough to find accommodations in the Jordaan, pick-up the tourist office brochure for a self-guided tour of this colorful area. This former working-class district is full of galleries, shops, and cafes.
Contact: VVV Amsterdam, Stationplein 10, ph. 266444

Free Concerts

Amsterdam's beautiful Vondel Park, with 120 acres of meadows, woods, and lakes, is the site for daily free concerts each summer. The open-air theater presents classical, jazz, and rock concerts, plus free plays.
Time: evenings, May-August
Place: Huygenstraat

The Royal Birthday

April 30th, the Queen's Birthday, is a grand time to be in Amsterdam. The festivities include a street fair at the Nieumarkt, fireworks, street dances, and free concerts.

Floating Flower Market

For over 200 years, residents have been buying flowers at a floating market on the Singel Canal. It's definitely worth a stroll, especial-

ly on a warm summer evening when the flower barges are illuminated.
Time: daily, 8am-8pm
Place: Singel, between Leidestraat and Muntplein

Botanical Gardens
Along the Kalfjeslaan dike, the Free University Botanical Garden contains an arboretum, tropical greenhouse, fern house, and a wild garden.
Time: Mon.-Fri., 8am-4:30pm
Place: Boechorststraat 8

Coronation Church
The imposing Gothic Nieuwekerk, the traditional chapel for the coronation of Netherland's monarchs, offers daily organ concerts.
Time: Mon.-Sat., noon-4pm; concerts at 3pm daily
Place: Dam

Arnhem

Sitting on the high north bank of the Rhine, Arnhem is really two towns in one—the rebuilt old city center, and the perimeter town of modern buildings. Contemporary Arnhem reflects change brought about by World War II fighting, which nearly leveled the city.

Decorative Arts
Perched high above the Rhine, the Arnhem Museum of Decorative Arts holds many surprises. After viewing the collection, which ranges from 17th-century painting to modern glass sculpture, don't miss the temporary exhibitions, which often generate much controversy in the community.
Time: Tues.-Sat., 10am-5pm; Sun., 11am-5pm
Place: Utrechtseweg 87

Breda

Beautifully situated amidst woodlands and moors, Breda has done an admirable job combining contemporary growth with historic preservation.

Walking Tour

The VVV tourist office conducts an instructive and amusing walking tour of the principal sights of Breda. The mile-long tour will tempt you to dally awhile and visit the Great Church, Breda Castle, and the narrow walkways of this woodland town.
Time: daily, May-Sept.
Place: VVV Willemstraat 17

Historic Garden Retreat

The restful Kruidentiun Begijnhof also has an herb garden that follows a 400-year old pattern. Culinary and medicinal plants share the garden with herbs used to thwart witchcraft.
Time: Mon.-Sat., 8am-6pm
Place: Katharinastraat 3

Delft

Delft is just the sort of picturesque town that one expects to see in the Netherlands—cobbled lanes, a maze of canals, arching bridges, and houses that look as though they haven't changed in 300 years. Delft is a romantic strollers' town, best explored on foot.

Delftware Demonstrations

Authentic Delftware is crafted at the Porceleyn Fles ("Porcelain Bottle"), where the blue and white dishes that have made Delft famous are still made the traditional way. The showroom has an exhibition of antique tiles, and there are demonstrations.
Time: April-Nov.: Mon.-Sat., 9am-5pm
Place: Rotterdamscheweg 196

Baroque Town Hall

Delft's 17th-century Stadhuis, designed by Hendrike de Keyser, is a faithfully restored monument to the great architect. The marble hall, portraits of the House of Orange, and traditional decor all contribute to the Dutch charm of this baroque town hall.
Time: Mon.-Fri., 9am-4pm
Place: Markt 80
Contact: ph. 126100

Carillon Concerts

The Nieue Kerk's 48-bell carillon plays regular concerts three days a week. Before the concert, be sure to visit the impressive mausoleum of William of Orange inside.
Time: Concerts: Tues.,Thurs., & Sat., 11am-noon. Church: daily, 8am-6pm
Place: Markt

Leaning Tower

The tower of the ancient Oude Kerk houses the nine-ton Bourbon bell (conceivably why the church tower has a pronounced list). The 13th-century edifice posseses many interesting tombs, including the elaborate memorial to Admiral Harpertz Tromp.
Time: Mon.-Sat., 8am-6pm; Sun., 2pm-6pm
Place: Oudekerkstraat 9

Gouda

The focal point of this tiny Dutch city is the well-preserved market square district. Gouda's historic cheese market draws a horde of visitors, but it's well worth the trip.

Majestic Church

The massive St. Janskerk, with the longest nave in the Netherlands, has an unusual wooden arched roof and dozens of magnificent stained glass windows. You can often hear recitals on the superb organ, too.
Time: Mon.-Fri., 8:30am-5pm; Sat. & Sun., 2pm-5pm
Place: Marketplein

Gouda by Candlelight

The best day to visit Gouda is December 18th, when the town Christmas tree is officially lit. There are free choir, carillon, and organ concerts in St. Janskerk, plus an evening candlelight procession.
Place: Markt
Contact: VVV, ph. 14284

Famous Cheese Market

Couda's reknowned cheese market is both a colorful tourist at-

traction and a serious commercial event. On market days, cheese balls are rolled through the streets to the Waagebouw (Weigh House) where they are sold. The ornate Waagebouw is also the site of demonstrations of local crafts.
Time: May 15-Sept. 15: Thurs., 9am-10am
Place: Markt 35

Haarlem

This ancient city, an important town when Amsterdam was still a sleepy fishing village, has a beautiful old town center, with narrow streets and Renaissance halls.

Grote Markt
Haarlem's medieval Grote Markt is one of the most elegant squares in the Netherlands. Once used as a jousting arena for Haarlem's Counts, the market place is dominated by the 14th-century St. Bavo's Church, ornate halls, and the noble Stadhuis. The streets surrounding the town center are lined with intriguing old shops, homes, and cafes.

Frans Hals Museum
The Frans Hals Museum is one of those truly special places that every visitor to the Netherlands should see. The museum, a former old men's home where Hals spent his final years, is a restored 17th-century townhouse with a handsome garden and courtyard. Besides paintings by Hals, Steen, van Ruysdael, and the Haarlem School, there are displays of furniture, jewelery, crafts, china, and an enchanting old dollhouse.
Time: Tues.-Sat., 10am-5pm; Sun. & Mon., 1pm-5pm; (free only from Nov.15-Feb. 15)
Place: Groot Heligiland 62
Contact: ph. 219059

The Hague (den Haag)

Although Amsterdam is the nation's capital, The Hague is the seat of government and the royal residence. In spite of recent suburban sprawl, The Hague remains an elegant city, full of parks, townhouses, and palaces.

Marvelous Mondrians
The Gemeente has the world's best collection of early works by Piet Mondrian. Donated in 1972 by a friend of the artist, the 250 paintings make this museum a must for modern art devotees. The rest of the permanent collection is also worth a peek; musical instruments, sculpture, and works by Kandinsky, Picasso, Degas, and Monet.
Time: Tues.-Sat., 10am-5pm; Sun., 11am-5pm
Place: Stadhouderslaan 41

Elegant Surprise
The little-known Bredius Museum is a gem. This 17th-century townhouse, home of the wealthy Bredius family, is still decorated with the family's draperies, carpets, silver, and porcelain, plus artwork by Rembrant, Breughel, van Dyke, and van Ruysdael.
Time: Tues. & Thurs., 2pm-5pm
Place: Prinsegracht 6
Contact: ph. 546200

Rosarium
The Hague's beautiful Rosarium, with it's seven rose gardens, is the site of an international rose festival every July 4th. This lovely park contains 350 varieties of roses from all over the world.
Time: daily, 8am-8pm
Place: Westbroekpark

Costume Museum
For a colorful tour of three centuries of fashions, visit the Costume Museum of The Hague. The far-ranging collection includes displays of regal clothing and Art Nouveau styles.
Time: Mon.-Sat., 10am-5pm; Sun., 1pm-5pm
Place: Lange Vijverberg 14

Japanese Gardens
The Hague is home to the Netherlands' only public Japanese Garden. Notable features of this oasis are a lovely traditional

teahouse, glorious Asian azaleas, oriental lanterns, and a rock garden.
Time: Mon.-Sun., 8:30am-8pm
Place: Clingendaelpark

s'Hertogenbosch (Den Bosch)

Den Bosch (as the locals call it) is the attractive capital of North Brabant Province. The town is justly celebrated for its sublime old town center, a magnificent Gothic cathedral, and a maze of old lanes.

Majestic Cathedral
St. Janskerk is a Gothic marvel constructed between 1350 and 1530. It has impressive religious art, wooden sculpture, and a lofty nave with 170 columns. The church's 48-bell carillon is played every Wednesday at noon. And don't miss the gargoyles.
Time: Mon.-Sat., 9am-5pm; Sun., 2pm-5pm
Place: Markt

Gilded Town Hall
One of Den Bosch's many gilded and gabled buildings is the 16th-century Stadhuis. This municipal edifice has a 38-bell carillon and a glockenspiel with knights who joust every hour.
Place: Markt 77

Hoorn

It's hard to imagine that this little town was an influencial city during the 17th century. As the headquarters of the wealthy Dutch East India Company, Hoorn's mariners pioneered worldwide exploration and trade. Today, Hoorn couldn't be more quaint. The town is loaded with squares, markets, canals, and ornate public buildings.

Craft Market
Hoorn features an entertaining folk market each summer. Hollanders in traditional folk costumes demonstrate venerable customs and dances. The most popular spectacle is the making

of Dutch clogs, which are handcarved from willow logs.
Time: June 11-August 31: Mon.-Sat., 9:30am-noon
Place: Marktplein

Walking Tour
Before you visit the folk market, get a free map and self-guided walking tour for the town. Be sure to see the charming harbor that once was the headquarters of the Dutch East India Company.
Time: Mon.-Sat., 9am-5pm
Place: Centralsquare

Kinderdijk

Windmills
To see Dutch windmills in action, the best place to go is the village of Kinderdijk, where you'll find the unique sight of 19 working windmills. All 19 mills are in operation on summer Saturdays.
Time: Late June-August: Sat., 1:30pm-5pm
Place: Laandijk

Leiden

Leiden, the home of the Netherland's oldest university, is crowded with many old buildings, museums and lovely quayside promenades.

Pilgrim's Haven
Leiden proudly maintains the Pilgrim Fathers Documentation Center, commemorating its heritage as a place of refuge for America's forefathers. You can visit the permanent exhibit of documents, which relate to the stay of the Pilgrims in Leiden from 1609 to 1619.
Time: Mon.-Fri., 9am-4:30pm
Place: Boisotkade 2a

Historic Tour
The VVV tourist office of Leiden sponsors a guided walking tour

of this handsome city. The tour includes peeks at quaint houses, dikes, and windmills.
Place: VVV, Stationplein 210
Contact: ph. 144846

Limmen

Tulip Collection
Flower lovers will find the Boschman Bulb Garden an interesting attraction. This specialized collection of tulip, daffodil, and hyacinth bulbs is renowned for its historical and scientific interest.
Time: April-mid June: Mon.-Sat., 9am-5pm
Place: Dusseldorpweg 81

Rotterdam

Virtually obliterated by Nazi bombing, Rotterdam has been rebuilt as an entirely modern city. With the biggest and busiest harbor in the world, Rotterdam has become an international business and transportation hub. Unlike most Dutch cities, there are few quaint homes or tree-lined canals, but you will discover an exciting metropolis of steel and glass—Europe of the future instead of the past.

Art Museum
The Boymans van Beuningen Museum is a gem. The collection of traditional and modern paintings, ceramics, decorative art, and sculpture has something to appeal to any taste. Bosch fans will be enthralled by his early works there, and don't miss the porcelain and glass exhibits.
Time: Mon.-Sat., 10am-5pm; Sun., 11am-5pm
Place: Mathenesserlaan 18
Contact: ph. 136006

Pilgrim's Port
The restored Delfshaven district is where the Pilgrims departed for the New World in 1620. The winding streets, gabled houses,

galleries, and the Pilgrim Fathers Church (Pelgrimvaderskerk) make this port an enchanting place to visit.
Time: Church: Mon.-Sat., 9am-5pm
Place: Voorstraat
Contact: ph. 774156

Pewter Factory
The ancient guildhouse of the Zakkendragershuisje (the Grain Carriers) has been converted into a workshop where craftsmen demonstrate traditional pewter casting techniques. Objects are cast from 17th-century molds and offered for sale.
Time: daily, 10am-5pm
Place: Voorstraat 13

Maritime Museum
Rotterdam's history is inexorably tied to the sea, and the Prins Hendrik Maritime Museum will give you a glimpse into the city's nautical past. The highlight is the detailed collection of ship models.
Time: Mon.-Sat., 10am-5pm; Sun., 11am-5pm
Place: Jacobsplein 8

Outstanding Gardens
The Trompengorg Arboretum has a rare collection of trees, plants, and shrubs from around the world. The gardens, first planted by the Smit family in 1820, lie along the Maas River dike.
Time: Mon.-Sat., 9am-8pm
Place: Honingerdijk 64
Contact: Free tickets are available from VVV, Stationplein 19, or VVV Information at the Central Railway Station, ph.136000

Scheveningen

Casino Tours
You don't have to risk one guilder to visit Holland's classiest casino. The Scheveningen Kurhaus offers entertaining guided tours on request. This lavishly restored gambling house is an architectural gem worth a visit, even if you have no interest in gaming.
Time: Mon.-Fri., 11am, 11:30am, & noon
Place: Gevers Deynootplein
Contact: ph. 546200

Utrecht

Although Utrecht has undergone a major (and controversial) facelift, it retains its appealing maze of winding streets and canals in the old city. This university town is one of the Netherland's liveliest cities, with friendly cafes and pubs all over.

Modern Art

The ancient Roman town of Utrecht, over 2,000-years old, has a very modern art museum. Hedendaags Kunst (Today's Art) is overlooked by most tourists, but it's a terrific art center, where no art produced prior to 1965 is exhibited.

Time: Tues.-Sat., 11am-5pm

Place: Achter de Dom 14

Norway

Norway

Alesund

At the top of fjord country, Alesund spreads across three coastal islands and a rocky fringe of skerries at the edge of the Norwegian Sea. With the snowcapped Sunnmore Mountains as backdrop and the rocky fjord landscape all around, Alesund abounds in breathtaking scenery.

Bird Sanctuary
Just southwest of Alesund on the rugged island of Runde, you'll find Norway's southernmost bird sanctuary. Amidst the cliffs and grottoes are the nesting places of nearly one million birds of 40 species. Contact the Tourist Office for directions.
Contact: Alesund Reiselivslag, Ronnebergsgate 15b, ph. 21202

Bergen

A delightful combination of old and new Norway, Bergen serves as the western gateway to the incomparable fjord country. Founded by King Olav Kyre in the 11th century, Bergen was Norway's capital and busiest port throughout the Middle Ages. Hanseatic merchants built impressive homes and warehouses along Bergen's quayside, and they're still there today—a row of tall, wooden buildings with pointed gables and sheltered courtyards. Modern

Bergen is a vibrant, charming town with attractive pedestrian zones, handsome architecture, and tree-lined boulevards.

Bergen Guide
Your first stop in Bergen should be the tourist office for a free copy of the *Bergen Guide*. This map-filled booklet is full of detailed information on a multitude of attractions.
Time: Mon.-Sat., 8am-10pm
Place: Torgalmenning
Contact: Turistinformasjonkontoret, ph. 211487 or 313860

Norwegian Art
The Rasmus Meyer's Collection, a fine museum of indigenous paintings, decorative arts, and furnishings, includes many works by Edvard Munch and paintings by Munthe, J.C. Dahl, and Harriet Backer. Backer.
Time: Mon.-Fri., 11am-4pm & Sun., noon-3pm
Place: Rasmus Meyer Allee

Romanesque Beauty
Bergen's most beautiful church, the Romanesque 12th-century Mariakirche, is also the city's oldest building. The carved and painted Baroque pulpit was a gift from Hanseatic merchants in the 16th century. During the summer, there are organ recitals each Thursday evening at 8:00 in the chapel.
Time: Mon.-Fri., 11am-4pm
Place: Dreggsalmenniger

University Museums
On Sydneshaugen Hill, overlooking the Puddefjord, is Bergen University, with the adjoining University Collections. The complex of buildings houses the Maritime Museum, the Museum of Cultural History, and the Natural History Museum.
Time: Mon.-Fri., 11am-3pm
Place: Olav Ryesvej
Contact: ph. 219626

Medieval Bergen
Bergen's foremost attraction is the old Hansa Merchant District at the harbor. The wooden houses and warehouses front a warren

of narrow alleys leading to courtyards and workshops, where local
artisans have shops and showrooms.
Time: Mon.-Sat., 9am-6pm
Place: Bryggen

Botanical Gardens
Founded in 1897, the Bergen University Botanical Gardens are
limited in area but rich in horticultural attractions.
Time: Gardens: daily, 8am-7pm; Greenhouse: Mon.-Sat., 9am-3pm
Place: Olav Ryesvej

Bodo

Although Bodo is considered a resort town, its principal attraction
is its proximity to the arctic wilderness. Flattened by German air
raids during World War II, Bodo was rebuilt entirely.

Midnight Sun
The Bodo Tourist Office can direct you to the Ronvikfjell overlook,
two miles from town, where you can enjoy an unobstructed view
of the midnight sun against the jagged peaks of the Lofoten Islands.
The sun doesn't set from early June until late July.
Contact: Bodo Reiselivslag, Dronningensgate lb, ph. 21240

Modern Cathedral
Bodo's striking Domkirke, built in 1956, contains vibrant stained
glass windows by Agen Storstein, handsome Nordic wallhangings,
and redwood carvings.
Time: Mon.-Fri., 9:30am-5pm & Sat., 9:30am-2pm
Place: Radhusplassen

Maelstrom
Twelve miles southeast of Bodo, Norway's famous Saltstraumen—a
narrow strait with roiling waters—links the Saltsfjord and Skjerstad-
fjord. Four times each day the tides force 100,000 million gallons
of water through the narrows, creating spectacular tidal waves,
whirlpools, and eddys.

Fredrikstad

Straddling the Glomma River at the mouth of the Oslofjord, Fredrikstad is a city with a dual personality. The new town is a modern industrial center, while the Old Town, dating back to 1660, is one of Scandanavia's best-preserved fortified towns.

Nature Reserve

The Ora Nature Reserve, on the eastern shore of the Oslofjord just below Fredrikstad, covers the river delta with its lush vegetation and abundant wildlife. The reserve is an important resting and feeding area for migrating waterfowl, as well as home for the rare northern water vole, otter, and North Sea seals.

Fortified Town

Within the turreted stone walls of Fredrikstad's Gamlebyen are restored and preserved 17th-century homes, shops, and barracks. In workshops along the quaint alleyways, you can watch weavers, glassblowers, and other artisans at work. Be sure to walk along the ramparts for terrific views of the Glomma River Valley.
Contact: Fredrikstad Turistkontor, Turistsenteret, ph. 20330

Hammerfest

The world's northern-most town, Hammerfest has become the base for Norway's arctic fishing fleet because of its sheltered, ice-free harbor. Destroyed by the Nazis, Hammerfest today is a colorful, modern town and a trading center for Finnmark Lapps.

Lapp Church

Hammerfest has a splendid modern church shaped like a Lapp tent. Instead of an altar, a glorious stained glass window has been installed as a focus for prayer. During weekday evenings in the summer, free concerts of sacred music are held in the chapel.
Time: Mon.-Sat., 9:30am-4pm
Place: Kirkegate
Contact: ph. 12185

Haugesund

Framed by a stretch of fjord coastline, Haugesund is a delightfully untouristy seaport.

Royal Tomb

Just a mile north of Haugesund is the Haraldshaug, the burial mound and tomb of Viking King Harald the Fairhaired. In 1872, a 60-foot high obelisk was erected at the mound to commemorate Harald's victory at the battle of Harfsfjord in 872 AD. See the tourist office for directions.
Contact: Turiskontor, Smedesundet 90, ph. 25255

Jevnaker

Historic Glassworks

At the southern end of the Randsfjord, the village of Jevnaker is home of Norway's oldest glass factory, the Hadelands Glasverk, established in 1765. Visitors can join free tours to see glassblowing, cutting, and etching still done by hand.
Time: Mon.-Fri., 9:30am-3:30pm
Contact: ph. 21577

Kirkenes

Iron Mines

Barely four miles from the Soviet-Norwegian border, Kirkenes is a bustling mining and ore-processing center. The tourist office is happy to arrange tours of the mines and processing plant, where millions of tons of iron ore are processed yearly. Also, the midnight sun there provides a memorable spectacle for more than two months, beginning late in May.
Contact: Turistkontor, Parkvejen 1, ph. 92294

Kongsberg

Kongsberg is an ancient silver mining town and still the seat of the Norwegian mint.

Rococo Church

Kongsberg's immense wooden Lutherankirke is a rococo surprise. Erected in 1750, the church's lavish decoration gives it a theatrical ambience. Along with the gilded boxes for visiting royalty and enormous silver candelabra, the impression is highlighted by *trompe l'oeil* which makes the wooden interior look like marble.
Time: Mon.-Fri., 9:30am-3pm
Place: Torget
Contact: ph. 731526

Laerdal

Stave Church

Near Laerdal, at the head of the Laerdalfjord, is the famed Borgund Stave church. Black with pitch and adorned with runic inscriptions, it was built in the mid-12th century. The gables with their dragon heads are reminiscent of Viking ship prows. Of Norway's 35 stave churchs, Borgund is probably the best preserved.
Time: Mon.-Fri., 10am-3:30pm
Contact: ph. 05-666101

Mo i Rana

The magnificent scenery around this Arctic town includes the neaby Svartsen Glacier, Norway's second-largest.

Steel Mill Tours

The Mo i Rana Tourist Office will arrange guided tours of the Norsk Jernverk Steelworks and Rolling Mill. The government-owned mill, Scandanavia's biggest steel plant, was financed in part by Marshall Plan funds in the early 1950's.
Contact: Turistkontor, Jernbaneplassen, ph. 50421

Molde

Molde is an attractive resort and commercial town. Largely destroyed during World War II, Molde was completely rebuilt in contemporary style. South and east of town, you'll find the peaks of the Romsdal Mountains and the breathtaking Rauma Valley.

Jazz Festival

Molde's annual Jazz Festival has been expanded in recent years to include many free companion attractions, including art shows, poetry readings, plays, concerts, and folk music.
Time: first week of July
Contact: Molde Jazz Festival, Boks 261, ph. 53233

Town Hall Tours

Built in 1967, Molde's Municipal Hall is one of the most striking modern town halls in Europe. The harmony achieved by blending marble, stone, wood, and greenery with cascades of light is both pleasant and functional. Tours of the facility are possible during business hours.
Time: Mon.-Fri., 9am-4:30pm
Place: Radhusplassen
Contact: ph. 52060

Modern Church

The eye-catching Moldekirke is Norway's largest modern church. Featuring dazzling stained glass, mosaics, and carved reliefs, the whitewashed brick church is a well-conceived example of modern Scandanavian ecclesiastical architecture.
Time: Mon.-Sat., 10am-4pm
Place: Radhusplassen ·

Oslo

Pine-covered mountains and the clear waters of Oslofjord provide a flawless setting for Norway's capital. Only one-fifth of the land within Oslo's boundaries is used for urban development; the remainder is forests, lakes, parks, and mountains. Miles of nature and cross-country ski trails are maintained inside Oslo's city limits.

Oslo has been inhabited for thousands of years, but its official history begins in 1050, when King Harald established a base for his Viking raiders at Oslo Harbor. Today, the city reflects a hodgepodge of architectural styles, with contemporary concrete and glass structures standing next to ancient stone buildings.

Postal Museum

Stamp collectors won't want to miss the Norwegian Postal

Museum's displays of stamps and three centuries of postal history.
Time: Mon.-Fri., 10am-3pm
Place: Dronningensgate 15

European Art
The National Gallery is renowned for its survey of 19th- and 20th-century Norwegian art, particularly the captivating Munch Hall. There is also a collection of art by Rubens, Rembrandt, El Greco, and other masters, plus a fine group by French Impressionists.
Time: Mon.-Fri., 10am-4pm; Sat., 10am-3pm; Sun., noon-3pm
Place: Universitetsgate 13
Contact: ph. 200404

Sculpture Park
Oslo's Frogner Park is home to the famous Vigeland Sculpture Park. Norwegian sculptor Gustav Vigeland used bronze, stone, and iron to create figures that depict the human life-cycle. The collection of 1,100 human and animal figures is the result of 40 years of work by Vigeland and his assistants.
Time: daily
Place: Kirkevei

Vigeland Museum
The former home and studio of Vigeland now houses a museum devoted to the sculptor, with thousands of sketches, plans, and woodcuts, along with castings and sculptures. During summer months, the Municipal Orchestra gives concerts in the courtyard on Wednesday evenings.
Time: Tues.-Sun., 1pm-7pm
Place: Nobelsgate 32
Contact: ph. 441136

Oslo Cathedral
Dramatically remodelled in 1950, Oslo's 17th-century Domkirke has a colorful, eclectic interior. Don't miss the silver sculpture *The Last Supper* in the Chapel of Our Saviour.
Time: Mon.-Fri., 10am-2pm; Sat., 10am-noon
Place: Stortorget
Contact: ph. 412793

Historical Relics

Affiliated with Oslo University, the Historical Museum of Oslo houses antiquities, ethnography, and numismatics. Among the Nordic antiquities, the ecclesiastical artwork and Viking artifacts are particularly memorable. You won't want to miss the Treasure Hall, with its hoard of gold and silver jewelry.
Time: Tues.-Sun., 11am-3pm
Place: Frederiksgate 2
Contact: ph. 416300

Botanical Garden

In 1814, King Frederik VI donated his estate at Toyen to Oslo University for use as a botanical garden. The collection of Norwegian alpine plants is unmatched.
Time: Garden: daily, 7am-8pm; Hothouses: Tues.-Fri. & Sun., noon-3pm
Place: Trondheimsveien 23

Weaver's Studio

Norway's most respected contemporary weaver, Sigrin Berg, welcomes visitors to her studio to see her work and design.
Time: Mon.-Fri., 10am-3pm
Contact: ph. 208041

Museums Galore

Oslo's Natural History Museum complex, divided into mineralogical, geological, paleontological, and zoological collections—plus a fascinating National Mining Museum—has something to interest any visitor.
Time: Tues.-Sun., noon-4pm
Place: Sarsgate 1

Parliament Tours

The Norwegian government offers free tours of the National Parliament building during the summer. The interesting tours are given in Norwegian and English.
Time: June 15-Sept. 15: Mon.-Sat., 11am, noon, & 1pm
Place: Karl Johansgate
Contact: ph. 427044

Royal Palace

Slottet, Norway's Royal Palace, isn't open to the public, but you may visit its lovely park during the day. Be sure to catch the changing of the royal guard daily at 1:30pm
Place: Karl Johansgate

Scandesign

Oslo's Crafts and Industries Association maintains a permanent exhibition of Norwegian art and design at the Forum. You'll find displays of home furnishings, textiles, glassware, and ceramics— all selected by a committee for their quality of design.
Time: Mon.-Sat., 9am-4pm; Sun., 9am-noon
Place: Rosenkrantzgate 7
Contact: ph. 333870

Monumental City Hall

The simple exterior of Oslo's Radhus belies the lavish interior of paintings, frescoes, sculpture, tapestries, and carvings. Henrik Sorenson's gigantic murals depict Norway's history and chronical the harshness of Nazi occupation. And don't miss the Swan Fountain in the courtyard. There are guided tours on Mon. and Wed. evenings between 6pm and 8pm
Time: Mon.-Sat., 10am-2pm; Sun., noon-3pm
Place: Radhusplassen
Contact: ph. 410090

Munch Museum

This modern museum houses the vast collection of paintings and memorabilia bequeathed to Oslo by Norway's greatest painter, Edvard Munch. Arranged chronologically, the exhibit charts Munch's changing style—from realism to macabre expressionism.
Time: Tues.-Sun., 10am-8pm
Place: Toyengate 53
Contact: ph. 673774

Decorative Art

Oslo's Museum of Applied Arts presents European decorative arts from the Middle Ages on. The real treasure of the Kunstin-

dustrimuseet is the 12th-century Baldishol Tapestry from an ancient Hedemark church.
Time: Tues.-Sun., 11am-3pm
Place: St. Olavsgate 1
Contact: ph. 203578

National Pageant
On May 17, Constitution Day, Oslo comes alive with pageantry. Paraders in folk costumes, flag-waving children, and brass bands march up Karls Johangate to the Palace to greet the royal family.

Ancient Church
Built in 1150, the venerable Gamle Akerskirke is the oldest stone church in Scandin avia in continuous use. Across the road from the small Anglo-Norman church is a cemetary with the tomb of Henrik Ibsen and the graves of many famous Norwegians.
Time: Church: May-Sept.: Mon.-Fri., 10am-noon
Place: Akersbakken 26
Contact: ph. 461168

Science and Industry
The Norsk Teknisk Museum is a terrific, hands-on exhibition of Norwegian scientific and industrial development. Along with Scandin avia's largest model railway, there are working models of oil rigs, hydraulic machinery, telecommunications, and power plants.
Time: Tues.-Sat., 10am-4pm
Place: Fyrstikkallen 1
Contact: ph. 675195

Municipal Museum
The 18th-century Frogner Manor houses Oslo's Municipal Museum, displaying decorative arts and home furnishings from old Oslo.
Time: Mon.-Fri., 10am-3pm
Place: Frognerveien 67
Contact: ph. 426676

Norwegian Crafts
You'll find woolens, ceramics, jewelry, traditional costumes, and a wide-ranging display of Norwegian handicrafts at Oslo's Husfliden. The non-profit shop and exhibition is run by the Associa-

tion for the Preservation of Norwegian Home Arts and Folk Culture. There are frequent demonstrations of rural handicrafts and folk arts on the lower level.
Time: Mon.-Fri., 9am-4pm; Sat., 9am-1pm
Place: Mollergaten 4
Contact: ph. 311695

Roros

Mining Museum
The little town of Roros owes its existence to the discovery of large deposits of copper in the area. Down the street from ancient miners' cottages, the visitor will find the Copper Mining Museum, which illustrates the mining and processing of copper as it was done in Roros for 300 years. The tourist office can arrange tours of the defunct Christianus Quintus mine during the summer.
Time: Tues.-Sat., 11am-3pm
Place: Bergmannsgatta
Contact: ph. 11165

Stavanger

Development of Norway's North Sea oil reserves has turned Stavanger into a Scandinavian boomtown. Fortunately, the historic harbor district and old town quarter have been preserved and protected.

Tourist Rambles
The Stavanger Tourist Bureau has developed a network of marked walking trails where one can ramble along fjords, down miles of sandy beaches, and in bucolic valleys.
Contact: Turistformasjon, Jernbaneveien, ph. 527254

Medieval Cathedral
Stavanger's 12th-century cathedral is Norway's second-largest church. The basilica has a richly carved Renaissance pulpit and Gothic sculpture.
Time: Mon.-Sat., 9am-9pm
Place: Konggate

Herb Garden

Two miles southwest of Stavanger, the Rogaland Folk and Archaeological Museum has established the new Ullandhaughagen Garden. The 300 species contained in the garden are mainly herbs and plants that are useful.
Time: daily, 8am-6pm
Place: Ullanhaugh
Contact: ph. 667773

Tromso

Cathedral of the Arctic

The Tromsdalen Church, erected in 1975, is known as the "Cathedral of the Arctic" because of its location and its design reminiscent of an iceberg. The church incorporates a dazzling stained glass window, 75-feet high. Located nearly 250 miles above the Arctic Circle, Tromso is bathed in the midnight sun from May 20 to July 15, but it remains completely dark from November 21 to January 21, except for the northern lights.
Time: June-Sept.: Mon.-Sat., 10am-noon & 3pm-5pm
Place: Bruvegan
Contact: ph. 84776

Trondheim

Trondheim seems perched on the edge of the world. Set on a peninsula on the shore of its namesake fjord, Trondheim is a town of medieval atmosphere and indomitable spirit that shines through the dark arctic winter.

Summer Madness

If you are lucky enough to be in Trondheim for the Midsummer Holiday, take the special tram from St. Olavsgate to the end of the line at Lian on Grakallen Mountain. Up there, a thousand feet above the city, celebrants erect bonfires around a small mountain lake and sing, dance, and carouse under the midnight sun.

Antiquated Fortress

Overlooking Trondheim's quaint old port, the small Kristiansten

Fortress affords fine views of the ancient Nidaros Cathedral, the old town, and the fjord.
Time: May-August: daily, 3pm-6pm
Place: Kristianstenbakken
Contact: ph. 25890

Voss

One for the Gipper
Voss's most famous son, Knute Rockne, is memorialized by a small park and monument located just below the railway station. If you visit lovely Voss, situated on the shores of Lake Vangs, you'll wonder why Rockne ever left.
Place: Jernebaneveien

Venerable Church
Many of Voss's older buildings were destroyed by Nazi bombing in 1940, but its Gothic church survived. Built in 1270, the stone church, with seven-foot-thick walls, boasts an unusual wooden tower, a Renaissance pulpit, carved Baroque rood screen, and an original stone altar.
Time: May-Sept.: Mon.-Sat., 9am-7pm
Place: Vangsgate

Fabulous Trails
The tourist office publishes guides to numerous marked paths in the spectacular Hordaland region. One challenging but rewarding hike is through the scenic Raundals Valley between Voss and Mjollf-jell. The hike along the wild ravine, following a river fed by glacial streams, is unforgettable.
Time: Mon.-Fri., 9am-4pm
Place: Vangsgate 81
Contact: ph. 11715

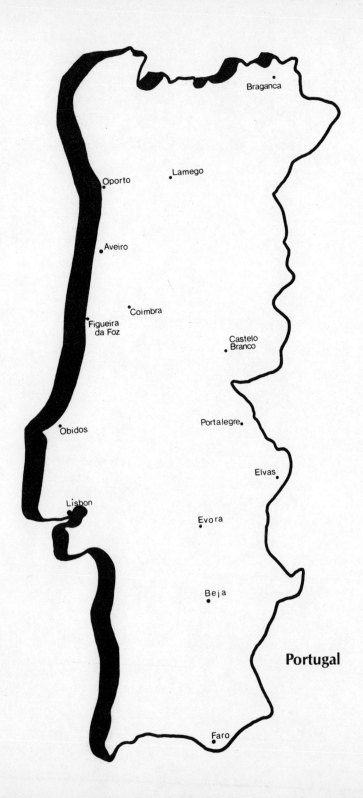

Portugal

Aviero

The "Venice of Portugal" is set on a vast lagoon, interlaced by numerous canals and united by low bridges. Separated from the sea by a barrier island of sand, Aviero is encircled by marshland, rivers, and sand dunes. The old town center, amidst a labyrinth of waterways, is crowded with quaint houses, fishing quays, and monuments.

Baroque Museum
Aviero's former Convent of Jesus, now a national museum, is a paragon of Baroque exuberance. Dating from the 15th century, the convent underwent a total renovation during the early 18th century. The chancel holds the extravagant tomb of King Alfonso V's daughter, who remained secluded at the convent the last 20 years of her life. The museum also displays an assortment of paintings, antiques, and statuary.
Time: Sat. & Sun., 10am-noon & 2pm-5pm
Place: Rua Santa Joana

Nature Reserve
A large area of marsh and lagoon on the northern edge of Aviero has been set aside for the Pateira de Fermentelos Nature Reserve.

The reed beds and salt marshes are rich habitats for waterfowl. Contact: Servico Nacional de Parques, Reservas e Patrimonio Paisagistico, rua da Lapa 73, Lisboa

Beja

Founded by the Romans, Beja suffered greatly during four centuries of Moorish occupation. Today, bright houses line the narrow Roman lanes of this market town, where colorful donkey carts still carry produce from the countryside through town.

Ancient Citadel
The ivy-covered walls of Castelo de Beja loom above Beja's streets. The massive fortress, constructed during the 13th century on the ruins of an earlier Roman fort, bears the scars of long neglect, but its marble keep, walls, and chambers are in good shape. The parapets offer a wonderful panorama of the city and the surrounding plateau.
Time: Sun., 10am-1pm & 2pm-6pm
Place: Rua Aresta Branco

Regional Museum
Set in the Convent da Conceicao, Beja's Museu Leonor is richly embellished with gilt carvings, colorful tiles, and glowing azulejo panels. The eclectic collection incorporates Visigoth sculpture, Roman artifacts, Moorish silverwork, and local costumes displayed on odd mannequins.
Time: Sat., 9:30am-1pm & 2pm-5pm
Place: Largo da Conceicao

Braganca

In the northeast corner of Portugal, the ancient town of Braganca overlooks its modern counterpart in the valley. The Dukes of Braganca, who ruled Portugal for three centuries, created this gem of medieval architecture.

Oldest Town Hall
Braganca's 12th-century Domus Municipalis is Portugal's oldest sur-

viving municipal hall. The spooky, Romanesque building is dimly lit by tiny arched windows and forms an irregular pentagon. The interior is one big hall, decorated by a simple carved frieze.
Time: Mon.-Sat., 10am-noon & 2pm-4pm
Place: Rua Dom Fernao

Wall Walks
For spectacular views of ancient Braganca and the surrounding mountains, climb one of the 18 towers and walk around the crenellated ramparts.
Time: always accessible

Coimbra
Clinging to the hillside above the Rio Modego, this romantic town is Portugal's most important educational center. Coimbra's University, the second-oldest in the world (established by King Dinis in 1290), is a labyrinth of alleys, arcades, and courtyards. Staunch traditionalists have preserved Coimbra's classic buildings and its enchantment.

Palace Museum
Named for a famous Portuguese sculptor, the Museu Machado de Castro has extensive collections of medieval statuary, gold and silver objects, Portuguese and Dutch paintings, and a series of spooky basement galleries of Roman origin, with displays of ancient statuary. Be sure to slip out to the west loggia for a sensational view of Coimbra.
Time: Sat. & Sun., 10am-1pm & 2pm-5pm
Place: Rua de Borges Carneiro
Contact: ph. 23727

Sublime Library
Coimbra's magnificent Biblioteca da Universidade is a Baroque masterpiece. The three lofty salons have floors of inlaid marble and ceilings decorated in a virtuoso display of false perspective. Bibliophiles will be awed by the collection of priceless books.
Time: Mon.-Fri., 9am-noon & 2pm-5:30pm
Place: Rua Guiherme Moreira

Fortress Cathedral

The mountainous Se Velha (Old Cathedral), built in the mid-12th century, is one of Portugal's most impressive Romanesque structures. The interior is enlivened by a flamboyant Gothic gilded altar and marvelous azulejos in the chapels.
Time: daily, 9am-6pm
Place: Praca da Se Velha

Academic Festival

The best time to visit Coimbra is at the end of May, when the academic year ends and the students celebrate the Fitas Festival. The revelry includes the burning of colorful college ribbons, midnight serenades, concerts, and parades, along with revelry sponsored by student "Republics."
Contact: Turismo, Largo da Portagem, ph. 25576

Elvas

This ancient walled town, just a few miles from the Spanish frontier, is known for its elaborate fortifications, Portugal's finest example of 17th-century military architecture. Today, donkey carts still labor up steep lanes, squeezing through ancient gates to tiny plazas.

Moorish Castle

The Elvas Castelo, constructed by Moors during the 12th century, was augmented by the Portuguese in the 15th century to restrain the interloping Spanish. The citadel's moldy ramparts offer a terrific panorama of Elvas, its bastions, and the countryside.
Time: Mon.-Wed. & Fri.-Sun., 9:30am-12:30pm & 2:30pm-7pm
Place: rua da Castelo

Civic Museum

The Museu Municipal Elvas features artifacts from Portugal's old colonial territories, antique weapons, paintings, and regional archaeological finds.
Time: Mon.-Fri., 9am-1pm; Sat., 10am-1pm
Place: Largo do Colegio
Contact: ph. 62236

Evora

This ancient town is a marvelous jumble of Portuguese history and culture. Every street is packed with architectural souvenirs of Evora's successive occupiers. The panoply of attractions in this provincial capital includes a Roman temple, a medieval university, and a Baroque palace.

Classical Temple

The graceful Corinthian columns of the Temple of Diana bear silent witness to Evora's Roman heritage. Little survives from the great Roman city except bits of mosaics, some statues, and the well-preserved temple of the Moon Goddess, used over the centuries as a warehouse, a garrison, and even a slaughterhouse.
Time: always open
Place: Largo Conde de Vita-Flor

Ancient Art

The Museu de Evora, housed in a former palace, is devoted to historic art, from Roman statuary to Renaissance painting. The lower galleries feature Roman, Arab, and medieval sculpture and reliefs. The upper halls display Portuguese religious art and Flemish altarpieces.
Time: Sat. & Sun., 10am-noon & 2pm-5pm
Place: Largo Marques de Marialva

Faro

Faro, capital of the Algarve, continues to be an attractive seaside resort, even though it is subject to hordes of European sun-worshippers. Set on Portugal's most southerly cape, Faro's protected bays have enticed travelers throughout the ages. The old town, with its ruined ramparts and ancient houses, is a tranquil place to steal away from the tourist bustle around the harbor.

Museum Tours

Faro's Museu Municipal provides tours of its diverse collections. The Archaeological Gallery contains interesting Roman finds from nearby Milreu excavations, along with African artifacts and ancient

weapons. The Ferreira do Almeida Art Collection includes religious art, antique furniture, and a stunning Roman mosaic.
Time: Mon., 9am-noon and 2pm-5:30pm
Place: Largo do Se
Contact: ph. 25404

Grisly Memorial
Behind the beautiful Igreja de Nossa Senhora do Carmo Church you can find Faro's strangest tourist attraction, the Capela dos Ossos. This "Chapel of Bones" is lined completely with skulls and bones of monks, nuns, and priests, unearthed from the adjacent cemetary. In startling contrast to this macabre chapel, the Carmelite Church in front is crowned by gilded domes and adorned with intricate lattice work.
Time: daily, 10am-1pm & 3pm-5pm
Place: Largo do Carmo

Nature Reserve
Faro overlooks the Ria Formosa Nature Reserve, an area of lagoons, barrier islands, cliffs, and mudflats. The Reserve is a renowned wildfowl breeding ground, and a Mediterranean-like flora adds color to the high ground.
Time: unrestricted access
Contact: Servico Nacional de Parques, Rua Justine Cumaro 5

Roman Ruins
The last enduring ruin of ancient Roman Milreu stands in the countryside north of Faro. All that remains are two sections of marble columns, a temple apse, and brick foundations. But it's worth the trek out to this first century AD town to see the colorful mosaics, especially the aquatic motifs in the public baths.
Time: daily, 8am-sunset
Place: five miles northeast on Rua Estoi (N2)

Figueira da Foz

Sunworshippers, gamblers, and fishermen co-exist in this seaside resort near Coimbra. Tourists head for the wide beaches that grace Figueira Bay and the new amusement quarter with its casino, cafes, and theaters. The old town shelters aromatic fishing quays, where racks of drying cod crowd the docks.

Villa of Delft
Few vacationers take the time away from the beaches or gaming tables to visit Figueira's most unusual attraction, the Casa do Paco. This old villa, once the vacation home of King Carlos V, contains the best collection of Delft tiles outside of the Netherlands. Nearly 7,000 colorful tiles are displayed.
Time: Mon.-Fri., 9:30am-noon & 2pm-5pm
Place: Largo Vitor Gueira 4
Contact: ph. 22159

City Museum
Located in the new public library, Figueira's Museu Municipal has an interesting collection of regional archaeological finds, antiques, sculpture, and paintings.
Time: Tues.-Sun., 9:30am-12:30pm & 2pm-5:30pm
Place: Rua Calouste Gulbenkian
Contact: ph. 22610

Lisbon

Legend has it that Lisbon was founded by Ulysses, but experts attribute the city's discovery to Phoenician traders in 1200 BC.

During the 16th and 17th centuries, voyages by da Gama, Cabral, and others made Lisbon the capital of the world's greatest maritime empire. Her explorers returned with riches from India, the Orient, Africa, and Brazil, while merchants, artists, and scholars flocked to Lisbon from every corner of Europe.

On All Saints Day in 1755, a cataclysmic earthquake struck while most of the city was in church. Within minutes, much of Lisbon lay in ruin. Fires burned for almost a week, and the lower town was inundated by a tidal wave. In the end, nearly 50,000 lay dead, and 2,000 years of Lisbon's heritage lay in ruin. Only the ancient Alfama, high in the hills, survived the holocaust.

But Lisbon rose from the rubble. Grand avenues, stately squares, new churches, homes, and palaces were built in a revolution of urban planning and renewal. The wide boulevards and clean 18th-century architecture is still very much in evidence in the Baixa district today.

During the past century, Portugal lost its great overseas empire, leaving the "Queen of the Tagus" merely the capital of a small, poor nation. Flooded with colonial refugees, Lisbon became increasingly dirty and crowded. But with the overthrow of the Fascist regime in 1974 and the resettlement of the refugees, Lisbon has begun to restore its self-confident air and captivating charm.

Foundation Collections
Set in a beautiful museum-park complex, the Calouste Gulbenkian Museum is one of the nation's best art collections, with great collections of Mesopotamian, Greco-Roman, and Egyptian antiquities, along with European and Islamic art.
Time: Sun., 10am-5pm
Place: Avenida de Berna 45
Contact: ph. 735131

Contemporary Arts
The Museu Nacional de Arte Contemporanea displays a varied collection of Portuguese painting and sculpture. The schools represented include 19th-century Naturalism and 20th-century Surrealism, Neo-Realism, and Abstractism.
Time: Tues.-Sun., 10am-5pm
Place: Rua Serpa Pinto 6
Contact: ph. 368028

Modern Art
The vanguard of Portuguese modern art is exhibited at Lisbon's swank Centro de Arte Moderno. The fashionable gallery has works by the nation's mainstream modern artists, as well as an exhibition hall for shows of more avant-garde work.
Time: Sun., 10am-5pm
Place: Rua Nicolau de Bettencourt
Contact: ph. 735131

St. George's Castle
Castelo de Sao Jorge, called the "Cradle of Lisbon" by residents, occupies an outstanding site above the Alfama. When Alfonso Henriques liberated Lisbon in 1147, he used the citadel as his

palace. Today, the castle's massive ramparts and towers shelter the tiny medieval Santa Cruz quarter and gardens populated by peacocks, swans, and flamingoes.
Time: daily, 8am-sunset
Place: Largo do Chao da Feira

Sacred Art

The Sao Roque Church also houses the Museum of Sacred Art. The elegant church has painted wooden ceilings and attractive azulejos, but its chief lure is the Chapel of St. John the Baptist. Built in Rome and shipped to Lisbon in 1750, the Chapel stands as a masterpiece of Baroque design. The altar is adorned with jewels, the columns are fronted with lapis lazuli, and the ceilings are embellished with silver and gold. The museum contains many treasures from the church, including vestments, enormous candelabra, and 16th-century paintings.
Time: Sun., 10am-noon & 2pm-5pm
Place: Rua da Misericordia
Contact: ph. 360361

Maritime Glory

Lisbon's Museu de Marinha contains hundreds of important naval relics, such as the anchor from Columbus' Nina, models of historic vessels, and historical exhibits. The Galliot Pavillion has lavish ceremonial galleys, like the one built in France for King Joao VI's wedding to Princess Carlotta in 1785.
Time: Wed., 10am-5pm
Place: Rua de Belem
Contact: ph. 612543

Star Gazing

Even if you don't speak Portuguese, you can enjoy the fascinating show at the Calouste Gulbenkian Planetarium, next to the Maritime Museum.
Time: Wed., 4pm, 5pm, & 6pm
Place: Rua de Belem
Contact: ph. 610192

Medieval Arts

The National Museum of Ancient Art has diverse collections of

European art, housed in an 18th-century palace and former convent. The first floor is given over to paintings by such masters as Bosch, Holbein, Durer, and Velasquez. In other galleries, you'll find gold and silver objects by French and Portuguese craftsmen. Don't miss the St. Vincent polyptych by Goncalves.
Time: Sun., 10am-7pm
Place: Rua das Janelas Verdes 95
Contact: ph. 664151

Folk Arts
Portuguese folk arts and crafts are displayed at the Museu du Arte Popular. Provincial halls show collections of costumes, furniture, toys, jewelry, paintings, and sculpture.
Time: Sat. and Sun., 10am-noon & 2pm-5pm
Place: Avenida Brasilia
Contact: ph. 611282

Period Palace
The Museum of Decorative Arts offers a vivid picture of the life of Portuguese aristocrats during the 17th and 18th centuries, with displays of period furnishings, tapestries, silver, and chandeliers.
Time: Sun., 1pm-5pm
Place: Largo das Porta do Sol 2
Contact: ph. 862183

Oceanography
The Vasco da Gama Aquarium and Museum has tanks with sea creatures from all over the world. The Oceanographic Museum consists mainly of stuffed fish and mammals, along with a marine laboratory.
Time: Wed., noon-6pm
Place: Avenida Marginal, Dafundo

Royal Carriages
Housed in the former riding academy of Belem Palace, the Museu Nacional dos Coches has a marvelous collection of coaches, carriages, and other royal conveyance dating from the 16th century.
Time: Sun., 10am-6:30pm
Place: Praca de Albequerque
Contact: ph. 628022

Obidos

This congenial town hovers above vineyard-clad hills, far from the sea coast it once defended. When its bay silted up long ago, Obidos faded in prominence, but the town has managed to sustain its medieval countenance and is one of Portugal's most charming places.

Child Bride

In 1444, in Obidos' Santa Maria Church, 10-year old King Alfonso V was wed to his 8-year old cousin Isabella. Santa Maria's interior walls are lined entirely with blue and white azulejos tiles in floral patterns, while the wooden ceiling is embellished with painted flowers and arabesques.
Time: daily, 9am-noon & 2pm-5pm
Place: Rua Direita

Municipal Museum

The small Museu Municipal has medieval and Roman archaeological finds, paintings by Josefa de Obidos, and souvenirs of the Anglo-Portuguese campaign against Napoleon in 1808.
Time: Wed., 10am-12:30pm & 2pm-5pm
Place: Rua Direita
Contact: ph. 95231

Wall Walks

The town walls, built by the Moors, provide terrific views of Obidos, the Royal Castle, the green countryside with creeky old windmills, and, on clear days, the sea. The easiest access is at the south end of Rua Direita.

Oporto

Set on granite tiers above the Rio Douro, Oporto's buildings seem in danger of sliding down to the river. Portugal's second city's fame derives from its wines and long history. Although urban renewal has deprived her of many ancient monuments, Oporto still has colorful old districts with steep lanes and crazy-quilt houses. To experience the real gritty charm of Oporto, wander freely around its riverside quarters of ancient arcades and homes.

Wine Tours

Across the Rio Douro in the Villa Nova de Gaia district, there are some 80 wine caves or lodges, where port wine is aged in barrels and bottles. Many of the old lodges provide guided tours of their cellars and bottling facilities, with a complimentary sample following the visit. Contact the tourist office or wine institute for information.

Contact: Turismo, Praca General Humberto Delgado, ph. 312740; or Port Wine Institute, Rua Ferreira Borges

Palace Museum

The Palacia das Carrancas now houses the Soare dos Reis Museum, Oporto's foremost art collection. There are galleries of Dutch, Italian, French, and Portuguese painting, sculpture, furniture, gold, and silver.

Time: Sun., 10am-1pm & 2pm-5pm
Place: Rua de Dom Manuel II
Contact: ph. 27110

Portalegre

Strategically located near the Spanish frontier, Portalegre reached its zenith during the 17th century through its successful tapestry studios and silk mills. Today, many fine Baroque townhouses and mansions remain.

Workshop Tours

Poralegre's Tapestry Workshop welcomes visitors for tours of its studios, weaving rooms, and exhibition hall.

Time: Mon.-Fri., 11am-1pm & 2pm-6pm
Place: Rua G. Fernandes

Spain

Spain

Alcala de Henares

Just 20 miles from Madrid, Alcala de Henares is built on the site of the Roman town of Complutum. Alcala values its renown as an intellectual center and as the birthplace of famous Spaniards such as Miguel de Cervantes, Catherine of Aragon, Emperor Ferdinand, and architect Bartolome Bustamante.

Old University

The beautiful Colegio de San Ildefonso, Cisneros' medieval university, still stands on the compact Plaza San Diego. The three-tiered Patio de Villanueva, with a small museum on the first level, surrounds a well adorned by the crest of the Cardinal. The Paraninfo Gallery is still used for the opening ceremonies of Madrid University semesters.
Time: Sun., 11am-1pm & 6pm-8pm
Place: Plaza San Diego
Contact: ph. 889-2694

Cardinal's Chapel

Adjoining the Old University, the 15th-century Capilla de San Ildefonso houses the mausoleum of Francisco Cisneros, sculpted

by Bartolome Ordonez. The lovely chapel's ceiling is evidence of lasting Moorish influence in Spain.
Time: Sat. & Sun., 11am-1pm & 5pm-7pm
Place: 2 Pedro Gunial

Algeciras

There are only two nice things to say about Algeciras: the view across the bay to Gibraltar is breathtaking, and the annual Fiesta de Algeciras is a blast. The Festival, held during the third week of June, attracts crowds from throughout the region for parades, dances, concerts, and spectacular fireworks on the final night.
Contact: Turismo, Plaza Conferencia, ph. 656761

Avila

Avila has been declared a national monument, and justly so, for this dramatic plateau town is encircled by massive 11th-century walls. The lasting grandeur of the town is due largely to the influence of two historic figures: Count Raymond of Burgundy, who conquered Avila from the Moors and built the walls, and the mystic Saint Teresa de Jesus, who was born behind the ramparts in 1515.

Wall Tours
Averaging 33 feet in height and running more than 1½ miles, the famous ramparts of Avila entirely enclose the ancient city center. The towers, gateways, and hundreds of embrasures create one of Europe's most medieval atmospheres. You can follow the sentry walk on your own or join a guided tour sponsored by the tourist office.
Contact: Turismo, Plaza de la Catedral, ph. 211387

Cathedral Bastion
Resembling an ancient fortress more than a church, Avila's Cathedral is literally embedded in the city's fortifications. Begun in 1135, the Cathedral was completed in in the 15th century. In

contrast to its grim exterior, the interior is decorated with attractive religious art.
Time: daily, 10am-1:30pm & 3pm-7pm
Place: Plaza de la Catedral

Saint's Birthplace
The Convento de Santa Terasa de Jesus, built on the site of St. Teresa's birth, has a lovely chapel embellished with Baroque decor.
Time: daily, 8am-1pm & 3:30pm-9pm
Place: Plaza de la Santa

Barcelona

Capital of Catalonia and Spain's second largest city, Barcelona is one of Europe's grandest cities. Fiercely independent and proud, the citizens of Barcelona have tenaciously maintained their Catalan identity and high standards of art and culture.

Established as a port town by the Phoenicians in 2500 BC, Barcelona flourished as Rome's most important Iberian port. During the Middle Ages, Barcelona rivalled Venice as a Mediterranean power.

Today, the sprawling city prospers as Spain's biggest port. With sidewalk cafes, excellent museums, and unique architecture, Barcelona offers many memorable experiences.

Royal Palace
The Museu Frederic Mares is devoted primarily to religious art. There's an important collection of polychrome wooden sculpture from the Middle Ages and the personal gallery of the museum's namesake, sculptor Frederic Mares.
Time: Sun., 10am-2pm
Place: Comtes de Barcelona
Contact: ph. 310-5800

Municipal History
Situated in the grand Casa Padellas, the Museu d'Historia de la Ciutat traces the development of Barcelona from its earliest set-

tlers through the 19th century.
Time: Sun., 9am-2pm
Place: Place del rei
Contact: ph. 315-1111

Picasso Collection

The Azuilar Palace is now home to one of the world's foremost Picasso collections. Over the decades, the artist donated hundreds of paintings, drawings, and etchings to the museum. Among the highlights is the wonderful *Harlequin*.
Time: Sun., 9am-2pm
Place: 15 Carrer de Moncada
Contact: ph. 319-6902

Gaudi's Garden City

Antonio Gaudi, the Catalan architect, artist, and designer, intended to create a garden city at the Parc Guell to demonstrate his vision of urban planning. Though his death reduced the scope of the project, the park is alive with Gaudi's verve and style.
Time: Park: daily, 9:30am-7:30pm; House: Sun., 10am-2pm & 4pm-7pm
Place: Placa de Lesseps

Exotic Civilizations

Divided into two sections, the Museu Etnologic presents exhibits exploring civilizations of Africa, Asia, and the Americas, plus a Hispanic section dedicated to various Spanish cultures.
Time: Sun., 10am-2pm
Place: Parc de Montjuic

Catalan Arts

The Museu d'Arte de Catalunya contains extensive collections of Catalan art. The holdings include rare Pyrenean frescoes, altarpieces, paintings, and statues, plus a gallery devoted entirely to Spanish ceramics.
Time: Sun., 9am-2pm
Place: Parc de Montjuic

Cordoba

Standing defiantly on a hilltop overlooking the Rio Guadalquivir, ancient Cordoba is a Moorish city of bright, whitewashed houses and enduring monuments to past glories. As early as the 8th century, Moslems established a caliphate in Cordoba, and the city grew to become one of the world's greatest metroplises, with half a million inhabitants. Blending Islamic, Christian, and Jewish cultures, Cordoba blossomed as a center of learning and science, and it remains a charming city.

Magnificent Mosque

The caprice of politics and history has converged in the famous Mezquita Catedral. Built on the site occupied by a Roman temple, a Visigoth church, and a mosque, the cathedral is a masterpiece of cultural amalgamation. After passing through the Patio de los Naranjos, one enters a forest of pillars, where 850 columns support hundreds of red and white arches. At the far end, the domed *mihrab*, or prayer niche, glitters with a gold mosaic. The center of the 8th-century mosque shelters the 16th-century Gothic cathedral. cathedral.
Time: Sun., 9:30am-1:30pm
Place: Cardenal Herrero

Medieval Legacy

In the heart of the ancient Juderia, or Jewish quarter, by the statue of the great philosopher Maimonides, there's a reminder of Cordoba's once-thriving Jewish community: a tiny 14th-century synagogue, adorned with Hebrew inscriptions and stucco decoration.
Time: Tues.-Sat., 10am-2pm & 4pm-7pm
Place: Calle Judios

Patio Festival

For centuries, Cordoba has celebrated the Patio Festival each May. The open-air patios, with their citrus trees and cool fountains, are an architectural holdover from Cordoba's Roman occupation. During the Festival, the patios, balconies, and grills of the city's homes are garnished with spring flowers.
Contact: Turismo, Plaza de Juda Levi, ph. 290740

Covadonga

National Park

Covadonga National Park is a region of rare scenic beauty, with dark forests, tall peaks, and clear glacial lakes. Nature trails throughout the park make exploring easy. For more information, contact the park office at Oviedo.

Contact: Parque Nacional de Covadonga, Servicio Provincial de Icona Calle Uria 10, Oviedo, ph. 213385

Guernica

During the Spanish Civil War, Nazi aircraft destroyed this historic town in the debut of massive bombing of civilian populations. Immortalized by Picasso, Guernica has been rebuilt largely in traditional style.

Basque Parliament

During the Middle Ages, Guernica was the focus of an independent Basque nation, and for centuries a parliament of landowners met there beneath a great oak. Remains of that tree, still a powerful symbol of Basque nationalism, stand next to the Casa de Juntas, which contains a Basque museum, archive, and council chamber.

Time: daily, 10am-7pm
Place: Calle Urioste
Contact: ph. 685-3558

Cave Paintings

Discovered in 1917, the Cuevas de Santimamine contain a variety of prehistoric art dating from the Paleolithic era. Wall paintings and engravings show bison, horses, and bears.

Time: Tue.-Sat., 10am-noon & 4pm-7pm
Place: three miles north of town

Jerez de la Frontera

Wine Tastings

There's not much to do in Jerez but sample the famous sherry and tour the wine cellars. Most the wine cellars, or *bodegas*, offer free

tours of their facilities and generous samples. A few major producers offering tours are Bodega Gonzales Byass (Manuel Maria Gonzales 12), Pedro Domecq (Calle San Ildefonso 3), and Bodega Sandermann (Calle Pizarro 10).
Time: Mon.-Sat., 9:30am-1pm

Harvest Festival
Jerez explodes in celebration during the second week of September, when the town rejoices in the "birth" of the new grapes. Each year the Fiesta de la Vendimia is dedicated to one of the nations that imports Jerez's sherry. There's a flamenco festival, contests, concerts, art shows, and, of course, prodigious wine consumption.
Time: second week in September

Leon

A beautiful city, Leon was the *de facto* capital of Christian Spain during the 11th century. The medieval quarter still has ramparts built on Roman foundations, old houses fronting narrow lanes, and ancient churches.

Royal Pantheon
Built into the medieval walls of Leon's old town, the Basilica San Isidro el Real houses the Asturian Royal Pantheon and the tomb of St. Isidore. An amalgam of Romanesque, Gothic, and Renaissance architecture, St. Isidro contains frescoes, elaborate caskets, and the extraordinary Dona Urraca chalice, composed of agate in gold with inlaid gems.
Time: Sun., 9am-2pm
Place: Plaza de San Isidro

Ancient Leon
Leon's Monastery of San Marcos shares its riverfront site with a hotel and the Municipal Museum of Archaeology. The museum displays artifacts from Roman times through the Middle Ages, with religious art and Limoges enamels.
Time: Thurs., 10am-2pm & 4pm-6pm
Place: Plaza San Marcos
Contact: ph. 237082

Lugo

Burned by the Moors in 714 and by Vikings in the 10th century, Lugo today is a restored town with an ancient heart and modern suburbs.

Wall Walks

One mile of stone walls 35-feet high surrounds Lugo's old town center. The wide sentry path is perfect for strolls around the city. Enter at Plaza de Pio XII.

Regional Museum

Lugo's Museo Provincial has exhibits ranging from Roman coins, tools, and sundials to displays of regional costumes and furnshings.
Time: Sat., 10am-2pm
Place: Plaza de la Soledad
Contact: ph. 231361

Madrid

Elegant, sprawling Madrid is the very heart of Spain. Geographically, Madrid stands at the center of the country, and politically, it is the nation's capital. Drawing talent from every corner of Spain, it's the trend-setter in culture, commerce, and intellectual life.

Dominating Spain for four centuries, Madrid is still a relatively young city. Superceding Toledo as the capital in 1516, Madrid experienced a golden age, still evident in Old Madrid's plazas, churches, and arcades.

Madrid today is a city of over four million inhabitants. The unavoidable growth has brough urban blight, pollution, and crime, but it hasn't erased the city's sensuous appeal.

Palace Collection

The lovely Palacio de Liria presents a collection of paintings by European masters, including Rembrandt, Goya, Botticelli, and Titian.
Time: Sat., 10am-1:30pm
Place: Calle Princesa 20
Contact: ph. 247-5302

Modern Art

In a park-like setting at the City University, the Museo Espanol de Arte Contemporaneo displays works by Picasso, Dali, Miro, and many other modern Spanish artists.
Time: Sun., 10am-3pm
Place: Ave. Juan de Herrera 2
Contact: ph. 449-7150

Maritime Museum

The most compelling reason to visit the Museo Naval is for a peak at Juan de Cosa's map of the New World, made on Columbus' first voyage. It's the first map to show the Americas. Other interesting exhibits include memorabilia from the Battle of Lepanto, antique navigational devices, and ship models.
Time: Thurs., 10:30am-1:30 pm.
Place: Cale Montalban
Contact: ph. 221-0419

Oviedo

Ancient History

Adjoining the eerie San Vincent Cloisters, Oviedo's Museo Arqueologic has a collection of pre-Romanesque Asturian art and architectural fragments. There are also regional prehistoric finds, Roman coins, ancient musical instruments, and glassware.
Time: Mon.-Sat., 10am-1pm & 4pm-6pm; Sun., 11am-1pm
Place: Plaza San Vincente
Contact: ph. 213385

Pamplona

Famous Festival

This ancient capital of Navarra has little for the tourist except the celebrated Fiesta de San Fermin, the "running of the bulls," immortalized by Hemingway in *The Sun Also Rises*. For seven days early each July, thousands of Spaniards and foreigners throng the streets in a frenzy of dancing, singing, drinking, and bull-dodging.

Besides the running of the bulls, there are fireworks, fairs, and Basque concerts.
Contact: Turismo, Calle Duque de Ahemada 5, ph. 124422

Regional Museum
If you come to Pamplona for San Fermin, don't miss the fascinating Museo de Navarra. Set in a 16th-century hospice, the museum contains finds from Roman Navarra, paintings, regional costumes, and antiques.
Time: free Sun. and on Fiesta days, 10am-2pm
Place: Santo Domingo

Santander
Santander is a very popular seaside resort, attracting Spaniards and foreigners alike. An ancient port, Santander was devastated by a storm and fire in 1941. Reconstruction following strict zoning plans has created a pleasant, modern port of gardens and seaside promenades.

Maritime Museum
Santander's tie with the ocean is explored at the Museo Maritimo. Featuring one of Spain's best aquariums, the museum has exhibits relating to the fishing industry, shipbuilding, and ocean trade.
Time: Tues.-Sat., 11am-1pm & 4pm-7pm; Sun., 11am-2pm
Place: San Martin de Abajo

Fine Arts
The Museo Municipal de Bellas Artes has a good collection of paintings by Spanish, French, Italian, and Flemish artists. Most noteworthy are the works by Goya and Zurbaran.
Time: Mon.-Sat., 11am-1pm & 5pm-8pm
Place: Calle Rubio
Contact: ph. 216120

Prehistoric Cantabria
Be sure to visit the Museo Provincial de Prehistoria y Arqueologia, which presents exhibits of prehistoric artifacts recovered from Cantabrian caves. The richest finds are from the late Paleolithic era, with scrimshaw-like carvings. One gallery is devoted to Roman oc-

cupation of the region, showing bronze statues, coins, and weapons.
Time: Tues.-Sat., 9am-2pm
Place: Calle Casimiro Sainz 4

Sevilla

Capital of Andalusia and Spain's fourth-largest city, Sevilla is a city of magnificent souvenirs of bygone grandeur. Steeped in history and legend, it has been inhabited since prehistoric times.

New World Archives

Students of history won't want to miss the Archivo General de Indias, housed in the 16th-century Casa Lonja. This collection of documents and memorabilia features Columbus' log books, maps of the New World, and the correspondence of Magellan, Cortes, Vespucci, and others who conquered the unknown. There are also intriguing shipping records and plans for new cities in the Americas.
Time: Mon.-Sat., 10am-1pm
Place: Ave de la Contitucion
Contact: ph. 221404

Tarragona

Rising in tiers above the Mediterranean, Tarragona's broad boulevards and popular resort hotels enfold ancient ramparts, pagan cemeteries, Roman aqueducts, and amphitheaters. By 45 BC, the Roman town of Tarraco had been raised to the status of an imperial capital by Julius Caesar, and its citizens were the first in Spain to gain Roman citizenship. Today, evidence of Roman settlement co-exists with medieval monuments and modern bustle.

Roman Forum

The remains of Tarragona's commercial forum make an impressive open-air museum. Even though the forum is bisected by a city street, the broken columns evoke the provincial prosperity of Roman times.
Time: Tues.-Sat., 10am-1pm & 4pm-7pm; Sun., 10am-1pm
Place: Calle Lerida

Praetorium Museum

The Museo Arqueologico houses a fine collection of Roman anti-quities. Adjoining the museum is the Pretori Roma, the birthplace of Pontius Pilate, whose father served as praetor of Tarraconensis in the first century BC.
Time: Tues., 10am-1pm & 4pm-8pm
Place: Plaza del Rei

Ancient Necropolis

Tarragona's enormous necropolis has yielded a variety of tombs, sarcophagi, and burial vaults. Dating from the 3rd to 6th centuries, this early Christian cemetery made use of earlier pagan burial sites. The Museo Paleocritia now houses many of the most fascinating items from the site.
Time: Tues., 10am-1pm & 4pm-7pm
Place: Ave. Ramon y Cayal

Valencia

Founded by Greek merchant-mariners, Valencia is Spain's third-largest city and capital of its namesake province. In this century, Valencia was the final Republican outpost to fall to the Fascists dur-ing the Civil War. The ancient Old Town has nearly been swallowed-up by ugly development, but there are still plenty of old churches, palaces, and museums to see.

Fiery Fiesta

Without a doubt, the best time to visit Valencia is between March 12th and 19th, when the city celebrates Las Fallas, an exciting car-nival. The city's districts compete to create the gaudiest papier-mache effigies, called *ninots*. Hundreds of these gigantic caricatures are displayed around town and then incinerated in a huge bonfire on the night of March 19. Throughout the week, there are parades, concerts, and fireworks.
Contact: Municipal Turismo, Plaza del Pais Valenciano, ph. 351-0417

Sweden

Abisko

National Park

Nearly 125 miles above the Arctic Circle, the Abisko National Park covers 12 square miles of wilderness on the shores of Lake Tornatrask. At the northern terminus of the Kingsleden Trail, the park is home to reindeer and remarkable flora, including tiny arctic orchids. The midnight sun is visible from Mt. Njulla in Abisko from May 30 to July 18.

Contact: Abisko Turiststasjon, ph. 40000

Borgholm

Borgholm is the only town of significant size on the resort island of Oland. From early spring to late fall, the pleasant old town is crowded with Swedish vacationers. Oland's mix of natural attractions and ancient archaeological sites has made the island a favorite for low-key holidays.

Castle Ruins

Sweden's most impressive castle ruin commands the high ground above Borgholm. Originally a medieval fortress, Borholm Castle was enlarged by King Gustav Vasa in the 16th century and destroyed

by fire in 1806. There are great views of Oland Island and the Kalmar Sound from the ramparts and towers.
Time: daily, 8am-10pm
Place: half a mile southwest of Borgholm

Royal Chateau
Two miles south of Borgholm is Solliden Manor, a royal summer residence. Built in 1903 for Queen Victoria, the gracious mansion is set in a lovely park. The Dutch Rose Garden is especially beautiful.
Time: June-Sept: daily, noon-2pm
Contact: ph. 12340

Eskiltuna

Sweden's noted steel industry had its origin at Eskiltuna in the 17th century, when earlier iron works were expanded at royal behest. Although it's a modern industrial city today, Eskiltura has preserved a morsel of its long heritage in the center of town.

Open-Air Museum
Six of Eskiltuna's early forges, established by Reinhold Rademacher in 1654, create the centerpiece of the city's open-air museum. Along with demonstrations at the iron and tin smithies, there is an interesting industrial museum, a zoo, and a garden in the adjoining Folkets Park.
Time: Mon.-Fri., 10am-6pm; Sat. & Sun., 10am-4pm
Place: Rademachergatan 50

Gallivare

Even though the town has little to offer in the way of tourist attractions, Gallivare makes a good jumping-off point for wilderness excursions in Swedish Lappland.

Iron Mine Tours
The arctic town of Gallivare owes its existence to the substantial iron ore deposits in the area. A Swedish government-owned mining company, Luossavaari-Kirunavaara AB, welcomes visitors to tour

the mining galleries by appointment. Above ground, the midnight sun is visible from June 1 to July 15.
Time: weekdays by appointment
Place: two miles north of Gallivare
Contact: ph. 21000

Goteborg (Gothenburg)

Goteborg may be Sweden's principal seaport and home to major industrial companies such as Volvo, but it's still known as the "Green City" because of its parks and gardens. Many travelers arriving by boat at the huge port make the mistake of rushing off without giving Goteborg a chance. Though Sweden's genial second city is a busy metropolis, it maintains a more languid social pace than many other major European cities.

Military Museum

The massive tower of the Skansen Kronan Fortress houses a military museum with a peerless collection of military paraphernalia from the 16th century to the present. There are marvelous views of Goteborg and the harbor from the fortress ruins, too.
Time: Tues.-Sat., 1pm-3pm; Sun., noon-3pm
Place: Skanstorget

Crown House

The Kronhus, built in 1643, is Goteborg's oldest building in continuous use. It has seen service as a military garrison, a warehouse, and a church, and it is now the Municipal Museum of Goteborg. Adjoining are the Kronhusbodarna, whose boutiques and galleries around a courtyard create a romantic, turn-of-the-century atmosphere.
Time: Tues.-Sat., 10am-4pm
Place: Kronhusgata

Botanical Garden

The principal features of Goteborg Botanical Gardens are a bamboo grove, a rock garden, and geometrical flowerbeds. The

hothouses contain orchids, tropical plants, and cacti, and there's a charming nature preserve.
Time: daily, 9am-sunset
Place: Carl Slottsbergsgatan 22

Museum of Industry
Goteborg's Industrial Museum displays the products of local factories and presents exhibits of Sweden's paper, wood, textile, and glass industries.
Time: Tues.-Sat., 11am-4pm; Sun., noon-4pm
Place: Gotaplatsen
Contact: ph. 135992

Fish Church
Don't miss Goteborg's unique Feskekorka (Fish Church) on the harbor canal. The Lutheran church looks like any other chapel from the outside, but the interior actually houses a seafood market where an auction is held daily at 7am.
Time: daily, 6am-4pm
Place: Rosenlunsgatan

Halmstad

Halmstad is a charming, unassuming city at the southern end of Sweden's "Gold Coast." Because of its proximity to the sandy beaches of the coast, Halmstad is rapidly becoming a summer resort.

Picasso Sculpture
On the bank of the River Nissan, Halmstad has erected an exciting Picasso sculpture, *Woman's Head*. The 650-year old town is noted for many city-sponsored works of art in its streets and buildings, including the Picasso and Carl Milles' fountain *Europa* in the market square.

Town Hall
Halmstad's Municipal Hall is decorated with remarkable mosaics by the Swedish Surrealists, an association of artists formed in the 1920's and known locally as the "Halmstad Group." The Town Hall

features a carillon with characters that change positions at 8am, noon, 6pm, & 9pm.
Time: Mon.-Fri., 9am-4:30pm
Place: Storatorget
Contact: ph. 111581

Jokkmokk

This old Lappland town on the Lulea River makes a good base for explorations of Europe's last true wilderness.

Lappland Festival
The Lapp, or Same, people hold an annual Winter Festival in Jokk-mokk, situated three miles above the Arctic Circle. The fair provides an excellent opportunity to meet the nomadic Lapps and to see the variety of their crafts.
Time: first week in February
Contact: Tourist Bureau, Porjusbagen 4, ph. 12140

Jonkoping

Matchstick Capital
Set on the southern end of Lake Vattern, Jonkoping achieved its fame as the world capital of matches in 1852 when J. E. Lundstrom began production of the safety match there. Today, the Swedish Match Company still makes matches, and the old plant has become a museum.
Time: June-Sept: Mon.-Fri., 10am-6pm; Sat., 11am-1pm
Place: Sturgatan 18
Contact: ph. 105543

Kiruna

World's Largest City
With an area of 7,000 square miles, Kiruna is the world's largest municipality. Sweden's northern-most city sits atop massive iron ore deposits, and the tourist office will arrange mine tours during the summer. The city boundaries include Mt. Kebnekaise, Sweden's

highest mountain. Travelers seeking the midnight sun can find fabulous views in Kiruna from May 31 to July 15.
Contact: Kiruna Turistbyra. Mangigatan 12, ph. 18660

Lapp Church
The wooden Katu Church, like many northern Scandinavian churches, is shaped to resemble a Lapp tent. It features an altar-piece painted by Sweden's Prince Eugen in 1812 and carved wood by Elgstrom and Erikkson.
Time: May-August: Mon.-Sat., 10am-5pm
Place: Villastigen

Leksand

Set in rolling hill country above lovely Lake Siljan, Leksand is both a popular resort town and a center of Dalarna folk culture. As the gateway to the Lake District, it makes a great starting point for exploration of the region's villages and hamlets. But be prepared for mobs of tourists (mostly European) in late June and early July.

Churchboat Races
Each July, Leksand hosts boat races unique to the Dalarna region. Churchboats, looking like minature Viking vessels, are propelled across Lake Siljan by 20 oarsmen dressed in colorful costumes. Following the races, fiddlers tune-up for a folk dance and music festival.
Time: first Sunday in July

Open-Air Museum
Just below Leksand's onion-domed 13th-century church is the Hembygard Open-Air Museum. Old timber homes, shops, and farm buildings have been transported from their original sites around Lake Siljan and reassembled at the museum. The collection ranges from barns to a stately 19th-century townhouse.
Time: June-August: Mon.-Sat., 10am-5pm
Contact: ph. 10186

Lessebo

Papermill Tours

Producing handmade paper since 1693, the Lessebo Papermill is the world's oldest continuous manufacturer of paper. Tours of the old mill reveal the ancient process of paper-making from pulp to finished product. Call ahead for an appointment.
Time: Tours: 10am, 1pm, & 2pm
Contact: ph. 50705

Linkoping

This ancient city is famous for its beautiful Cathedral and for the "Bloodbath of Linkoping," when, in 1600, Catholics were executed in the town's main square.

Harmonious Cathedral

Linkoping Cathedral was begun in the mid-12th century in Romanesque style and altered in the 16th century in Gothic style. The interior reflects a harmonious blend of various styles, including a 16th-century Dutch altarpiece and contemporary tapestries.
Time: Mon.-Sat., 9am-5pm
Place: Storatorget

Ancient Abbey

Seven miles northwest of town, you'll find the medieval Vreta Cloisters, once a Cistercian nunnery. The restored cloister chapel is noted for several monuments and tombs of important figures. Unfortunately, most of the buildings have fallen to ruin, but many walls and foundations are still in evidence.
Time: Mon.-Sat., 10am-4pm
Place: Motola Road
Contact: ph. 120279

Lund

Lund is a splendid town, rich in Old World character and charm and lively because of its large student population.

Romanesque Cathedral

Standing in the heart of town, Lund's 11th-century Cathedral is the oldest and finest Romanesque building in Sweden. Its principal treasure is the famous 14th-century astronomical clock, with medieval characters and religious figures that whir into action daily at noon and 3pm. Trumpets blare, knights clash, and the Three Wisemen march.

Time: daily, 8am-6pm
Place: Kyrkogatan

University Garden

The University Botanical Garden, founded in 1760, contains a unique shrub collection, medicinal herbs, annuals, and glasshouses with over 7,000 tropical plants from around the world.

Time: Gardens: daily, 7am-9:30pm; Greenhouses: daily, 1pm-3pm
Place: Ostra Vallgatan 20

Spring Festival

The most exciting time to visit Lund is on April 30, when the entire student population celebrates Walpurgis Eve, a rollicking salute to spring's arrival. The merrymaking includes bonfires, torchlight parades, lusty sing-a-longs, and all-night dances—a Scandanavian bacchanalia not to be missed.

Time: April 30
Place: Tegners Plats

City Map

Lund's Tourist Office supplies a free map of southern Sweden's most charming medieval town, plus a guide to Lund's museums, exhibits, and special events.

Time: Mon.-Fri., 9am-5pm
Place: St. Petrikyrkogata 4
Contact: ph. 124590

Cultural History

Lund's Kulturhistoriska Museet includes one of Sweden's best open-air museums. Farmsteads, homes, workshops, stores, churches, and manorhouses from all over southern Sweden have been transported there and reassembled in the heart of old Lund. There are also col-

lections of textiles, folk art, and Viking artifacts on display.
Time: Oct.-April: Wed., noon-4pm
Place: St. Annegata & Tegner Plats

Malmo

Facing Copenhagen across the Oresund, Malmo is Sweden's third-largest city and the capital of Skane, but it seems more like a friendly small town than a great city. Malmo's Old Town, bounded by canals in the heart of the city, preserves much of the city's original character while integrating modern shops and restaurants.

Amusement Park

Every summer, Malmo's population heads for Folkets Park, the largest and oldest recreation center in Sweden, with a zoo, an open-air theater, carnival rides, dancehalls, a puppet theater, and several restaurants.
Time: May-Sept.: free Mon.-Fri.
Place: Admiralsgatan
Contact: ph. 70990

Moated Castle

A lovely park, with long avenues of linden trees, a Japanese garden, and a children's zoo, surrounds the 15th-century Malmohus Castle. Today, the moated fortress houses the Malmo Municipal Museum, with collections of northern European paintings, archaeology, and natural history.
Time: Castle: daily, noon-4pm. Park: daily, 8am-sunset
Place: Malmohusvagen
Contact: ph. 103830

Baltic Gothic

Malmo's finest ecclesiastic building is the handsome St. Petri Kyrka. Built in Baltic Gothic style, the copper-roofed church is noted for its Baroque altar, carved pulpit, and Gothic wall paintings.
Time: Mon.-Fri., 9am-5pm
Place: Kalendegatan

Forest Park

Pildamms Park was created on the site of Malmo's Baltic Exhibi-

tion of 1914. More than 20,000 trees were planted around the lake, while the pavillions were transformed into exhibition halls. There is also a zoo, an open-air theater, and a stadium.
Place: Fersenvag

Mora

This delightful Dalarna town is situated between Lakes Siljan and Orsa. Less crowded than nearby Rattvik, Mora makes a pleasant stop in the Lake District.

Handicraft Center
Mora has restored an entire district of homes and shops to their traditional appearance. Many of the shops sell local handicrafts, folk art, and regional costumes.
Time: Mon.-Sat., 9:30am-5pm
Place: Hantverksbyn
Contact: ph. 15200

Ski Marathon
Each year, thousands of spectators and 12,000 contestants descend on Mora on the first Sunday in March for the 53-mile Wasaloppet Ski Marathon. The racers ski from Salen to Mora, commemorating King Gustav Wasa's trip to Mora in 1521.

Norrkoping

Baltic Curiosity
The port of Norrkoping on the Baltic Sea is a surprising place to find an extensive cactus garden, but the Karl Johans Cactus Park has a collection of 25,000 cactus plants.
Time: daily, 8am-6pm
Place: Karl Johans Parkvagen
Contact: ph. 123910

Venerable Church
Norrkoping's oldest building is the 12th-century Ostra Eneby

Church. It contains rare Scandinavian tapestries, medieval ceiling paintings, and a lovely marble font.
Time: Mon.-Sat., 10am-4pm
Place: Drottinggatan
Contact: ph. 129620

Orebro

Renaissance Castle
The Orebro Lan Provincial Government is housed in the fairytale Orebro Castle. Built on the foundations of a 12th-century fortress, the castle, with its four round towers, sits on an island in a bend in the River Svarta.
Time: Mon.-Fri., 9:30am-3:30pm
Place: Kungstan
Contact: ph. 130760

Marshal's Church
In 1810, Napoleon's Marshal, Jean-Baptiste Bernadotte, was named King by the Swedish Riksdag in the Nikolaikyrka. Ruling as King Karl Johan, he led Swedish troops against the French. The church also contains the tomb of Sweden's legendary hero, Engelbrekt Engelbrektsson.
Time: Mon.-Sat., 9am-5pm
Place: Stortorget

Ostersund

Pagan Island Relics
Linked to Ostersund by two bridges, Froso Island is the site of Iron Age burials and the northern-most rune stone in Sweden. Erected in 1050, the stone is found at the old Frosobru. The island also provides spectacular views of Jamtland, Lake Storsjo (which is said to harbor a Loch Ness-type monster), and, on clear days, mountains on the Norwegian border.
Contact: Turistbyra, Radhusgatan 29, ph. 110320

Rattvik

Rattvik, a charming, year-round resort town, is the center of Dalarna folk culture and one of the prettiest towns on the lake.

Dalarna Handicrafts

Rattvik is home of the Swedish Hemslojd Craft Association for the region. Visitors can see displays of local woodcarving, weaving, metalwork, and little Dalarna horses (particularly the grey ones, a specialty of Rattvik).
Time: Mon.-Fri., 9am-4pm; Sat., 9am-1pm
Place: Torget
Contact: ph. 10645

Sigtuna

Ancient Capital

You'll find it hard to imagine that diminutive, idyllic Sigtuna was once the religious and political capital of Sweden. Founded nearly 1,000 years ago, Sigtuna, with its relics of Viking and early Christian heritage, is one of Sweden's oldest towns. Scattered around town, the ruins of St. Per, St. Lars, and St. Olafs Churches bear witness to Sigtuna's past glory.
Contact: Turistbyra, Storagatan, ph. 50451

Stockholm

Beautifully situated on 14 islands separated by broad canals, wide bays, and swift narrows, Stockholm is a truly handsome city. At the heart of the capital, the contest between old and new is striking: the cobbled narrow lanes and medieval buildings of Gamla Stan are joined by a short bridge to the ultra-modern city center of steel and glass skyscrapers. Nature and urban planning have combined to make Stockholm a showplace capital, with a multitude of historic monuments, comfortable neighborhoods, cultural attractions, attractive pedestrian zones, and marvelous views in every direction.

Brewery Tour

Pripp's Brewery provides a tour and multi-media show illustrating

brewing through the ages. Visitors to the Bryggerimusset should make an appointment for the tour.
Time: Mon.-Fri., 10am-4pm
Place: Voltavagen 29
Contact: ph. 981500

Changing of the Guard
The changing of the guard at Sweden's Royal Palace has occurred every day since 1523. Military units from all over Sweden share the honor and responsibility of guarding the Renaissance castle and the gregarious king.
Time: Mon.-Sat. at noon & Sun. at 1pm
Place: Slott courtyard
Contact: ph. 118551

Cultural Center
Stockholm's modern Kulturhuset, located in a downtown skyscraper, hosts exhibitions of modern art, handicrafts, concerts, readings, and art studios. Visitors are also welcome in the library, with its foreign and domestic periodicals and music room. Everything is free.
Time: Tues.-Sun., 11am-6pm
Place: Sergelstorg 3
Contact: ph. 141120

Free Concerts
Throughout the summer, the city of Stockholm sponsors free concerts in many city parks. There is daily entertainment on the open-air stage in the downtown Kungstradgarden during July and August. While you're there, stop by the Sweden House next to the park for a free copy of *This Week in Stockholm*, a guide to free entertainment and events in town.
Time: daily, 8am-7pm
Contact: Sverigehuset, Hamnagatan 27, ph. 227000

Fine Arts
The National Museum of Art houses Sweden's largest collection of fine and applied arts. The painting gallery contains works by

many Dutch and Flemish masters, French Impressionists, Scandinavian artists, and rare Russian icons.
Time: free on Tues., 10am-9pm
Place: Sodra Blasieholmshammen

Historic Gardens
The Bergius Botanical Garden was established by Jonas Bergius, a pupil of the famed botanist Carl Linnaeus. Since its founding, the garden has expanded to contain tens of thousands of plants, all arranged according to geographic origin.
Time: daily, 8am-sunset
Place: Frescati

Ceramics Center
The Gustavberg Company has been producing beautiful porcelain and stoneware for 200 years in Stockholm. Their old studios and workshops, along with an interesting exhibition center, welcome visitors for free guided tours by appointment.
Time: May-Sept.: Tues.-Fri., 10am-4pm; Sat., 11am-2pm
Contact: ph. 07-663-9100

Modern Arts
The Museum of Modern Art and Photography has one of Europe's leading collections of contemporary art. The permanent collections, with works by Dali, Picasso, and Warhol, is augmented by controversial special exhibits.
Time: free on Thursdays, 11am-9pm
Place: Svenskundsvagen
Contact: ph. 244200

Noble Sanctuary
Situated just behind the Royal Palace, the venerable Storkyrka is Stockhom's Cathedral. Dating from the late 13th century, the Storkyrka was remodeled in Baroque style in 1740. Near the ornate silver altar, where Swedish monarchs are crowned, is the distinguished statue *St. George and the Dragon* by Berndt Notke.
Time: daily, 9am-6pm
Place: Storkyrkabrinken

Postal Museum
Housed in a quaint old building in Gamla Staden, Sweden's Post Museum has a priceless collection of stamps and displays surveying the history of postal service from medieval times to the present. Philatelists won't want to miss the rare 1847 Mauritus.
Time: Mon.-Fri., noon-3pm; Sat., 10am-2pm
Place: Lilla Nygatan 6
Contact: ph. 781-1755

Studio Exhibit
Set in Bellvue Park, the Carl Eldh Atelier Museum, in the artist's former studio, provides an excellent introduction to the sculptor's work.
Time: May-Sept.: Tues.-Sun., noon-4pm
Place: Logebodavagen 10

Transportation Nostalgia
Anyone can get behind the wheel of a historic tram, trolley, or bus at Stockholm's Tramway Museum. This entertaining exhibition demonstrates the development of public transportation in Sweden's capital, with retired vehicles, photographs, and other displays.
Time: Mon.-Sat., 10am-5pm; Sun., 1pm-5pm
Place: Odenplan T-Bana Station

Royal Library
Situated in Humlegarden Park, the Swedish Royal Library possesses, among its collection of books and illuminated manuscripts, the 8th-century Codex Aureus, a Latin translation of the Gospels.
Time: Mon.-Thurs., 8:45am-8pm; Fri., 8:45am-6pm
Place: Humlegarden at Sturegatan

International Center
The city of Stockholm provides a free center for international visitors and residents alike. There is a reading room (Swedish and foreign periodicals), a music room, cooking facilities, a photo lab, and plenty of practical information from the helpful staff.
Time: Mon.-Sat., noon-8pm
Place: Valhallavagen 142
Contact: ph. 634389

German Church

Amid the maze of narrow streets, old homes, and historic squares of the Gamla Staden, St. Gertrude's German Church preserves the style of 17th-century Stockholm. Built in 1642, the interior contains an extraordinary alabaster and ebony pulpit and an ornate Baroque altar.

Time: Mon.-Sat., 10am-3pm
Place: Skomakaregatan

Uppsala

Most North American visitors make Uppsala a daytrip destination while staying in Stockholm, or they miss the city entirely. Too bad, because Uppsala is one of Sweden's most interesting towns. With Sweden's oldest university, the nation's largest Cathedral, and a stupendous castle, Uppsala is deserves a long, leisurely visit.

Provincial Museum

The Upplands Provincial Museum displays folk art, handicrafts, and artifacts illustrating the cultural history of Uppsala and the Upplands region. Movie buffs will recognize the museum as a set from the film *Fanny and Alexander*.

Time: Mon.-Sat., 11am-4pm
Place: Erikstorg 10
Contac: ph. 161825

Regal Cathedral

At 390-feet high and 390-feet long, the twin-towered Uppsala Cathedral is Sweden's largest church. Among the prominent figures entombed here are St. Erik (in an impressive gilt reliquary), King Gustav Vasa (in an immense marble tomb), the philosopher-theologian Swedenborg, and the botanist Carl Linnaeus.

Time: May-Sept: Mon.-Sat., 8am-8pm & Sun., noon-8pm; Oct.-April: Mon.-Sat., 8am-6pm & Sun., noon-6pm
Place: Fyristorg

Spring Festival

On Walpurgis Eve (April 30), students, alumni, and townspeople celebrate the arrival of spring with a torchlight procession,

speeches, singing, bonfires, and all-night revelry.
Contact: Turistinformation, Kungsgatan 44, ph. 117500

Linnaeus Garden
In 1787, Carl Linnaeus created the Uppsala University Botanical
Garden in the garden of the Royal Castle. Today, glasshouses con-
tain plants from the time of Linnaeus, an extensive collection of
Scandanavia alpine plants, and a lovely rose garden.
Time: May-Sept.: daily, 9am-7pm; Oct.-April: daily, 9am-3pm
Place: Villavagen 8

Ancient Library
The Uppsala University Library, Sweden's largest library, contains
more than two million volumes, including 30,000 rare manuscripts.
The supreme treasure is the *Codex Argenteus*, a 6th-century translation of the Gospels into Old Gothic. This priceless volume, the only
extant manuscript in Old Gothic script, is illuminated in gold and
silver letters and bound in silver. Other uncommon works include
a Venetian medieval map of Europe, the *Codex Uppsalenisis*, and
the *Deretum Concilii Uppsalenisis.*
Time: Mon.-Sat., 9am-6pm
Place: Drottninggatan

Pagan Capital
Just three miles north of town is Gamla Uppsala, once the capital
of pre-Christian Sweden. There are a series of burial mounds of
the 5th- and 6th-century Yngve kings—Egil, Adel, and Aunn. Nearby, the 12th-century stone church once served as a cathedral and
was built over an ancient Norse temple. In the 12th and 13th century, Swedish monarchs were crowned there, though today the
church is unimposing.
Place: Vattholmavagen

Open-Air Museum
Just north of the aged church at Gamla Uppsala is the Disgarden
Open-Air Museum, composed of old homes and farm buildings
brought from locations around Uppland and reassembled there.
Time: June-August: daily, 9am-5pm
Place: Vattholavagen

Vaxjo

Regional Museum

The Smaland Provincial Museum has a collection of regional art-work and an excellent section on glassmaking in Sweden and abroad. In the same building, you'll find the Utvandrarnas Hus (Emigrant's House), an exhibition devoted to Swedish immigration to America. There's also a research center for Swedish-Americans in search of their roots.

Time: Mon.-Sat., 9:30am-5pm
Place: Jarnvagsgatan
Contact: ph. 25000

Ystaad

Ystaad, one of Sweden's best-preserved medieval towns, flourish-ed as a major fishing port and benefitted from a lucrative smuggl-ing trade with mainland Europe. Every corner of this old Skane town seems to have a half-timbered house, an ancient church, or a good museum.

Friars Abbey

Amidst the narrow maze of Ystad's medieval lanes lies the Grabrodra Klostret, Sweden's best-preserved monastic house. Con-structed in 1267, the Franciscan Friary was used after the Refor-mation as a school, hospital, workhouse, and distillery. The cloister contains an interesting ecclesiastic collection and the 13th-century St. Peters Chapel.

Time: Mon.-Fri., 11am-4pm
Place: Klostret
Contact: ph. 77000

Time-Honored Landmark

The town watchman still sounds his horn each hour from the tower of St. Maria Church. A Baroque restoration endowed the 13th-century church with a white and gilt interior noted for its wood-carvings and decor.

Time: Mon.-Sat., 9am-6pm
Place: Stortorget

Nationwide

Kingdom of Glass

King Gustav Vasa brought the first glassblowers to Sweden from Venice in 1555, but it was German immigrants who established the center of Sweden's glass industry in Smaland. This Sylvan province is today home to three-fourths of Sweden's glassworks. More than 20 of these establishments welcome visitors. Listed below are some of the more interesting and accessible glassworks. Most are open weekdays from 9am-3pm.

Kosta-Boda, Kosta—ph. 04-785-0300
Sea Glasbruk, Kosta—ph. 04-785-0310
Orrefors, Orrefors—ph. 04-813-0300
Maleras Glasbruk, Orrefors—ph. 04-813-1100
Bergdalaglas, Houmantorp—ph. 04-781-8065

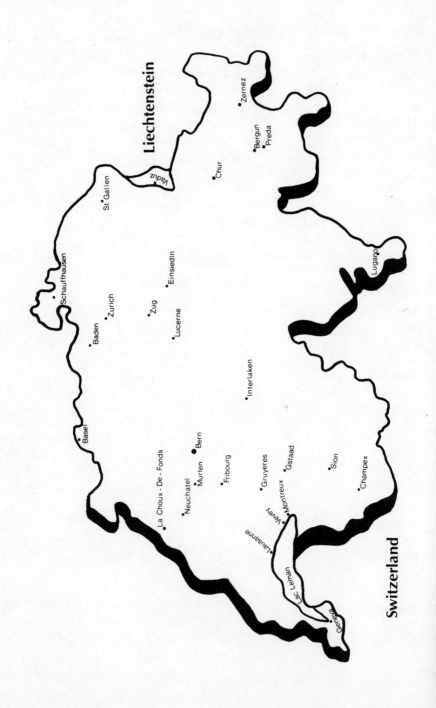

Liechtenstein

Zernez

Bergun
Preda

Chur

St. Gallen

Vaduz

Schauffhausen

Lugano

Zurich

Einsiedln

Baden

Zug

Lucerne

Interlaken

Basel

Bern
Murten

La Choux - De - Fonds

Fribourg

Gruyeres

Gstaad

Sion

Champex

Neuchatel

Montreux

Vevey

Lausanne

Lac Leman

Geneva

Switzerland

Switzerland
(and Liechtenstein)

Baden

Baden is an untouristy spa town with a rich history pre-dating the Romans, who called it *Aquae Helvetiae*. The old town quarter is a warren of narrow lanes, gabled homes, shops, and galleries.

Bailiff's Castle

Guarding the right bank of the Limmat above the Holzbrucke, Baden's ancient Landvogtieschloss today houses a diverse historical collection. This 15th-century castle served as the residence of local officials from 1415 until 1798. Now its keep and public halls display selections of antiques, Roman relics, and folk costumes of Canton Aargau.

Time: March-Jan.: Tues.-Sun., 10am-noon & 2pm-5pm
Place: Sonnenbergstrasse
Contact: ph. 225318

Historic Citadel

Commanding a rocky prominence above the old town, Schloss Stein is an impressive castle ruin with panoramic views of Baden, the Canton Aargau, and beyond. The 13th-century castle has been uninhabited since 1712, when it was partially demolished by the army of Canton Bern.

Basel

Switzerland's second-largest city straddles the Rhine at the convergence Switzerland, Germany, and France. Although it lacks the alpine beauty of other Swiss cities, Basel sparkles as a center of art and culture, with 25 museums, the nation's oldest university, and a venerable old town quarter.

City Tours

Your first stop in town should be the Tourist Office, where you can get a free city map and a brochure outlining self-guided walking tours of Basel. Be sure to get a copy of *This Week in Basel*, which covers most events and attractions in the city. For longer walks in and around Basel request *Treffpunkt Postauto*, a booklet describing a dozen excursions utilizing the ubiquitous yellow post buses.
Time: Mon.-Fri., 8am-noon & 1:30pm-6pm; Sat., 8am-noon
Place: Blumerain 2
Contact: ph. 253811

Fine Arts

Basel's Kunstmuseum, one of Europe's best collections of fine art, features the world's largest collection of Holbein paintings, 15th- through 20th-century European paintings, and a gallery of post-Impressionist works.
Time: Sat. & Sun., 10am-5pm
Place: 16 St. Alban Graben

Town Hall Tours

Built in 1510 and restored at the turn of the century, Basel's red sandstone Rathaus is adorned with guild crests and frescoes. Guided tours of the ornamented state rooms can be arranged by prior appointment on Sundays throughout the year.
Contact: Rathaus, Marktplatz, ph. 218549

Cherry Orchard Museum

Set in an 18th-century mansion, the Haus zum Kirschgarten has period furnishings, antique timepieces, porcelain, and marvelous tapestries. Don't miss the old cellar with its gigantic cask, built to hold 2,500 gallons of wine.
Time: Sat. & Sun., 10am-noon & 2pm-5pm
Place: 27 Elizabethenstrasse

Historic Basel
Basel's Historisches Museum houses exhibitions on regional life from the prehistoric era to modern times. Displays include Roman pottery and statuary, items from pagan graves, ecclesiastical art, mementoes of Erasmus (who died in Basel in 1536), and stained glass. Part of the collection is displayed in the church's 14th-century salt cellars.
Time: Sat. & Sun., 10am-noon & 2pm-5pm
Place: Barfusserplatz
Contact: ph. 220505

Towering Gothic
Facing the Munsterplatz, Basel Cathedral is a grand 12th-century building, rebuilt in Gothic style in the 14th century. Formed of glowing red sandstone and crowned by slender twin spires, the Munster is topped by a splendid tiled roof. Of special interest inside the cathedral are bas-reliefs honoring St. Vincent and the monumental tombstone of Erasmus.
Time: April-Oct.: Mon.-Fri., 10am-6pm; Sat., 10am-noon & 2pm-6pm; Sun., 1pm-5pm
Place: Munsterplatz

Winter Carnival
On the first Monday in the Lenten season, a genial madness pervades this usually reserved town. The annual Fasnacht Carnival is a three-day binge of processions, costumed dances, and merrymaking fueled by prodigious drinking. For details and dates, contact the tourist office.

Jewish Museum
Displaying items relating to European Jewish life and religion, the Judische Museum features memorabilia of Theodore Herzl and the first Zionist Congress of 1897, which he organized in Basel.
Time: Mon., Wed., & Sun., 3pm-5pm
Place: 8 Kornhausgasse

European Antiquities
The Basel Antikenmuseum has an outstanding collection of antiquities ranging from pre-Hellenic Greece to the Roman era.

Sculpture, jewelry, and art from various cultures are on display.
Time: Sat. & Sun., 10am-noon & 2pm-5pm
Place: St. Alban Graben

Bern

Founded in 1191, Bern, with its winding arcades, curious painted fountains, and engaging clocktowers, is today honored as a "World Landmark City." Although Switzerland's capital has many contemporary buildings, strict zoning has kept the heart of town entirely medieval. Built on a steep peninsula and set against the stunning backdrop of the Bernese Oberland, this enticing capital has charm and verve.

Municipal Mascots
Most visitors head for Bern's famous Barengraben (Bear Pits), where the city's pampered mascots have been quartered since 1480. Legend has it that when Duke Berhold founded the city in the 12th century, he decided that the town would be named for the first animal killed on his next hunt. Today, bears appear on everything from local chocolates to the Cantonal flag. Stop on the Nydeggbrucke, just before the Bear Pit, for a marvelous view of the river gorge and old Bern.
Time: always open
Place: Nydeggbrucke

National Parliament
Politically-minded travelers will want to visit the Swiss Parliament, or Bundeshaus. Guided tours are provided except when Parliament is in session, and then you can watch the proceedings from the visitors' galleries.
Time: tours on the hour Mon.-Sat., 9am-noon & 2pm-4pm
Place: Bundesplatz
Contact: ph. 618522

Natural History
The Naturhistorisches Museum is one of the best natural history museums in Europe. Dioramas simulate natural habitats of Euro-

pean, African, and arctic animals. The museum's upper floor displays minerals, geology, and palaeontology.
Time: Wed. & Sat., 9am-noon & 2pm-5pm; Sun., 2pm-5pm
Place: Bernastrasse 15
Contact: ph. 431664

Garden Panoramas
Just below the Barengraben, the Rosengarten provides marvelous views of the heart of the medieval town. Established in 1914, the gardens now are planted with azaleas, rhododendrens, and hundreds of varieties of roses.
Time: daily, 9am-6pm
Place: Aargauerstalden

Historical Treasures
The Bernisches Historisches Museum is a must visit, if only for a peek at the spectacular booty captured from the Duke of Burgundy's army in 1476. The collection included Flemish tapestries, embroideries, and standards. You'll also find 18th-century furnishings, folk art, and costumes, along with archaeological finds of Stone Age Berner Oberland.
Time: Tues.-Sat., 9am-noon & 2pm-5pm; Sun., 10am-noon & 2pm-5pm
Place: Helvetiaplatz 5
Contact: ph. 431811

Landmark Tower
Built in 1191, Bern's monumental Zytgloggeturm (Clocktower) served as the city's western gate until 1250. In 1527, a fantastic astronomical clock was installed on the east face of the tower. At four minutes before every hour, the medieval tomfoolery begins with the jester's jig, followed by costume bears who lead the parade of knights and animals until the Golden Knight hammers out the hour.
Place: Kramgasse

Fine Art
The Kunstmuseum contains a worthy collection of European painting from the 14th through 20th centuries, with works by Monet, Picasso, Matisse, and Rousseau. It also has the world's greatest

assemblage of works by Paul Klee, with 2,500 paintings and drawings tracing Klee's stylistic development. Works by contemporary Swiss artists are also displayed.
Time: Sun., 10am-noon & 2pm-5pm
Place: Hodlerstrasse 12
Contact: ph. 220944

Gothic Cathedral
Although construction began in 1421, the Cathedral of St. Vincent was not completed until 1893. The tympanum over the main portal is the church's most remarkable architectural feature. Inside, the principal attractions are the stained glass windows. Those in the chancel date from the 15th century, while the macabre "Dance of Death" window is a 20th-century work based on 16th-century designs.
Time: Tues.-Sat., 10am-noon & 2pm-4pm
Place: Munsterplatz

Botanical Garden
Bern's University Botanical Garden, though it covers only five acres, includes fine collections of alpine plants arranged geographically, as well as glasshouses.
Time: daily, 8am-6pm
Place: Altenbergrain 21

Communications Museum
With one of the world's best collections of international postage stamps, plus displays exploring the development of Switzerland's postal and electronic communications systems, the Schweizerisches PTT Museum makes a diverting attraction.
Time: Tues.-Sun., 10am-noon & 2pm-5pm
Place: Helvetiaplatz 4

La Chaux-De-Fonds

Nature Reserve
La Chaux-De-Fonds is the gateway for the popular Vallee du Doubs Nature Reserve, a region of steep wooded slopes, shimmering lakes, and cascading falls, close to the French frontier. In the spring and

summer, wildflowers blanket the meadows and mountainsides. Contact: Office du Tourisme, Ave. Leopold Robert, ph. 233610

Chur

Residents of Chur boast that their's is the oldest city in the nation. Diggings indicate a small community lived in Chur in 3000 BC. Modern Chur, an important crossroads for trade and transportation, is a good base for exploring southeastern Switzerland.

Walking Tours

Chur's Tourist Office has created two infallible self-guided walking tours of the medieval quarter. Green and red footprints have been painted on the city sidewalks (starting at the train station square) to coincide with the two routes described in a free brochure. Each stroll takes the visitor over streets trod for centuries. The routes are timed to last about an hour, but you'll probably want to tarry longer.
Time: Mon.-Fri., 9am-noon & 2pm-6pm; Sat., 9am-noon
Contact: Verkehrsverein fur Graubunden, Ottostrasse 6, ph. 221360 or 221818

Splendid Cathedral

Crowned by a curious belfry, the Cathedral of Our Lady is a splendid 12th-century church, built on the site of an ancient temple. The dimly lit interior contains a carved triptych and an eerie pagan sacrificial stone, leftover from the first tenants at that address. To reach the cathedral and the neighboring Bishops Palace, you must first climb a flight of stairs and pass through the Hoftor Gate, a relic of ancient Chur.
Time: Mon.-Sat., 9am-noon & 2pm-6pm
Place: Hofplatz

Mountain Rambles

The Graubunden is Switzerland's largest, least-populated canton. With nearly 7,000 miles of marked hiking trails—past glaciers, forests, and remote villages—the Graubunden is Switzerland at its loveliest. Chur's tourist office supplies free maps and brochures detailing routes throughout the canton. Many trails originate and terminate at train stations or bus stops. A favorite is the spectacular

(and mostly downhill) hike from the tiny village of Preda to the gorgeous village of Bergun.
Contact: Verkehrsverein fur Graubunden

Einsiedeln

Magnificent Monastery
Einsiedeln is famed throughout Europe for its remarkable Baroque monastery. The imposing, graceful Klosterkirche, built between 1720 and 1734, is Switzerland's greatest and most frequented pilgrimage place. Inside, the interior is largely the work of the renowned Assam brothers, who covered the church in vivid frescoes and stucco. A moving chapel at the entrance occupies the place of St. Meinrad's martyrdom and protects the venerated Black Madonna of Hermits. An object of special devotion for handicapped or ill pilgrims, the Madonna attracts tens of thousands of believers each year.
Time: daily, 9am-6pm
Place: Klosterplatz
Contact: ph. 532510 or 534488

Fribourg

Divided by the River Sarine gorge, this town is also bisected by a linguistic boundary. It's "Freiburg" on the German-speaking right bank and "Fribourg" on the Francophone left bank. Too often overlooked by travelers, medieval Fribourg is one of Switzerland's prettiest towns.

Gothic Beauty
Majestic St. Nicholas Cathedral watches over the rooftops of old Fribourg. Although its first stone was laid in 1283, the church wasn't completed until the 17th century. Interior highlights include a rose window, Baroque chapels, and a 19th-century organ. Recitals are held on the famous organ during the summer months.
Time: daily, 8:30am-6pm
Place: St. Nicholas
Contact: ph. 813175

Botanical Garden
Planted at the turn of the century, the University Botanical garden comprises nearly four acres, with alpine plants, floral beds, and modern glasshouses.
Time: Mon.-Sat., 8am-5pm
Place: 3 rue A. Gockel

Geneva

A vibrant town of parks and lakeside promenades, Geneva is a true international city, with some 150 international organizations in residence. Handsome boulevards around the lake are lined with trendy shops, classy department stores, and contemporary architecture.

Ironically, Geneva owes much of her cosmopolitan atmosphere to the austere Reformation leader, John Calvin, who directed the city's 16th-century Protestant revolt, which attracted religious refugees from all over Europe. The new residents helped to develop Geneva's reputation as a center of learning, philosophy, and art.

Spilling down to the shore of Lac Leman, the old town quarter is a cluster of restored buildings along narrow lanes. Comfortably human in scale, Geneva remains an accessible city, easily explored on foot.

Classic Timepieces
Befitting Geneva's status as a watchmaking center, the Musee de l'Horlogerie, devoted to the history of time measurement, displays historic timepieces from sundials to enameled wristwatches. There's also a reconstructed clockmaker's workshop, authentic to the last detail.
Time: Tues.-Sun., 10am-noon & 2pm-6pm; Mon., 2pm-6pm
Place: 15 route de Malagnou
Contact: ph. 367412

Natural History
The Musee d'Histoire Naturelle is one of Europe's best natural history museums. The varied collections are greatly enhanced by dynamic vivariums and aquariums. The upper floor is devoted to

the geology and minerology of Switzerland and to palaeontology.
Time: Tues.-Sun., 10am-5pm
Place: 11 route de Malagnou
Contact: ph. 359130

Municipal Symbol
The Jet d'Eau, Geneva's lovely city trademark, shoots a plume of
dancing water more than 450 feet in the air above Lake Geneva.
This fountain, in operation from May to October, dates from 1890
and is visible for miles around. The Jet's precise workings are a
secret, but we do know that it spurts lake water at 150 miles per
hour.
Place: Quai Gustave Ador

Library Museum Complex
The Library of Geneva contains 1.5 million books and two fine
museums: the Jean-Jacques Rousseau Museum and the History of
the Reformation Collection. Located in the Salle Lullin, the Rousseau
exhibit displays manuscripts, mementoes, and the death mask of
the renowned philospher and writer. The Musee de la Reformation exhibits materials relating to the Reformation.
Time: Mon.-Fri., 9am-noon & 2pm-5pm; Sat., 9am-noon
Place: Promenades des Bastions
Contact: ph. 208266

Art and History
Geneva's most popular museum, the Musee d'Art et Histoire,
presents an eclectic range of collections encompassing civilization from prehistoric times to the present. The Archaeological Section is dedicated to Middle Eastern and Mediterranean civilizations.
Fine arts are represented by European paintings, including works
from the Italian Renaissance, Dutch schools, and modern artists
such as Picasso and Renoir.
Time: Tues.-Sun., 10am-noon & 2pm-6pm
Place: 2 rue Charles Galland
Contact: ph. 290011

Saved by the Soup
One of the most interesting times to visit Geneva is on December
11th for the celebration of l'Escalade, when the city commemorates

the thwarting of a sneak attack in 1602. As legend has it, when soldiers attempted to scale Geneva's ramparts, a Mrs. Royaume poured a kettle of boiling soup on them, and their howls alerted the city guard. Today, the event is remembered with torchlight processions and costume parties that last till the wee hours.

Literary Giant
Les Delices, the home of Voltaire from 1755 to 1765, has become a museum and research center devoted to the literary giant. Institute Voltaire exhibits manuscripts, correspondence, pictures, and furnishings of the French author, along with portions of his art collection.
Time: Mon.-Fri., 2pm-5pm
Place: 25 rue des Delices
Contact: ph. 447133

History of Science
The Musee de l'Histoire des Sciences presents a collection of instruments and memorabilia of famous Swiss scientists, physicians, and mathematicians, all displayed in a villa once owned by the Bartholomi family.
Time: Mon.-Sat., 2pm-6pm
Place: 128 rue de Lausanne
Contact: ph. 316985

Classic Porcelain
Musee de l'Ariana, housed in a villa built for the author Revilliod, has one of Europe's best collections of porcelain, pottery, and ceramics. The focus is on Meissen, Delft, and Sevres, but you'll also find Oriental pieces and modern ceramics.
Time: Tues.-Sun., 10am-noon & 2pm-5pm
Place: 10 Avenue de la Paix
Contact: ph. 333944

Garden Conservatory
Adjoining the Parc de l'Ariana, the Botanical Garden and Conservatory dates from the early 19th century. The manicured grounds

include a charming aviary, tropical greenhouses, and a deer park.
Time: Garden: April-Oct.: daily, 7am-6:30pm; Nov.-Feb.: daily,
8am-5pm; March-April: daily, 8am-6pm. Glasshouse: daily,
9am-11am & 2pm-4:30pm
Place: 192 route de Lausanne

Gruyeres

Walking into the fortified hilltop village of Gruyeres (no cars allowed)
is like strolling back to the Middle Ages. In this fairytale setting of
cobblestone lanes lined with 15th-century houses, you can easily
imagine Switzerland in a bygone era.

Cheesy Show

The local cheese-making cooperative operates a model dairy to
demonstrate the production process of their famous product. After
touring the facility, you can watch experts fashioning huge wheels
of the creamy cheese.
Time: Mon.-Sat., 8am-10am & 1:30pm-3pm; Sun., 8am-1:30pm
Place: Pringy
Contact: ph. 28022

Gstaad

Alpine Wildlife

Although Gstaad is best known as a winter playground for
celebrities, this rather ordinary town is located between two of
Switzerland's most popular nature reserves. The Vanil Noir Reserve,
about five miles northwest of Gstaad, is between two 7,500-foot
peaks. Three miles southeast of Gstaad, the Gelten-Iffigen Nature
Reserve offers an alpine landscape with mountain lakes, waterfalls,
and glaciers. South of the 9,000-foot Laufbodenhorn, archaeologists
have uncovered evidence of human occupation from the
Palaeolithic era, making this the earliest-known site of human
habitation in Switzerland.
Contact: Verkehrsvereien Gstaad, Hauptstrasse, ph. 41055

Interlaken

Situated between the Thunersee and Brienzersee, Interlaken has long been a mecca of the Bernese Alps. Even though the town has become touristy over the years, it remains a great base for lake trips and mountain excursions.

Idyllic Hikes
One of the best mountain hikes accessible from Interlaken is the day-long Rundwanderungen, an easy circular hike from the town to Alp Gron. For a free booklet detailing this and two dozen other walks around the Berner Oberland, stop by the tourist office. Contact: Verkehrsverein Berner Oberland, Jungfraustrasse 36, ph. 222621

Lausanne

Even Neolithic lake-dwellers had the good sense to settle on the shore of Lake Geneva. Today, Lausanne climbs in tiers above the lake, in a setting few cities can match. With views of the French Alps across the lake and a gentle climate, this capital of Canton Vaud is a favorite stop for European travelers.

A mix of ancient and modern makes Lausanne an exciting city to visit. The historic medieval town center, known as La Cite, has cobbled streets and steep alleyways, connected by unusual,covered stairways. The Vidy District, hugging Lac Leman, is rich in Roman ruins. Modern Lausanne is connected with its port of Ouchy by Switzerland's shortest and steepest subway system.

Ancient Artifacts
The Roman Ruins Museum displays objects discovered at the excavations of port Lousana. If possible, visit this small but enlightening museum after you see the uncovered site.
Time: Tues.-Sat., 2pm-5pm
Place: Chemin du Bois de Vaux

Town Hall Tours
Lausanne's restored 17th-century Hotel de Ville, with its Renaissance-style facade and animated clock, is worth a visit. Each

weekday afternoon, free guided tours are provided of the municipal chambers.
Time: Mon.-Fri., 2:30pm-4:30pm
Place: Place de la Palud
Contact: ph. 237333

Museum Complex
Along with Lausanne University and the Cantonal Library, there's a complex of fine museums housed in the Palais de Rumine, including a museum of archaeology, zoology, and geology.
Time: Tues.-Sun., 10am-noon & 2pm-5pm
Place: place de la Riponne
Contact: ph. 228332

Gothic Beauty
Perched on a terrace 500 feet above the lake, Notre Dame Cathedral, begun in 1175, is Switzerland's pre-eminent Gothic building. In the midst of the medieval La Cite, Notre Dame is adorned with intricate reliefs and statuary and crowned by picturesque towers. The interior features 13th-century choir stalls, fine murals, and the beautiful rose window *Imago Mundi*.
Time: Mon.-Sat., 7am-6pm; Sun., 2pm-6pm
Place: Place de la Cathedral

Old Lausanne
Next door to the Cathedral, the former Bishop's Palace has been transformed into a museum. The Musee de l'Ancien Eveche presents a portrait of old Lausanne, with exhibits from prehistoric to contemporary times.
Time: Tues.-Sun., 10am-noon & 2pm-6pm
Place: 2 Place de la Cathedral
Contact: ph. 221368

Alpine Gardens
Established in the late 19th century, Lausanne Botanical Garden overlooks Lac Leman and the Savoy Alps. Within its landscaped acres you'll find a colorful array of alpine flora.
Time: March-Oct.: daily, 8am-noon & 2pm-7pm
Place: 14 bis Avenue de Cours.

Ancient Castle

The imposing Chateau St. Maire was the residence of the Bishop of Lausanne and the Bernese Governor. Now the seat of the Cantonal government, the castle has some interesting decor, including rare frescoes uncovered during restoration. Walk out on the terrace for a grand view of Lausanne, the lake, and the Alps.
Time: Mon.-Fri., 8am-11am & 2pm-5pm
Place: Avenue de la Universite

Lucerne

Lucerne is storybook pretty, everyone's notion of how a Swiss city should look. Shadowed by snowcapped peaks and encircled by 14th-century walls, the old town is a district of cobbled lanes lined with old homes and ancient buildings. Even when swamped with the sightseers who come in droves in the summer, Lucerne is well worth the hassle.

Rampart Walk

Early morning is the best time to climb the ancient city wall for panoramas of Lucerne and the lake. Only nine of the original 30 watchtowers still stand, but you can climb inside and get a unique perspective on medieval fortifications.
Time: May-Oct.: daily, 8am-8pm
Place: St. Karliquai to Museggstrasse

City Symbols

Built in 1333, the flower-trimmed Kappelbrucke is Europe's oldest standing wooden bridge. The interior is decorated with paintings of the history of Lucerne and its patron saints. Flanking the bridge, the huge Wasserturm has been used as a prison, a torture chamber, and a warehouse. A little further up the river, Lucerne's other covered bridge, the Spreuerbrucke, was built in 1408. Inside, the gables are adorned with a macabre series of paintings called the *Dance of Death*.

Alpine Mardi Gras

Every February, Lucerne dispells the chill of winter with a weekend of revelry. The celebration includes all-night dances, costumed processions, concerts, and general hoopla. Normally staid Luzerners

wear masks to hide their pre-Lenten indiscretions. For exact dates and a schedule of organized events, see the folks at the tourist office.
Time: Office hours: Mon.-Fri., 8am-noon and 2pm-6pm; Sat., 9am-noon
Place: Pilatusstrasse 14
Contact: ph. 285252

Resplendent Rococo
The modest facade of Lucerne's Jesuitenkirche belies the exuberant interior. This lovely church was the first Jesuit church built in Switzerland. Inside, the nave is overlaid with frescoes and the altar is decorated with sumptuous pink marbles.
Time: Mon.-Sat., 9am-noon & 2pm-5pm
Place: Bahnhofstrasse

Poignant Memorial
Be sure to see the exquisite Lion Monument, on the edge of the old town. This memorial honors a complement of Swiss Guards killed by revolutionary mobs in Paris in 1792. The 30-foot long lion is carved directly into the cliff.
Time: always accessible
Place: Denkmalstrasse, off of Lowengartenstrasse

Lugano
Lugano, the gem of Switerzand's "Riviera," is an ideal year-round resort. Not officially part of Switzerland until 1803, it has retained an Italian atmosphere, with romantic piazzi, outdoor cafes, and elaborate balconies.

Architect Remembered
The villa of designer Wilhelm Schmid is today a municipal museum dedicated to the work of the adventurous artist. Along with Schmid's paintings and furnishings, the museum maintains an archive of his books and papers.
Time: irregular hours—call for details
Contact: ph. 238350

Magnificent Frescoes
Set on a lakeside piazza, the Chiesa di Santa Maria degli Angioli

is a Franciscan church with two of Bernardino Luini's finest frescoes. *The Crucifixion* and *The Virgin with Child* have been compared to the works of da Vinci.
Time: Mon.-Sat., 9am-noon & 2pm-5pm
Place: Piazza Luini
Contact: ph. 214664

Montreux

Festival du Jazz
With its opulent hotels and villas, lakeside promenades, and alpine vistas, Montreux is a choice venue for the annual Festival du Jazz. Lasting nearly three weeks each July, the international music fest presents many free concerts along with the schedule of expensive shows. For information on the festival, which also provides free campgrounds, write well in advance to the festival office.
Contact: Festival du Jazz, Case 97, CH-1820 Montreux, Canton Vaud

Murten

As one of Switzerland's best-preserved medieval towns, bilingual Murten\Morat has saved many of its picturesque old buildings.

Forbidding Fortress
The imposing lakeside castle, built by Duke Peter of Savoy, is a hulking eminence dominating the quaint Altstadt of Murten. Its inner courtyard affords excellent views of the Murtensee and the Jura mountains.
Time: Tues.-Sun., 9am-5pm
Place: Schlossgasse

Wall Walks
There are unsurpassed panoramas of the castle, the old town, the lake, and the mountains from the ancient city ramparts, built during the 13th and 14th centuries. For information on guided wall walks, contact the tourist office.
Contact: Office di Tourism, Schlossgasse 5, ph. 813175

Neuchatel

A small city with an air of self-satisfied prosperity, Neuchatel maintains a link with its heritage in the traffic-free Ville Ancienne, a historic district of old homes, defensive towers, and fountains. Along the lake, the city's broad thoroughfares are lined with dignified sandstone villas.

Chocolate Tour

Chocoholics won't want to miss the free tour of the Suchard Chocolate Factory. Call the tourist office to arrange a visit to see how those delectable treats are made.
Contact: Office du Tourism, Place Numadroz, ph. 254242

Chateau Complex

Revealing few traces of its original 12th-century architecture, the Chateau anchors a complex of medieval ramparts, terraces, cloisters, and a Gothic church with a curious group of medieval statuary. The unusual Gothic memorial to the Counts of Neuchatel dates from the 14th century and is found in the choir.
Time: daily, 8am-8pm
Place: 23 rue du Chateau
Contact: ph. 223610

Swiss Archaeology

The Musee Cantonal D'Archeologie presents artifacts from excavations around Lac de Neuchatel. Many of the finds were discovered at La Tene, a significant Iron Age site on the lake.
Time: Tues.-Sun., 2pm-5pm
Place: 7 rue Du Peyrou
Contact: ph. 250336

Modern Gardens

Founded in 1954, the University Botanical Garden contains greenhouses, an alpine garden, and an artificial peat bog.
Time: April-Oct.: daily, 8am-6pm
Place: 11 rue Emile-Argand

Tours and Hikes

For a wealth of free brochures and information on hikes, walking tours, castles, and nature reserves in the region, visit the

Neuchatelois Cantonal Tourist Office. Ask for the particularly helpful booklet, *Neuchatel Tourist Guide*.
Contact: Office Neuchatelois du Tourism, 9 rue du Tresor, ph. 251789

St. Gallen

Founded in 612 by the Irish monk Gallus, St. Gallen's famous monastery has enjoyed renown as an intellectual center since the 8th century. Today, St. Gallen is the hub of Swiss cotton and embroidery industries. The Old Town has preserved its medieval atmosphere, with twisting, narrow lanes, tiny squares, and old houses.

Historic Abbey
The Domkirche, built in 1765, is one of Switzerland's finest Baroque buildings. The interior is a marvel of Baroque style from the famous Voralberg School of design. Surmounting the great rotunda, there's a dome adorned with paintings on a mellow red background. The cathedral chancel is a masterpiece of design, with delicate grillwork, a moving altar, and carvings of sensuous beauty.
Time: daily, 9am-5pm
Place: Gallus Strasse

Botanical Tours
St. Gallen's Botanical Garden offers free guided tours each Sunday, given by local experts.
Time: Gardens: Sun.-Fri., 9am-noon & 1:30pm-5pm; Tours: Sun., 10am & 3pm
Place: 69 Brauerstrasse

Woodland Walks
The regional tourist office will supply a booklet with route descriptions and maps for ten walks around St. Gallen. Hiking is easy in these alpine foothills, and the area offers a varied landscape with wandering rivers, broad plateaus, lakes, and hills.
Contact: Nordostschweizerisches Verkersvereinigung, 1 Bahnhofplatz, ph. 226262

Schaffhausen

Visitors to the nearby Rheinfalls often overlook Schaffhausen's other attractions. Its Old Town, built on terraces above the rushing Rhine, reflects the prosperity of medieval merchants who settled there to take advantage of the city's location on the river.

Old Town and Tower

Dominated by the Munot, a 16th-century fortified tower, the Altstadt is still rich in medieval character and atmosphere. From the Munot's ramparts, you can see the lower town's fine old houses and fountains and the revered Munster.
Time: Tower: May-Sept.: daily, 8am-8pm; Oct.-April: daily, 9am-5pm
Place: Munotstrasse

Eclectic Collection

Housed in the former All Saints Abbey, the Museum zu Allerheiligen contains a diverse collection, including ancient manuscripts, artifacts from regional excavations, period furnishings, industrial displays, jewelry, and much more.
Time: Tues.-Sun., 10am-noon & 1:30pm-5pm
Place: Baumgartenstrasse
Contact: ph. 55141

Sion

This 2,000-year old town, high in the Rhone Valley, is dominated by two rocky peaks, each crowned by a medieval citadel.

Wine Tours

Provins Valais, the local wine cooperative, proudly shows off its immense wine cellar complex. The varieties distributed under the Provins Valais label (and periodically offered in tasting sessions) range from the Fendant to Pinot Noir. Call the tourist office to arrange for a visit.
Contact: Union Valaisanne du Tourisme, 6 rue de Lausanne, ph. 222898

Town Hall

Built in 1657, the pink Hotel de Ville is not to be missed. At the

entrance, there's an elaborate door and ancient Roman inscriptions, and inside, the Council Chambers are lavishly appointed. A special feature of the Town Hall is the much-photographed astronomical clock.
Time: Mon.-Fri., 9am-11am & 2pm-4:30pm
Place: Rue du Grand-Pont

Castle Ruins

During the 13th century, Sion's Prince-Bishops built a fortified chateau on the Tourbillon peak to defend their domain from encroachment by the House of Savoy. Much of the structure was destroyed by fire in 1788, but the remains are impressive. The panorama of the Valais, particularly in early morning and at sunset, is stunning.
Place: Rue des Chateaux

Zernez

National Park

Zernez is the gateway to Switzerland's most important national park. Established in 1909, the Swiss National Park has become a model for wildlife and landscape conservation. Adjacent to the Stelvio National Park in Italy, the park occupies over 40,000 acres in the Engadine and has many 11,000-foot peaks separated by deep valleys and snowfields. The best time to visit is early summer, when the wildflowers and alpine plants produce an unmatched display. The Park House provides demonstrations and guided walks in the summer.
Time: Park House: June-Oct.: Mon-Sat., 9am-noon & 2pm-6:30pm
Contact: Nationalparkhaus, ph. 81300

Zug

Preserving many of its old neighborhoods along Lake Zugersee, Zug has retained a pleasant medieval character, with lakeside promenades that offer superb views of the mountains of central Switzerland.

Art and History

Build in 1503, Zug's Rathaus presents exhibits dedicated to local history and artisans, with displays of regional costumes, paintings, and prized relics of the Battle of Arbedo in 1422.
Time: Mon.-Fri., 9am-noon & 1:30pm-4pm
Place: Kolinplatz
Contact: ph. 210078

Gothic Church

The beautiful facade of St. Oswald's Church is decorated with remarkable carvings on its King's Door. The interior is noted for its painted vaulting, unusual statues, and gilded triptychs.
Time: Mon.-Sat., 9am-noon & 2pm-5pm; Sun., 2pm-5pm
Place: Grabenstrasse

Zurich

Switzerland's largest city and an international financial center, Zurich's roots go back to 3000 BC. Today, Zurich is a colorful city of waterfront promenades, parks, and handsome boulevards. The city's most famous street, the Bahnhofstrasse, is a pedestrian zone leading through the heart of the old town. And Zurich's romantic Altestadt is made for aimless exploration.

Outstanding Museum

The Schweizerisches Landesmuseum, housed in an immense castle-like building, illustrates Swiss culture and history from prehistoric times to the present. Displays include artifacts of Switzerland's early lake-dwellers, Roman militaria, toys, folk costumes, models of Swiss villages, paintings, and much more.
Time: Tues.-Sun., 10am-5pm
Place: 2 Museumstrasse
Contact: ph. 221-1010

Precious Porcelain

Zurich's Zunfthaus zur Meisen-Keramische contains a treasure of European porcelain. An extension of the Landesmuseum, this old

guildhall has beautiful rococo rooms packed with porcelain items from the 18th and 19th centuries.
Time: Tues.-Sun., 10am-noon & 2pm-5pm; Mon., 2pm-5pm
Place: 20 Munsterhof

Kids' Heaven
Franz Carl Weber, owner of the famous toy shops, has opened a charming museum, the Spielzougmuseum, in the Altestadt to exhibit his collection of antique toys.
Time: Mon.-Fri., 2pm-5pm
Place: 15 Fortunagasse
Contact: ph. 211-9305

Fine Arts
Set in a modern exhibition hall, the Zurich Kunstmuseum displays paintings and sculpture from the 13th through the 20th centuries, with such luminaries as Munch, Monet, Degas, Rodin, Cezanne, and Picasso.
Time: Wed., 2pm-5pm; Sun., 10am-5pm
Place: Heimplatz
Contact: ph. 251-6765

Spring Festival
All of Zurich turns out on the third weekend in April for the Sechselauten, a celebration that symbolically banishes winter and greets spring with parades, bands, fireworks, and general carousing. The festival culminates in Bellevueplatz with the burning of Boogg, a giant cotton snowman.
Contact: Verkehrsverein Zurich, 15 Bahnhofstrasse, ph. 211-4000

Legendary Cathedral
According to legend, Zurich's Grossmunster was founded by the Emperor Charlemagne, whose horse knelt at the site where three saints had been martyred. Overlooking the Limmat, the Cathedral's gilded twin towers are an enduring city landmark. The austere interior is enlivened by modern stained glass windows designed by August Giacometti.
Time: daily, 9am-4pm
Place: Limmatquai
Contact: ph. 475232

Chagall Windows

Standing on the left bank of the Limmat across from the Grossmunster, the Fraumunster's greatest attraction, is a set of stained glass windows by Marc Chagall. Dating from the 13th century, the Fraumunster replaced an abbey founded there in 853 by Emperor Ludwig, grandson of Charlemagne.

Time: Mon.-Sat., 9am-6pm; Sun., noon-6pm
Place: Munsterhof

Rare Plants

Descended from Switzerland's first botanical garden, the modern University Garden of Zurich is a spacious park with rare plants from around the world. There's also an unusual complex of plastic domes with tropical and desert plants and a wildflower display. The park is quite popular with Zurichers.

Time: Garden: daily in summer, 7am-7pm; in winter, 7:30am-6pm.
Glasshouses: daily, 8am-11:30am & 1pm-4pm
Place: 107 Zollikerstrasse
Contact: ph. 251-3670

Nationwide

Independence Day

All of Switzerland celebrates the Swiss National Day on August 1, in commemoration of the first Helvetic Confederation in 1291. There are parades, concerts, fireworks, torchlight processions, and bonfires throughout the nation. Some of the most exciting and moving celebrations are held in mountain villages and small towns.

Liechtenstein

Vaduz

Postal Museum

No philatelist will want to miss Liechtenstein's world-renowned Postal Museum. Stamps from the principality are among the world's most beautiful and precious—they are often reproductions of art masterpieces found in the prince's collection.

Time: Mon.-Sat., 10am-6pm
Place: Stadtle 37
Contact: ph. 07-521443

Mountain Hikes

Liechtenstein maintains over 200 miles of marked hiking trails and footpaths. Many go through alpine meadows and forests and above the timberline for unobstructed views of the Alps. The tourist office can provide maps of trips to prehistoric settlements, Roman ruins, castles, and mountain summits.

Contact: Liechtensteinische Fremdenverkehrszentrale, St. Floringsgasse, ph. 07-566288

Prince's Palace

Schloss Vaduz is the residence of the Prince of Liechtenstein. Though you can't gain admittance to the castle's interior, the grounds and gardens are open to the public. The visit is lovely, with a panoramic view of Vaduz, the countryside, and the surrounding Alps.

Time: 8am-sunset
Place: Schloss Strasse

West Germany

Aachen

Much of Aachen's 2,000-year history was obliterated by World War II bombings, but this town of kaisers and kings still radiates imperial grandeur. Its proximity to the Netherlands and Belgium also gives Aachen an international flavor.

Charlemagne's Cathedral

The Kaiserdom, begun in 800 by Charlemagne, is an unusual blend of Carolinian and Gothic architecture. Besides the brilliant stained glass windows, the Dom is known for the marble throne of Charlemagne and the golden reliquary that holds his remains. And don't miss the Shrine of Ste. Marie, an elaborate 13th-century reliquary.
Time: daily, 7am-7pm
Place: Pontstrasse
Contact: ph. 33491

Augsburg

Augsburg refuses to be overshadowed by neighboring Munich. Two thousand years of wealth and prominence have graced the city with architectural monuments of every period and style. Its medieval splendor is evident in the Old Town, where the noble

Maximillianstrasse, Germany's finest Renaissance thoroughfare, is lined by mansions, fountains, and churches.

Palace Galleries

Adorned with baroque and rococo decoration, Augsburg's fantastic Schaelzer Palais houses the city's art collection. The galleries of the 18th-century palace display masterpieces of European Renaissance and baroque art. Works by Durer, Rubens, Tiepolo, Veronese, and more are displayed.
Time: Tues.-Sun., 10am-5pm
Place: 46 Maximillianstrasse
Contact: ph. 324-2171

Renaissance Hall

Twin towers frame the entrance to Augsburg's Renaissance Rathaus. This huge civic hall, built in 1620, incorporates the old Perlach Tor in the design. Serious World War II damage necessitated a lengthy restoration project.
Time: daily, 10am-6pm
Place: Rathausplatz, Maximillianstrasse

Swabian Silver

Works by regional silversmiths and goldsmiths are on display, along with Swabian and Bavarian sculpture, at the Maximillian Museum. You'll also find exhibits on the history of old Augsburg.
Time: Tues.-Sun., 10am-5pm
Place: 24 Phillipine Welser-Strasse

Public Housing

One of Augsburg's special attractions is the Fuggerei. Built by the wealthy Fugger family in 1519, this housing project for the poor has been occupied for over 450 years. The residents still pay a token rent of 1 Rhenish mark a year and are expected to pray for the Fugger family.
Place: Jacoborvorstadt
Contact: ph. 36026

Ancient Church

The thousand-year old Dom Kathedrale should be on every visitor's itinerary. The 11th-century bronze doors tell the story of creation,

and the stained glass in the south nave is said to date from the early 12th century. Be sure to see the altar paintings by Hans Holbein the Elder.
Time: Mon.-Sat., 8am-6pm; Sun., 2pm-5pm
Place: Karolinenstrasse

Berchtesgaden

Berchtesgaden is one of Bavaria's tourist hot spots, with good reason. Few places in Germany offer such spectacular scenery, so be prepared for summertime crowds.

Mountain Hikes

Berchtesgaden makes an excellent base for hikes in the National Park and Wildlife Reserve. The tourist offices can provide maps of mountain walks.
Place: Tourist Office, Konigsseerstrasse 2
Contact: ph. 08-652-5011

Berlin

Despite its post-war division and tense position as a geopolitical island, Berlin remains on the cutting edge of German culture. Germany's largest city is a vital and creative place, as active and lively as ever, presenting an array of architectural styles within its surprisingly expansive borders. The city has everything from modern shops along the trendy Ku'damm to vast baroque palaces.

Philharmonic Hall

The home of the renowned Berlin Philharmonic Orchestra, this unusual and controversial hall is open for visits, as long as no concerts or rehearsals are going on.
Time: Mon.-Sat., 1:30pm-3pm; Sun., 2:30pm-3:30pm
Place: Kemperplatz
Contact: ph. 269251

Reichstag

Completely restored after wartime devastation, the former parliament building now houses an exhibit of 20th-century German

history. The Reichstag's location near the Berlin Wall makes it a good spot for viewing East Berlin.
Time: Tues.-Sun., 11am-5pm
Place: Platz der Republic

Flea Market
You can find one of Europe's most unusual flea markets at Nollendorfplatz. Everything from antiques to old clothes is sold in this former el station. The shops are housed in subway cars from the 1920's and '30's.
Time: Wed.-Mon., 11am-9pm
Place: Nollendorfplatz

National Gallery
Designed by Mies van der Rohe, the National Gallery has a terrific collection of 19th- and 20th-century art.
Time: Tues.-Sun., 9am-5pm
Place: Potsdammerstrasse 50
Contact: ph. 2666

Schloss Charlottenberg
Berlin's other great museum complex is found at the Charlottenberg Palace. With museums of Egyptian, Roman, Greek, and decorative arts, there's something to please any visitor. Be sure to see the famous bust of Nefertiti.
Time: Sat.-Thurs., 9am-5pm
Place: Schlossstrasse
Contact: ph. 32011

"Ich bin ein Berliner"
Students of history will want to visit the Schoneberg Rathaus, where John F. Kennedy made his famous speech in 1963. The tower affords an excellent view and contains a replica of the Liberty Bell, presented to the city by the occupation governor General Lucius Clay.
Time: Wed., Sat., & Sun., 10am-3pm
Place: John F. Kennedy Platz
Contact: ph. 783-3318

Avant-Garde Art
Berline's Kunste Akademie is on the cutting edge of international modern art. The exhibitions are always worth seeing.
Time: Tues.-Sun., 11am-8pm
Place: Hanseatenweg 10

Architectural Archives
The Bauhaus Archive has a collection based on the well-known Bauhaus School of design. This intriguing museum, with architectural models, furniture, textiles, and household products, testifies to the enthusiasm and imagination of Bauhaus designers and architects.
Time: Mon., 11am-5pm
Place: Spandauerdamm at Schlossstrasse
Contact: ph. 26118

Dahlem Museum Center
One of Europe's great museum complexes can be found at the Dahlem Center. Among the many exhibition halls in the complex are the Museum for Oriental Art, the Painting Gallery, the Ethnographic Museum, the Etching-Print Gallery, and the Sculpture Gallery.
Time: Tues.-Sun., 9am-5pm
Place: Lannstrasse and Arnim Allee
Contact: ph. 83011

Tiergarten
The oldest and largest of Berlin's parks, the Tiergarten began as a royal game preserve in the early 16th century. Destroyed in World War II, the park was restored in the 1940's and '50's with the planting of more than a million plants and trees.
Time: daily, sunrise to sunset
Place: 17 Junestrasse

Bremen

Germany's oldest maritime city, still calling itself a Free Hanseatic City, is an enjoyable cultural center. Outside of the compact city center, Bremen is blessed with many neigborhoods and districts which make excellent diversions from the tourist merry-go-round of big cities.

Town Hall

The Bremen Rathaus has an elegant Renaissance facade and beautiful public reception rooms. The guided tour includes the Golden Chamber, Great Hall, relics, and an amazing model warship.
Time: Mon.-Fri., 10am, 11am, and noon; Sat., 11am
Place: Markt
Contact: ph. 321212

Medieval Bremen

Discover medieval Bremen by strolling through the restored Schnoor District, remodelled during the 1920's.
Contact: Tourist Office, Bahnhofplatz, ph. 36361

Botanical Park

Covering nearly 100 acres, Bremen's Botanical Garden contains more than 8,000 varieties of plants and is known for the rhododendron collection and variety of Asian plants in the greenhouse.
Time: daily, 7:30am-sunset
Place: Marcusallee 60

Celle

Stallion's Parade

The most important event of the year in the town of Celle is the Stallion's Parade. Horses have played an important role in the life of Celle since 1735, when the Royal Stud farm was established there. Today the town is famous for its Provincial Stud Farm and its racing horses. The parade, horse show, and races are just a few of the festivities each October.
Time: first Sunday in October
Contact: Verkehrsverein, Schlossplatz 13, ph. 23031

Preserved Town

Celle has preserved its medieval heritage in the Alt Stadt, particularly in the area of Kalandgasse and Poststrasse.

French Gardens

Created in the 16th century, the Franzosischer Garten is a charming spot, with a promenade through an avenue of linden trees and a lake for rowing. Apiculturists will find the Institute of Bee Research there an interesting attraction.
Time: daily, 8am-sunset
Place: Wehlestrasse

Dinkelsbuhl

Children's Festival

Each July, Dinkelsbuhl celebrates the time during the Thirty Years War when Swedish forces were convinced by the town's children to spare their village. The week of festivities includes a children's pageant, concerts, and a parade.
Time: July 13-20

Town Walk

With gabled homes, half-timbered buildings, and medieval walls, Dinkelsbuhl is a jewel of a town. When you visit, be sure to stop by the tourist office for information on the free tour of the town walls.
Contact: Verkersamt, Marktplatz, ph. 3013

Dortmund

Rhineland-Westphalia's largest city is a center of industry, brewing, and commerce. Severely bombed during World War II, Dortmund has rebuilt its attractive old town center, around the ancient Alter Markt.

Brewery Tours

Beer enthusiasts will find nirvana in Dortmund. The annual production of Dortmund's breweries even exceeds the output of Munich's brewmasters. Tours of production facilities with complimentary tastings can be arranged through the city's brewers' association.
Contact: Dortmunder Bierbrauer Verband, Karl Marx Strasse 56, ph. 528973 or 140341

Panorama
High above the Ruhr River Valley, the ruins of the ancient Castle Hohensyburg provide a setting for panoramic views of the Ruhr region and Dortmund. The earliest building on this rocky height was a Saxon bastion built in the 8th century.
Place: Ardeigebirge

Dusseldorf

Capital of North Rhineland-Westphalia, Dusseldorf is a stylish city of wide avenues, spacious parks, and elegant shops. The heart of the modern city is the swank Konigsallee, laid out on the former city moat and lined with boutiques, cafes, and galleries. Dusseldorf's rebuilt Altstadt, on the Rhine's bank, is crowded with pubs, beergardens, and old shops.

Japanese Garden
Dusseldorf seems an unlikely location for a renowned Japanese Garden, but there it is nonetheless. Included in the Nordpark along the Rhine, this serene garden was designed by Japanese master gardeners in the early 1970's. The remainder of the park, restored after extensive damage in World War II, is a fantasy of fountains, flowers, pools, and canals.
Time: daily, 9am-sunset
Place: Stockum

Elector's Church
Fans of baroque will want to visit the historic court church of St. Andreas in the Alt Stadt. Built in the 17th century, this church contains the mausoleum of the Electors of the Palatinate.
Time: Mon.-Sat., 8:30am-5:00pm; Sun., 2pm-5pm
Place: Kasernenstrasse
Contact: ph. 350505

Essen

Ancient Cathedral
The biggest surprise in ultra-modern Essen is the old Musterkirche. Dating from the 9th century, the Munster's special treasures include

the 900-year old Golden Madonna and many elaborate reliquaries.

Time: Mon.,-Sat., 8am-5pm; Sun., 1pm-5pm
Place: Burgplatz

Design Center
A fascinating permanent show of award-winning industrial designs makes the Haus Industrieform an interesting detour.
Time: Mon.-Sat., 9am-5pm; Sun., 11am-5pm
Place: Steelerstrasse
Contact: ph. 20421

Frankfurt Am Main

Don't expect too much of busy Frankfurt. Nearly bombed out of existence during WWII, it has restored few of its historic districts. But there are some attractive pedestrian zones, the lively Sachsenhausen quarter, and the rebuilt Romerberg. If possible, avoid the seedy area around the train station, one of Europe's few high crime sections.

Sculpture Gallery
The Stadtische Galerie Liebieghaus presents sculpture from many eras and civilizations. There are exhibits of Roman, Greek, and Egyptian works, as well as sculpture from the Middle Ages to the 18th century.
Time: Tues.-Sun., 10am-5pm
Place: Schaumainkai 77
Contact: ph. 638907

Leading Museum
Frankfurt's Stadelisches Kunstinstitut ranks among Germany's finest art museums. The collection incorporates works by Bosch, Durer, Botticelli, Rembrandt, Rubens, Picasso, Renoir, Cezanne—and on and on. If you visit Frankfurt, this museum is a must.
Time: Sun., 10am-5pm
Place: Schaumainkai 63
Contact: ph. 617092

Neither Rain Nor Sleet...

Communications through the ages is explored at Frankfurt's Bundespost Museum. Exhibits cover everything from papyrus missives, a reconstructed 19th-century post office, stamp-making machinery, and stamp collections.
Time: Tues.-Sun., 10am-4pm
Place: Schaumainkai 53

Stock Exchange

Travelers interested in high finance will enjoy a visit to Frankfurt's Stock Exchange. Completely rebuilt after WWII, the exchange has a spectators' gallery overlooking the trading floor.
Time: Mon.-Fri., 11am-1:30pm
Place: Borsenplatz
Contact: ph. 219-7383

Botanical Gardens

The Goethe Botanical Garden, which adjoins the Gruneburgpark and the Palmengarten, contains an extensive planting of alpine and ornamental flora. There are educational tours of the geographic groupings.
Time: Mon.-Sat., 8am-sunset; Sun.,9am-1pm
Place: Siesmayerstrasse 72
Contact: ph. 212-3939

Free Concerts

Each Sunday during the summer, free concerts are presented in the court of the Frankfurt Historical Museum. Jazz, pop, and classical music are featured.
Time: June-August: Sunday evening
Place: Sallgasse 19
Contact: ph. 212-3370

Freiburg im Breisgau

Freiburg is one of Germany's most appealing towns. Off the tourist beat at the edge of the Black Forest, Freiburg has restored its exceptional Altstadt to its pre-war splendor. This lively university town sits at the foot of its own mountain and is threaded by unique streams—the Bachle—which belonged to the town's medieval water system.

Rhine Museum

Housed in an ancient abbey, Freiburg's Augustiner Museum contains a collection of medieval art of the upper Rhine region, along with religious art from the Munster. A special treasure of the museum is Grunewald's *Miracle*.
Time: Wed. & Sun., 10am-5pm
Place: Salzstrasse
Contact: ph. 216-3289

Castle Ruins

The Schlossberg has striking Black Forest scenery and romantic castle ruins, and there are marvelous views of Freiburg from the Kanonenplatz lookout.

Grafenau

National Park

Grafenau is the gateway for Bayerischerwald National Park. This park, with numerous clear streams, is unusual in that it's almost entirely wooded. You'll find marked trails throughout the park, and naturalists lead tours from June through September.
Contact: Nationalpark Bayerischerwald, Freyunger Strasse 2

Hamburg

The Free and Hanseatic City of Hamburg is one of Germany's most modern and exciting cities. Its status as a Federal State and as the nation's largest port testify to its importance. Second only to Berlin in size, Hamburg is a city of elegant neighborhoods, expansive parks, cultural centers, bustling commerce, and popular entertainment of every sort. Very little of Hamburg's ancient heritage survived the Great Fire of 1842 or WWII, but it's still a city of many faces, preserving what's left of its past and creating an attractive future.

Botanical Gardens
Hamburg's University Botanical Garden contains more than 20,000 varieties of plants from all over the world. Germany's most modern garden has beautiful greenhouses, an alpine garden, and many specialized exhibits.
Time: Mon.-Sat., 8am-6pm.; Sun., 9am-5pm
Place: Flottbeck
Contact: ph. 324758

Old Hamburg
Little of historic Hamburg survived WWII, but you can find a glimpse of old Hamburg at the Krameramtswohnungen. This cultural center, in the shadow of St. Michaelis, was originally a community built for the widows of members of the Merchants' Guild.
Place: Krayenkamp 10

Trumpeting Watchman
Every day at 10am and 9pm, the city watchman blows his horn from the tower of St. Michaelis church. You can enjoy the same view that he has by climbing the clocktower yourself.
Time: Mon.-Sat., 9am-4:30pm
Place: Neanderstrasse

Another Walk on the Wildside
The curious and courageous tourist won't miss a visit to Hamburg's St. Pauli district. After sundown, this district comes to life with crowds attracted to the music, neon, and sex clubs. Not recommended for the prudish or fainthearted.

Free Map
The Hamburg Tourist Office will provide a free map and guide to this enormous city.
Time: daily, 7am-10pm (summer)
Place: Hauptbahnhof
Contact: ph. 241234 or 326917

Hamelin

On the right bank of the River Weser, Hamelin is rich in folklore and fine Renaissance architecture. Many of its old houses are adorned with pinnacled gables and attractive scrollwork.

Pied Piper

Hamelin is home to the famous Pied Piper legend. Each summer the *Rattenfangerspieler*, a re-enactment of the legend, is staged in the streets of the town. The piper, dressed in his colorful costume, plays his flute and leads the dancing town children away, never to return.
Time: June-Oct.: Sunday at noon
Place: Hochzeitshaus on Osterstrasse
Contact: ph. 26182

Piper's Clock

Even if you can't make it to Hamelin for the play, be sure to see the fanciful Pied Piper glockenspiel on the Hochzeithaus. The beautiful Rathaus was once used by the people of Hamelin for weddings and other ceremonial occasions.
Time: the clock & carillon play at 7am & 5:30pm
Place: Osterstrasse 2

Hannover

Virtually bombed out of existence during the war, Hannover has been largely rebuilt in modern fashion, and what remained of the old town center was painstakingly restored. Today, this capital of Lower Saxony is a commercial center and transportation hub.

Arts and Antiquities

Hannover's Kastner Museum has a collection of Egyptian, Roman, and Greek artifacts, as well as European decorative arts.
Time: Tues.-Fri., 10am-4pm; Sat. & Sun., 10am-6pm
Place: Trammplatz 4
Contact: ph. 168-2730

Super Fountain

Among the unusual features of the Herrenhausen Garten, you will find the loftiest garden fountain in the world. There are other special

fountains, gilded statuary, a grotto, cascades, pavillions, and the Sylvan Theater.
Time: daily, 8:30am-sunset
Place: Herrenhauser Allee

Grand Town Hall

With its domed tower, the immense Rathaus looms above Masch Lake. The impressive interior houses models of old Hannover and examples of municipal art, and the dome affords a fine panorama.
Time: Mon-Fri., 9am-5pm
Place: Trammplatz
Contact: ph. 168-2319

Gothic Landmark

The restored Gothic Marktkirche has been a landmark since the 14th century. Fortunately, the wartime destruction spared the carved altar and 15th-century baptismal font.
Time: Mon.-Sat., 8am-5pm
Place: Marktplatz

Eclectic Gardens

Another of Hannover's many distinctive gardens is the former royal Berggarten. The first greenhouse was erected on the site in 1665; the modern greenhouses contain a collection of desert, tropical, and decorative plants. More unusual is the park's mausoleum, containing Britain's George I and his family.
Time: daily, 8am-7pm
Place: Herrenhauserstrasse

Windmill Park

Hannover's postwar rebuilders created a beautiful English garden around the city's Lake Anna, with old wooden windmills transplanted from the city center.
Time: daily, 8am-sunset
Place: Hermann Lons Park, Kirchroerstrasse

Heidelberg

Heidelberg is Germany's oldest and best-known university town. One of the few German cities spared from wartime bombings, it preserves many medieval and Renaissance buildings and monuments. However, the town has become swamped with tourist commercialism and is best appreciated during the off-season.

Fabulous Ruin
High above old Heidelberg you will find Germany's most pictures-que castle ruin, the Schloss Heidelberg. The grounds provide fan-tastic views of the town and the River Neckar. Each summer, free concerts are held in the castle courtyard.
Time: daily, 8am-10pm
Place: Schlossstrasse

Medieval Manuscripts
Heidelberg's University Library, founded in the 14th century, houses a wealth of medieval treasures. The highlight of this ancient col-lection is the *Mannessische Codex*, an illuminated 14th-century manuscript of poetry and song.
Time: Mon.-Sat., 10am-5pm
Place: Grabenstrasse

Free Maps
Stop by the Tourist Office at the Hauptbahnhof for free city maps and brochures of events in and around town.
Time: Mon.-Fri., 9am-7pm; Sat.-Sun., 2pm-7pm
Place: Hauptbahnhof
Contact: ph. 21341 or 21881

Fireworks Spectacle
On Saturdays in the summer, Heidelberg puts on a pyrotechnics display that draws huge crowds. It's well worth a detour to see this grand show.

Heilbronn

Wine Festival
The center of an important wine-producing region, Heilbronn celebrates a raucous Harvest Festival each September. The

highlight, of course, is the chance to sample the wines from local vineyards.
Time: mid-September
Contact: Verkehrsamt, Rathaus, ph. 562270

Kassel

Much of Kassel's historic legacy went up in flames during World War II, but the city of parks and gardens that rose from the rubble is a pleasant commercial, cultural, and administrative town.

Fairytales and Folklore

The Bruder Grimm Museum, located in the Bellvue Palace, contains manuscripts, letters, and original illustrations of Jacob and Wilhelm Grimm. The famous brothers lived and worked in Kassel for 30 years.
Time: Tues.-Fri., 10am-1pm & 2pm-5pm; Sat. & Sun., 10am-1pm
Place: Schone Aussicht 2
Contact: ph. 787-4059

Provincial Museum

Kassel's Hessisches Landesmuseum contains an eclectic collection which includes medieval clocks, antique scientific equipment, folk art, and the unique Tapetenmuseum, a museum of wallcoverings from the 16th century to the present.
Time: Tues.-Sun., 10am-5pm
Place: Bruder Grimm Platz 5
Contact: ph. 12787

New Gallery

The Neue Galerie presents German and international art from 1750 to the 1980's. German Impressionists and Expressionists, as well as the Romantic School, are well-represented.
Time: Tues.-Sun., 10am-5pm
Place: Schone Aussicht 1
Contact: ph. 15266

Cologne (Koln)

Cologne's skyline is dominated by the spires of its magnificent cathedral. Germany's fourth-largest city has been a commercial center since Roman times—almost 2,000 years ago. Completely devastated by World War II bombing, Cologne has risen to become a center once again of German art and culture.

Grand Cathedral

Begun in 1248 but not completed until 1880, the Kolner Dom is a must for any visitor to Germany. A masterpiece of Gothic architecture, the Cathedral contains art treasures such as the Dombild triptych, the gold Three Kings reliquary, and the Gero Cross. Free organ concerts are held Tuesday evenings in the summer.
Time: daily, 8am-7pm
Place: Am Dom
Contact: ph. 221-3345

Carnival

The most exciting time of the year to visit Cologne is during the uproarious Carnival. The festivities include masquerades, processions, parades, and dances—all culminating with Rosenmontag, when the whole city turns out to enjoy the flamboyant activities.
Time: early Feb.
Contact: Verkehrsamt, Am Dom, ph. 221340

Mainz

Mainz, capital of the Rhineland-Palatinate, is an ancient town with a rich heritage. Although seriously damaged during the WWII, Mainz has restored many historic sites while blending new buildings into the cityscape. This 2,000-year old city is also a center of the Rhine wine trade.

Central Rhine Museum

The Mittelrheinische Landesmuseum provides an entertaining look at Mainz and the central Rhineland from prehistoric times to the

present. Roman antiquities dominate the collections, which also include the city's art gallery.
Time: Tues.-Sun., 10am-5pm
Place: Grosse Bleich 49
Contact: ph. 232955

Guttenburg Museum

Rare books, including a Guttenburg Bible, and a replica of Guttenburg's printing shop are the highlights of this unique museum. There is also an interesting exhibition of the history of printing.
Time: Tues.-Sat., 10am-6pm
Place: Domplatze
Contact: ph. 28371

Medieval Sculpture

The imposing Cathedral of St. Martin houses some of Germany's most famous medieval statuary and sculpture. Don't miss the rococo choir stalls and the bishops' tombs.
Time: Mon.-Sat., 8am-5pm
Place: Domplatze

Munich (Munchen)

Munich, capital of Bavaria, lies at the crossroads of the continent. The city is sophisticated and earthy, with a friendly, beergarden sociability. Following tremendous World War II destruction, Munich chose to reconstruct its buildings to their original plans. In Munich, architecture can be enjoyed in all is forms—from Gothic to Art Nouveau, and from Renaissance to International Modern.

Munich's Multi-Museum

The Munich City Museum is really six museums under one roof. Besides the Museum of City History, with old and modern city models, you can enjoy the German Museum of Brewing, with everything you ever wanted to know about beer; the 25,000 puppets of the Puppet Theater Museum; the Film Museum, exploring Munich's role as a film capital; the Musical Instruments Museum;

and the Museum of Photography, covering the history of documentary photography and film technique.
Time: free Sun., 9am-4:30pm
Place: St. Jakobs Platz 1
Contact: ph. 233-2370

Fanciful Church
Be sure to see the little Church of St. Johann Nepomuk, also called the Asamkirche. It's one of Germany's most fantastic rococo creations.
Time: daily, 8am-6pm
Place: Sendingerstrasse

Glockenspiel
Munich's much-loved glockenspiel springs into action every morning at 11am, high above the Marienplatz on the facade of the Neues Rathaus. The mechanical knights and dancing characters represent a tournament held in 1567 to celebrate a royal wedding.
Time: daily, 11am
Place: Marienplatz

Great Gallery
One of the world's great art museums, the Alte Pinakothek, contains a treasure of European paintings from the 14th to the 19th century. The gallery houses masterpieces by Rubens, Durer, Bosch, Titian, Rembrandt, and most of Europe's great masters.
Time: free on Sun., 9am-4:30pm
Place: Barer Strasse 27
Contact: ph. 2-380-5215

Bavarian Beer
Spaten, one of Munich's biggest brewers, provides a guided tour of their production facilities. Visitors learn the beer-making process from harvesting grain to bottling the brew. Of course, there's free beer at the end of the tour.
Time: Mon.-Fri., 10am-4pm
Place; Mars Strasse 48
Contact: ph. 5122

BMW Tours
Housed in a modern museum, BMW presents films, videos, slide shows, and displays of modern technical achievements. There are over 100 cars, motorcycles, and planes on display. The high point of the museum is the film on movement.
Time: Mon.-Sat., 10am-5pm
Pance: Petuelring 130
Contact: ph. 3-895-3307

English Garden
One of Europe's largest inner-city parks, the Englischer Garten was created in 1793 at the suggestion of American ambassador Benjamin Thompson. It has a Japanese teahouse, a Chinese pagoda, cafes, pavillions, riding trails, and lakes. On sunny days, local nature lovers bare all on the park lawns.
Place: Koningenstrasse

Bavarian Porcelain
Amidst the gardens, lakes, waterfalls, statues, and palaces of Nymphenburg, you will find the Royal Porcelain Factory of Bavaria. The displays present the art of porcelain manufacturing as it was practiced there in the 18th century. After watching the artisans create delicate ceramics, visit the museum of antique porcelain from the palace.
Time: Mon.-Fri., 9am-noon & 1pm-5pm.; Sat. 9am-noon
Place: Manzingerstrasse
Contact: ph. 12081

Electrical Magic
In Germany, the name Siemens is synonomous with electrical energy. At the Siemens Museum you will find models, diagrams, audio-visual shows, and exhibits exploring the development of electrical technology. It's a fun, educational museum.
Time: Mon.-Fri., 10am-4:30pm
Place: Prannerstrasse 10
Contact: ph. 234-2660

Bavarian Arts
The Bavarian National Museum is a vast collection of art, jewelery, tapestries, costumes, stained glass, and ceramics from southern Ger-

many. The museum is famous for its extensive collection of nativity scenes.
Time: free on Sun., 10am-4pm
Place: Prinzergentenstrasse 3
Contact: ph. 21681

New Masters
Munich's Neue Pinakothek is an architectural sensation housing a collection of 19th-century art. Delacroix, Van Gogh, Turner, and Gauguin are all represented.
Time: free Sun., 9am-4:30pm
Place: Barer Strasse 29
Contact: ph. 2-380-5195

Old Peter
The beauty of St. Peterskiche will captivate even the most jaded tourist. Affectionately called "Alte Peter," Munich's oldest parish church is a rococo gem. Don't miss the grisly relic of St. Mundita in a side chapel—you won't soon forget her!
Time: Mon.-Sat., 8am-6pm
Place: Rindermarkt

Blue Rider Group
The gallery in the Lenbach Villa is a must for admirers of Vassily Kandinsky and the Blue Rider Group. The treasure of this gallery is the world's largest collection of early works by Kandinsky, plus works by Klee, Macke, and Marc.
Time: free on Sun., 10am-6pm
Place: Luisenstrasse 33
Contact: ph. 521041

Never Forget
Dachau, the suburban site of the infamous concentration camp, is a chilling sidetrip from Munich. The museum, memorials, barracks, and campground only hint at the magnitude of the crime.
Time: daily, 9am-5pm
Place: Alte Romerstrasse, Dachau

Modern Art
The Gallery of Modern Art is one of the world's leading museums

of 20th-century art. This collection includes Pop, Surrealist, Cubist, Expressionist, and Photorealist works by modern masters.
Time: free on Sun., 9am-4:30pm
Place: Prinzregentenstrasse 1
Contact: ph. 292710

Mineral Marvels

Minerals from all over the world are on display at the State Collection for Mineralogy. The most interesting section details the use of crystals in industry and art.
Time: free on Sun., 9am-4:30pm
Place: Theresienstrasse 41
Contact: ph. 23941

Classical Art

The State Collection of Classical Art and the Glyptothek comprise Germany's greatest collection of classical art. The museum has Greek, Roman, and Etruscan jewelry, vessels, and implements. The Glyptothek's array of Greek and Roman statuary is stunning.
Time: both free on Sun., 10am-4:30pm
Place: Konigsplatz
Contact: ph. 598359 or 286100

Passau

Situated at the confluence of the Danube, the Inn, and the Ilz, Passau is a lovely town, more Tyrolian than German in character and charms. The quaint old town is overshadowed by the twin towers of St. Stephandom and the medieval Veste Oberhaus fortress.

Huge Organ

Passau's 15th-century St. Stephendom is home to the world's largest church organ, with 17,000 pipes and 208 stops. You can hear daily recitals on this colossus in the summer.
Time: May-Sept.: recitals daily at noon
Place: Domplatz
Contact: ph. 51408

Beautiful View

There is a gorgeous view of the meeting of the Danube and the

Inn Rivers—and of Passau—from the Mariahilf Pilgrimage Church in the Innstadt district.
Place: Mariahilfberg

Rothenburg ob der Tauber

Medieval Town Tour

Rothenburg is Germany's best-preserved medieval town. Start with a walk around the town on the city walls, then stop by the Marktplatz to see the Town Hall and the glockenspiel. Next, visit St. Jakobskirche to see the stained glass and the impressive altar. After touring the rest of this medieval gem, climb the hill to the Burggarten for a magnificent overview.

Mighty Drink

Each September, Rothenburg celebrates Der Meistertrunk Festival, which commemorates the mighty drinking feat that saved the town. In 1631, the Burgomeister saved the day by consuming three liters of wine in one drink on a challenge from the commander of the invading army. During the festival, the event is re-enacted in a pageant. You can also see the tale retold everyday on the clock of the Ratstrinkstube on the hour from 11am to 3pm and at 9pm and 10pm.
Time: festival: early Sept.
Place: Marktplatz
Contact: Verkehrsamt, Rathaus, Marktplatz, ph. 2038

St. Goar

Rhine in Flames

In September, St. Goar and its sister city St. Goarhausen stage the spectacular *Rhine in Flames* fireworks and light show. The impressive pyrotechnical display is guaranteed to please.
Time: third Sat. in Sept.
Contact: Verkehrsamt, Heerstrasse 15, ph. 2383

Stuttgart

Stuttgart, capital of Baden-Wurttemberg, is not the concrete jungle one expects of an important industrial city. Within Stuttgart's city limits, nearly three-fourths of the land is gardens, vineyards, orchards, and woodlands.

Provincial Museum

Housed in the ancient ducal palace, the Wurttembergisches Landesmuseum explores Swabian art and culture through the ages. It also contains collections of musical instruments, sacred art, clocks, and costumes.
Time: Tues.-Sun., 10am-5pm
Place: Schillerplatz

Mercedes-Benz Museum

The Mercedes-Benz Works houses the distinctive Daimler-Benz Museum. The collection includes the first Daimler-Benz cars, motorcycles, aircraft engines, and the first motorboat, along with the history and development of the company.
Time: Mon.-Fri., 9:30am-5pm
Place: Mercedesstrasse, Unterturkheim
Contact: ph. 172578

Outstanding Gallery

The Stuttgart Staatsgalerie has a fine collection of paintings ranging from medieval art to 20th-century abstract expressionists. Among the noteworthy works are paintings by Monet, Renoir, Rembrandt, Picasso, and Klee.
Time: Tues.-Sun., 9:30am-5pm
Place: Konrad Adenauer Strasse 32
Contact: ph. 212-5108

Bible Museum

Stuttgart's unique Bible Museum has more than 3,000 Bibles from 80 countries. The treasure is a 1545 Luther Bible.
Time: Tues.-Sat., 10am-4:30pm
Place: Ballingerstrasse 31
Contact: ph. 720030

Folk Festival

The Cannstatt Folk Festival begins with a parade of brass bands and traditional Swabian costumes. During the two weeks of

festivities, there is much drinking, eating, and a grand fireworks display.
Time: last week of Sept.
Place: Bad Cannstatt Kurpark
Contact: ph. 299411

Trier

Today, Trier is a pleasant provincial city, but 2,000 years ago it was known as the "second Rome." For centuries it remained one of Europe's leading cities, a place where Latin, Germanic, and Celtic cultures met and mingled.

Roman Antiquities
The Rheinischer Landesmuseum presents one of the finest collections of Roman antiquities outside of Italy. There are remarkable mosaics, ceramics, coins, and sculpture, along with displays of Frankish glass, pottery, and jewelry.
Time: Mon.-Fri., 9:30 am-4:00 pm; Sat. & Sun., 9:30 am-1:00 pm
Place: 40 Ostallec
Contact: ph. 718448

More Great Books
from Mustang Publishing

Europe: Where the Fun Is by Rollin Riggs & Bruce Jacobsen. No hotels, no museums, no historic sights. Just the best bars, nightclubs, restaurants, beaches, flea markets—just the fun stuff, in all the major cities of Europe. A terrific supplement to the major guidebooks. *Named one of the 25 best European travel guides by "Changing Times" magazine.* **$8.95**

Essays That Worked: 50 Essays from Successful Applications to the Nation's Top Colleges by Boykin Curry & Brian Kasbar. Applying to college? Dread the application essay? This book can help. With 50 outstanding essays from schools like Yale, Duke, and Wesleyan—plus lots of helpful advice from admissions officers—this book will challenge and amuse any college applicant. *"Fifty essays, each one a winner"—New* York Times. **$8.95**

Essays That Worked—For Business School by Curry & Kasbar. The essay is often the most critical part of the business school application. With 50 successful essays and lots of practical advice from admissions officers from Harvard, Stanford, Wharton, and others, this book will assist and inspire any hopeful MBA. **$8.95**

The Student's Guide to the Best Summer Jobs in Alaska by Josh Groves. Thousands of young adults head for Alaska each summer, seeking jobs in the lucrative fishing industry. This book offers the most accurate and thorough information on the Alaska summer job scene available. *"Highly recommended"—The Tartan, Carnegie-Mellon Univ.* **$7.95**